COLLECTED
POEMS

Books by Galway Kinnell

POETRY

What a Kingdom It Was / *1960*

Flower Herding on Mount Monadnock / *1964*

Body Rags / *1968*

First Poems 1946–1954 / *1971*

The Book of Nightmares / *1971*

The Avenue Bearing the Initial of Christ into the New World:
    Poems 1946–64 / *1974*

Mortal Acts, Mortal Words / *1980*

Selected Poems / *1982*

The Past / *1985*

When One Has Lived a Long Time Alone / *1990*

Three Books / *1993*

Imperfect Thirst / *1994*

A New Selected Poems / *2000*

Strong Is Your Hold / *2006*

PROSE

Black Light / *1966*

Walking Down the Stairs: Selections from Interviews / *1978*

How the Alligator Missed Breakfast (for children) / *1982*

TRANSLATIONS

Bitter Victory (novel by René Hardy) / *1956*

The Poems of François Villon / *1965*

On the Motion and Immobility of Douve
    (poems by Yves Bonnefoy) / *1968*

Lackawanna Elegy (poems by Yvan Goll) / *1970*

The Poems of François Villon (second version) / *1977*

The Essential Rilke (with Hannah Liebmann) / *2000*

EDITION

The Essential Whitman / *1987*

Galway Kinnell

COLLECTED POEMS

INTRODUCTION BY

Edward Hirsch

Houghton Mifflin Harcourt

Boston   New York   2017

For information about permission to reproduce selections from this book, write
to trade.permissions@hmhco.com or to Permissions, Houghton Mifflin Harcourt
Publishing Company, 3 Park Avenue, 19th Floor, New York, New York 10016.

www.hmhco.com

Library of Congress Cataloging-in-Publication Data is available.
ISBN 978-0-544-87521-0

Printed in the United States of America
DOC 10 9 8 7 6 5 4 3 2 1

These poems were originally published in the following journals and magazines:
American Poetry Review: "Jubilate." *Catamaran Literary Reader:* "The Sulphur
Baths at Esalen." *The New Yorker:* "Turkeys," "Astonishment," "I, Coyote, Stilled
Wonder," "The Silence of the World," "Gravity."

When One Has Lived a Long Time Alone, copyright © 1990 by Galway Kinnell.
Used with permission of the Knopf Doubleday Publishing Group, a division of
Penguin Random House LLC.

CONTENTS

What a Kingdom It Was (1960)

Flower Herding on Mount Monadnock (1964)

ix

Body Rags (1968)

The Past (1985)

When One Has Lived a Long Time Alone (1990)

Imperfect Thirst (1994)

Strong Is Your Hold (2006)

v

Last Poems (2010–2014)

INTRODUCTION

LIKE WALT WHITMAN, his major precursor, Galway Kinnell was a poet of wide-ranging sympathies, deep immersions, who threw himself into the flux. He, too, was "mystically physical." He was socially engaged and identified strongly with people in trouble, the fraught and suffering, the injured and dying, the wounded body politic. He was keenly aware of the nonhuman world — he wrote some of the finest animal poems of our era — and defended the rights of the earth in an increasingly technological time. He was obsessed by transience, the need to live in our bodies, and relied on personal experience to try to transcend the self. He found a way to incorporate a humane politics into his large, inclusive, free-verse poems, many of them in sequences, and often adapted a religious vocabulary — one of his defining influences was the King James Bible — for secular ends. He sacramentalized experience.

Much of Kinnell's poetry is an intense personal testimonial in the face of death. "The subject of the poem is the thing which dies," he asserts in his essay "The Poetics of the Physical World." In one of the most telling moments of his work, he turns and makes a promise to his infant daughter:

Little sleep's-head sprouting hair in the moonlight,
when I come back
we will go out together,
we will walk out together among
the ten thousand things,
each scratched in time with such knowledge, *the wages*
of dying is love.

Kinnell confronts the inevitability of death with a fragile yet fierce protectiveness, which extends not only to his daughter but also to what the Taoists call "the ten thousand things."

In an equally revealing moment from *The Book of Nightmares* the poet finds a poem suddenly writing itself out on a blank white page. His hand becomes a vehicle: "its title," he states, "the dream / of all poems and the text / of all loves — 'Tenderness toward Existence.'" Tenderness is an extremely rare quality in modern poetry — it was pretty much banished by the modernists determined to extricate poetry from what they considered nineteenth-century sentimentalities. Suspicious of too much feeling, which they considered "romantic" or "womanly," they sought hardened finishes, the coldness of sculpture. But Kinnell celebrates and capitalizes Tenderness, which is directed outward toward all of Existence, with a sacred embrace.

Despite his sacramental stance toward the physical world, Kinnell vehemently rejected Christianity, especially the Christianity of his childhood. He did not look back on it fondly. "I would speak of injustice," he declares emphatically in his early poem "First Communion," "I would not go again into that place." He disliked theological dogma, and yet the language of religion continued to resonate with him, hence his revision of Romans 6:23, recasting "For the wages of sin is death" as *"the wages / of dying is love."* Think of titles like "The Supper After the Last," "The Avenue Bearing the Initial of Christ into the New World," and "The Dead Shall Be Raised Incorruptible." I agree with the literary historian David Perkins that "God was absent from his cosmos but not from his emotions."

Throughout his work Kinnell explored the existential consequences of his position — the death of God, the loss of faith — and made a poetics out of it. He recognized that a luminous spark in us makes it possible to dream of paradise, to invent the realm of eternity, a world outside of time. "But there is another kind of glory in our lives which derives precisely from our inability to enter that paradise or to experience eternity," he argues in "The Poetics of the Physical World." "That we last only for a time, that everyone and everything around us last only for a time, that we know this, radiates a thrilling, tragic light on all our loves, all our relationships, even on those moments when the world, through its poetry, becomes almost capable of spurning time and death."

There are lightning-like instances of transcendence in Kinnell's poems, many incandescent moments, but there is also a tragic awareness that they inevitably dissolve back into time, which is irreversible. He needed to consecrate what is fleeting, unstable, evanescent. I find a credo, a capsule moment, in his tiny poem "Prayer," a haiku-like gem with a triple use of the word "is," the verb of being. It states the hunger and affirms the quest:

> Whatever happens. Whatever
> *what is* is is what
> I want. Only that. But that.

Reading over Kinnell's work as a whole, one finds that he was essentially looking for ultimate meaning, which he could not find in a provisional universe. What he could create was a poetry that embraced our earthly hold, the bonds of connection, the nature of being. His ambition was overarching. He dreamed of a true poem of embodiment, one that would incorporate as much of the available world as possible.

That dream is realized as these *Collected Poems,* the single work he was writing all his life, his *Leaves of Grass.* It could be described as *Tenderness toward Existence.*

Born in 1927, Kinnell came of age in the late forties and early fifties during the era of the New Criticism, with its strong predilection for poetic complexity and impersonality. Like many poets of his generation, he began by writing in rhyme and meter, regular stanzas, fixed forms, and later moved into more open forms. A parallel evolution takes place in the work of Robert Bly, James Wright, and W. S. Merwin, with whom he is often grouped, as well as Adrienne Rich, Philip Levine, Donald Hall, and others. Nonetheless, readers who know only his most well-known poems of the sixties and seventies can be forgiven for feeling a kind of cognitive dissonance on encountering this early work, which shows a determined apprenticeship to the traditional craft of poetry. Here is a committed free-verse poet, a follower of Whitman, an heir to D. H. Lawrence and Theodore Roethke, initially writing in the seventeenth-century mode of the English metaphysical poets, which turned out to be alien to his budding neoromantic sensibility.

Still, it is compelling to see him arduously wrestling with the forms — establishing and breaking up meters, finding and concealing rhymes — and searching for his true subjects. "The death-haunted, tragic Kinnell had already spoken," his friend and mentor Charles Bell later noted, though it would take years to recognize. W. B. Yeats was Kinnell's most enduring touchstone from this period — he thought of the Irish maker as "poetry itself" — though in the mid-to-late fifties he came to feel that for "modern poets — for everyone after Yeats — rhyme and meter, having lost their sacred and natural basis, amount to little more than mechanical aids for writing."

Kinnell found his method and his voice when he abandoned prescribed forms and moved into more improvisational free-verse structures, organic forms. He embraced Coleridge's idea that a work of art is like a living organism, especially a plant, which originates in a seed, continues to grow, and evolves spontaneously from within, effecting "its own secret growth." The metaphor of form that develops naturally appealed to his sensibility. Consequently, his best poems unfold according to an evolving inner logic and assume an architecture all their own. He savored words — their weights, their sounds, their exact meanings — and listened to his own poems as they developed. He downplayed technique and distrusted overly technical or academic discussions of poetry, but he was also a tireless, obsessive, and lifelong reviser of his own poems. One could sometimes see him revising a piece at the podium at the beginning of a poetry reading. He substituted words, slashed phrases, changed line breaks, realigned stanzas. He couldn't help himself. There was some music that he heard in his head, some rhythm that he experienced in his body, and then tried to get down on the page.

Kinnell began to explore longer, looser, somewhat jagged free-verse structures in the last section of *What a Kingdom It Was* (1960), most notably in his moving elegy for his brother, "Freedom, New Hampshire," and in his breakthrough long poem, "The Avenue Bearing the Initial of Christ into the New World," which stakes his Whitmanian claim, though without Whitman's optimism. He purposefully links the first letter of Christ's name to a dirty, chaotic street in Manhattan's Alphabet City, and thus gives a sacred aura to the world of African Americans, Puerto Ricans, and Jewish immigrants on New York's Lower East Side.

Kinnell's postmodernist poem, which unfolds over the course of a single day, doesn't progress in an orderly or chronological fashion through its fourteen parts. It cuts and weaves, eschewing narrative, describing a cauldron of activity. It seems astonished by its own lists, how many shops it names, how much daily life it needs to describe. Ezra Pound's collagist method from *The Cantos* was one point of departure, but as the poet and critic Clive James once noted, "It is the Ezra Pound poem that Pound himself could never have written." It is more vernacular, quotidian, democratic. It views history from street level.

T. S. Eliot's "The Waste Land" was another starting point. Like Hart Crane, Kinnell used some of Eliot's cut-up methods to respond to Eliot's negative vision of the urban realm and create an anti–Waste Land of celebration and sorrow. "Avenue C" has a strong kinship to Allen Ginsberg's poems of the fifties, especially "Howl," one of its models. It is a poem without illusions about poverty, especially sympathetic to Jews from Eastern Europe living in a post-Holocaust world ("The promise was broken too freely / To them and to their fathers"). I love the way it finds beauty on an ordinary, gritty, overlooked avenue, and then builds to a crescendo in the last section:

> From the blind gut Pitt to the East River of Fishes
> The Avenue cobbles a swath through the discolored air,
> A roadway of refuse from the teeming shores and ghettos
> And the Caribbean Paradise, into the new ghetto and new paradise,
> This God-forsaken Avenue bearing the initial of Christ
> Through the haste and carelessness of the ages,
> The sea standing in heaps, which keeps on collapsing,
> Where the drowned suffer a C-change,
> And remain the common poor.

Kinnell launched with one of our major urban midcentury poems, but most of his subsequent work is grounded in the countryside. He believed that poetry should be rooted in the physical world, a form of embodied knowledge, and most of that knowledge came to him in rural surroundings. His poems are animated by the wind, the woods, the night sky, the morning sun. A frog pond, a burnt landscape, a mountainside bursting with flowers. The Northeast Kingdom of Vermont. Animals are never very far away in his often ruined, semiwild landscapes. I would say that he anticipated green or eco-poetry, not just because his poems show great sensitivity to the natural world itself, a place that is other than human, but also because they challenge the idea of our dominion over nature. He recognized the complicated interrelationship between nature and humankind.

Kinnell's poems are shadowed by his knowledge of how hard it is to inscribe the natural world. There is a key to his thinking in the poem "On the Oregon Coast" where he recalls a dinner with the poet Richard Hugo. At one point the conversation turned to the subject of personification, the attribution of human qualities to inanimate objects, animals, or ideas.

> We agreed that eighteenth- and nineteenth-century poets almost
>   *had* to personify, it was like mouth-to-mouth resuscitation, the
>   only way they could think up to keep the world from becoming
>   dead matter.
> And that as post-Darwinians it was up to us to anthropomorphize
>   the world less and animalize, vegetablize, and mineralize ourselves
>   more.
> We didn't know if pre-Darwinian language would let us.

Kinnell's sympathetic view of eighteenth- and nineteenth-century poets (think of such holy eccentrics as Christopher Smart, William Blake, John Clare) runs contrary to John Ruskin's notion that personification, or what Ruskin called "the pathetic fallacy," was a morbid romantic and Victorian phenomenon, a mode that produces "in us a falseness in all our impressions of external things." Rather, Kinnell suggests, the personalizing mode was a desperate measure to try to show that the world is alive in all its parts. It was not a way of deadening nature but of trying to embody it. But that method is no longer available to "post-Darwinians," who must find a new language to bring ourselves closer to the natural world, not by humanizing it, but by naturalizing ourselves.

Kinnell was influenced in the sixties and seventies by the notion and practice of the deep image. In his polemical essay "A Wrong Turning in American Poetry" (1963), Robert Bly distinguished Imagism, which he dismissed as "Picturism," from the psychological kind of image American poetry needed, which concentrated inner and outer energies, uniting the psyche and the cosmos. The models were Spanish and Latin American surrealists (Federico García Lorca, Pablo Neruda, César Vallejo); the impulse was Jungian. The idea was to break down the icy formalism of the fifties. Like his friend James Wright, another poet of the "emotive imagination," Kinnell answered the call. He collapsed the ironic distance between the poet and the poem, embracing the torrid heat of experience. The poet Richard Howard described this work as "ordeal by fire." We are not made for transcendence like the phoenix, Kinnell argues in "Another Night in the Ruins," but must surrender to our own creative destruction in time.

> How many nights must it take
> one such as me to learn
> that we aren't, after all, made
> from that bird that flies out of its ashes,
> that for us
> as we go up in flames, our one work
> is
> to open ourselves, to *be*
> the flames?

There is something archaic in Kinnell's image-centered poems, something primitivist in his procedure, a way of thinking both very old and very new. This is especially evident in his totemic animal poems, "The Porcupine" and "The Bear." The animals in these poems seem very much themselves, yet they also take on a symbolic or representative character. They are figures of the body, who are both like and unlike us. What is striking is how the speaker in these poems moves from describing the animals into becoming one with them. Imaginatively, the poet leaps into their dying bodies. He enacts a psychological regression or shamanistic flight — living with the animals, fusing and dying with them, and waking up with a new consciousness of his own bodily presence, animal knowledge. The conclusion of "The Bear" ponders the mystery of his journey as he wonders "what, anyway, / was that sticky infusion, that rank flavor of blood, that poetry, by which I lived?"

Kinnell is a postromantic poet in the way he seeks a primordial energy — exalted, trance-like starts, regenerative dramas. There is a tremendous mystic propulsion in his work, a longing to overcome our individual isolation, to find some long-lost unity, to join graveolent animals, earthly elements. And yet he also recoils from that need, which entails a loss of self, a dissolution of identity. We desire merging and fear extinction. His poems repeatedly enact that dual feeling or impulse, what he calls a "kinship and separation between ourselves and what is beyond us."

I don't want to underestimate the existential dread that underlies many of the poems in Kinnell's signature books: *Flower Herding on Mount Monadnock* (1964), *Body Rags* (1968), and *The Book of Nightmares* (1971). There is a dark-night-of-the-soul quality to many of these lyrics, which often begin in the middle of the night ("Poem of Night," "Middle of the Way") and/or in the ruins ("Ruins under the Stars," "Another Night in the Ruins"). The salve or response to terror, his characteristic gesture, is to turn from this nighttime dread to the renewable morning world. "How many nights / have I lain in terror, / O Creator Spirit, maker of night and day," he begins one of his spiritually oriented poems,

> only to walk out
> the next morning over the frozen world,
> hearing under the creaking of snow
> faint, peaceful breaths . . .
> snake,
> bear, earthworm, ant . . .

The poem takes one more turn when he looks up at "a wild crow crying *'yaw yaw yaw'* / from a branch nothing cried from ever in my life." Here he ends on an oddly surreal image that undercuts the consolation of morning.

An overpowering dread is the starting point for *The Book of Nightmares,* which struck American poetry like a thunderclap. Part of its appeal was the way that Kinnell used and transformed his own experience. He was not trying to delve into a personality, like, say, Robert Lowell or John Berryman, but to generalize a self, like, say, Whitman or Rainer Maria Rilke. In an essay called "Poetry, Personality, and Death" (1971), Kinnell spoke of a poetry in which "the poet seeks an inner liberation by going so deeply into himself — into the worst as well as the best — that he suddenly finds he is everywhere." That's the strategy for an archetypal personal journey across a particularized landscape, like Wordsworth's "Prelude" or Roethke's "North American Sequence." Keats called it "the egotistical sublime."

The Book of Nightmares is a book-length sequence of ten poems, each one in seven parts, a sort of magical formula. It takes its epigraph, its ten-part structure, and its literary inspiration from Rilke's *Duino Ele-*

gies, which Kinnell later cotranslated. He originally drafted a long poem to be called *The Things* ("Praise this world to the angel, not the unsayable one . . . ," Rilke instructs himself in "The Ninth Elegy." "Tell him of things"), which undergirds *The Book of Nightmares.* Throughout the sequence he struggles to hold on to physical things, to stay the changing world. His true subject is time's passing, which he looks at with radical innocence and horror, as if for the first time.

In one sense, *The Book of Nightmares* is a father's book. The sequence is framed by the birth of the poet's children — his daughter Maud in the first poem ("Under the Maud Moon") and his son Fergus in the final one ("Lastness"). It begins with him lighting a small fire in the rain and singing "one of the songs I used to croak / for my daughter, in her nightmares." It describes the anxiety of a parent who now suffers his own nightmares, not just worry over his own death, which is palpable, but the additional fear of losing or leaving a child. It is thus partly a work of self-instruction, or as he puts it at the beginning of the journey:

Listen, Kinnell,
dumped alive
and dying into the old sway bed,
a layer of crushed feathers all that there is
between you
and the long shaft of darkness shaped as you,
let go.

Here Kinnell starts to page through his book of night fears and counsels himself to surrender to existence, to face death head-on and live with it.

Everything is rent, broken, or torn in *The Book of Nightmares.* There is an occluded journey up a mountain, which hints at a plot, but mostly the protagonist immerses himself in the dying world. He feels divided against himself. Death figures everywhere in the passage, much of it natural, some institutional or man-made (the Vietnam War bursts to the surface in the sixth poem). There is a longing throughout for an original harmony, a prenatal oneness, the world from which we came, the one into which we will disintegrate, but there is also a terror of it. He is lit by the recognition that "Lastness / *is* brightness." The psychological goal: to move through the ruins to find grounds for affirmation. This directive to his small son closes the poem:

> Sancho Fergus! Don't cry!
>
> Or else, cry.
>
> On the body,
> on the yellowed flesh, when it is
> laid out, see if you can find
> the one flea that is laughing.

In retrospect, it is possible to see that with *Mortal Acts, Mortal Words* (1980) Kinnell started to become preeminently a poet of blessing, if not of gaiety then of transfigured dread. This turn distinguishes him from most of his contemporaries. His poems invariably acknowledge an impending darkness, the deep emptiness beyond, a sort of inner desolation, the constant drumbeat of death, whose work never ends. But they also respond with increasing clarity to the power and beauty of fragile things, impermanent moments. For example, I don't know of a more instructive anti-suicide poem than "Wait" ("Wait, for now. / Distrust everything if you have to. / But trust the hours. Haven't they / carried you everywhere, up to now?"). Or a clearer assertion of this redemptive leap than the close of "Goodbye," his grief-stricken elegy for his mother:

It is written in our hearts, the emptiness is all.
That is how we have learned, the embrace is all.

Beginning with *Mortal Acts, Mortal Words,* Kinnell also began to explore less splintered, more consecutive and integrated lyrics, some of them a single sentence or stanza. He combines lyrical and narrative values, often extending the duration of a moment through long, snaking sentences that twist and turn over the course of many lines. Look at the opening of "Fergus Falling" and "After Making Love We Hear Footsteps," which enact what Yeats called "a passionate syntax for passionate subject-matter." Some of Kinnell's one-sentence poems are also his most iconic and celebratory, such as "Saint Francis and the Sow" ("sometimes it is necessary / to reteach a thing its loveliness") and "Blackberry Eating," which connects the sensual pleasure of picking and eating blackberries with the way that words sometimes fall "almost unbidden" from the tongue.

Kinnell continued to pursue the physical world until it yielded a kind of spirit flowing through the body. As he explained in part two of "There Are Things I Tell to No One":

I say "God"; I believe,
rather, in a music of grace
that we hear, sometimes, playing
from the other side of happiness.

Time and again, Kinnell tells us, this music is as close as we'll come to paradise, a song we sing to heal ourselves.

Kinnell's obsessive meditations on time take on a retrospective glow in *The Past* (1985). "Here I sat on a boulder by the winter-steaming river and put my head in my hands and considered time — which is next to nothing, merely what vanishes, and yet can make one's elbows nearly pierce one's thighs," he recalls in the first poem, "The Road Between Here and There." In a way, that road marks the passage of the entire book as Kinnell's imagination turns to childhood memories, to men, including himself, getting older and weaker, to friends who have died, some of them poets, like James Wright, Muriel Rukeyser, Robert Hayden, Richard Hugo ("This one or that one dies but never the singer"), to watery landscapes from the past, which at times seemed eternal ("Here / waves slap not in time but in / evanescence, a rhythmless medium").

Writing about *The Past,* Robert Bly observed that Kinnell "often refers to a transformative power that gives radiance to the gross life of flesh; and transfigures the flesh because the radiance comes from beyond the flesh. He imagines and represents two movements: the movement down into earthly body, dirt, appetite, gross desire, death; and a movement toward sunlight, time, fulfillment, lily blossoms, purity, narcissus flowers, beauty, opening." Kinnell often divides these two movements or desires, a conversation between two sides of himself, into different poems, which speak to each other, but he combines them in the last poem of the book, "The Seekonk Woods." At one point he looks down and states, "I want to crawl face down in the fields / and graze on the wild strawberries." The next moment he looks up and asserts:

> I want to lie out
> on my back under the thousand stars and think
> my way up among them, through them,
> and a little distance past them . . .

Kinnell's longing is palpable, but he rejected any philosophy that rejected the body, a too-easy transcendence, a suspicious upward movement. He recognized the danger of leaving our physical lives behind. And yet he also loved those moments when things shined with a seemingly transcendental light. This explains the extravagant assertion at the end of "The Olive Wood Fire" when he recalls holding his young son in the glimmer of a fire burning low at night: "In my arms lay Fergus, / fast asleep, left cheek glowing, God." Here God operates not so much as a supreme being — the speaker is not worshiping his son — but as a metaphor for the embodiment of something he feels is sacred, a moment freed from chronological time. Kinnell appropriates a supreme name for a secular experience, which he considers holy and cannot otherwise describe.

Against the relentless pressure of loss, the past getting longer, the future looming, Kinnell recurs to those epiphanic junctures when chronology seems to collapse and the world, through its poetry, appears "to spurn time and death." Some of those are regained in memory. Thus the close of his beautiful poem "That Silent Evening":

> Then I will go back
> to that silent evening, when the past just managed
> to overlap the future, if only by a trace,
> and the light doubled and cast
> through the dark the sparkling that heavened the earth.

Kinnell consolidated his achievement with his final three books: *When One Has Lived a Long Time Alone* (1990), *Imperfect Thirst* (1994), and *Strong Is Your Hold* (2006). This phase commences in late middle age with a deep, nearly debilitating loneliness and guilt, sometimes poignant and rueful, as in the sequence of ten thirteen-line sonnets, "When One Has Lived a Long Time Alone." Each of these one-sentence poems begins and ends with the same title phrase, which takes on a haunting resonance. Here he dwells "among regrets so immense the past occupies / nearly all the room there is in consciousness." At other times, however, Kinnell treats the subject of disfiguring loneliness with comic zeal, as in the poem "Oatmeal," wherein he recommends breakfasting with an imaginary companion, in this case John Keats, who just happens to explain how he wrote "Ode to a Nightingale."

The poems in Kinnell's last books often press down on uncomfortable personal truths. They burrow down into the unconscious, as in psychoanalysis, and tend to bring up something glimpsed or experienced a long time ago, something ugly or painful, sometimes small, other times large. The memory implicates him; the poems are infused with a guilt he is trying to expiate. The work of the pen is memory, he suggests in his proem "The Pen": "This Ideal pen, with vulcanite body, can't resist dredging up the waywardness of my youth." These poems are gutsy, honest, discomfiting. They repeatedly evoke something shameful or seemingly shameful — one is called "Holy Shit." The method tends to be stichic; the poems unspool in long, unbroken sections, like the poems of his friend and colleague Sharon Olds, who explores similarly fraught territory. One feels in them the pressure of consciousness bearing down, of a thirst that cannot be filled, of time running out.

> How much do I have left of the loyalty to earth,
> which human shame, and dislike of our own lives,
> and others' deaths that take part of us with them,
> wear out of us, as we go toward that moment
> when we find out how we die . . .
> ("The Striped Snake and the Goldfinch")

My favorite of these guilt-ridden poems of reckoning, the one I wish I had written, is called simply "Shelley." Here Kinnell remembers that when he was twenty the only truly "free spirit" he looked up to was the quintessential romantic poet Percy Bysshe Shelley, the advocate of "atheism, free love, the emancipation / of women, and the abolition of wealth and class." The poem recounts the wreckages of Shelley's life, the list of women and children that he used up and loved, discarded and destroyed in his quest for art, his "pursuit of Eros." The deaths of children, almost inadvertently left behind, is harrowing reading. The poem ends not by romanticizing Shelley but by condemning him — and also the speaker's younger self: "and in those days, before I knew / any of this, I thought I followed Shelley, / who thought he was following radiant desire." Kinnell mines the gap here between what romantically minded poets think they are doing in the name of art and what damage they are actually doing. Radiant desire doesn't excuse personal failings; it has consequences for everyone involved. He is laying out an ethic of art's relationship to life.

Something unexpected also enters Kinnell's late work: a sudden sustaining happiness, moments of contentment, renewed joy, love achieved. His final collection takes its title and spirit from Whitman ("Strong is your hold O mortal flesh, / Strong is your hold O love") and stakes a fresh claim: "I, who so often used to wish to float free / of earth, now with all my being want to stay" ("The Stone Table"). There are elegies to friends — James Wright, Jane Kenyon, and others — and a backdrop of public tragedy ("When the Towers Fell"), but also a sense of deep attachment — to the beloved, to the earth itself. The last poem of his last published book moves beyond regret and ends with a simple question:

> Doesn't it outdo the pleasures of the brilliant concert
> to wake in the night and find ourselves
> holding each other's hand in our sleep?

A sense of deep astonishment animates Kinnell's final poems. "The present pushes back the life of regret," he concludes. "It draws forward the life of desire." The poet in old age continues to hold on to things, to respect the earth, to be amazed by the world, despite the fact that he everywhere hears the call of goodbye. His own life is ending, the days are sadly numbered, but he continues to praise the way that poetry sings the world into being.

"Jubilate," Kinnell's homage to the eighteenth-century English poet Christopher Smart, is perhaps the most surprising of these poems. This anecdotal work looks back on and recounts a communal poets' reading and celebration of Smart's "Jubilate Agno" ("Rejoice in the Lamb") that Kinnell organized at a church in the late seventies. Kinnell's homage incorporates many lines from Smart's euphoric poem, which is more than a thousand lines long, and cleverly links each of the twenty-one poets to the passage he or she was given to read. He explains that Smart — "this profligate, drunken, devout, mad polymath" — composed his "Magnificat," as he himself called it, between 1759 and 1763 while locked up in St. Luke's Hospital for the Insane and then the "less bedlamic" asylum at Bethnal Green. Now contemporary poets were reciting Smart's grand, unfinished masterpiece. "Some poets were attracted to passages they knew / for their own reasons," Kinnell notes in "Jubilate," such as Etheridge Knight, "who, like Kit Smart, had done time," and Allen Ginsberg, "who remembered / that in writing 'Howl' he had communed / with the genius of Kit's madness," and Muriel Rukeyser, "who once wrote her own Smartian vow: / 'Never to despise in myself what I have been / taught to despise, and never to despise the other.'"

So many of these poets have since died that "Jubilate" becomes a collective elegy. It transforms into a poem of friendship, of kinship through poetry, which connects the living and the dead, and it builds to a rousing conclusion:

> For all those who were there, at the Church
> of the Transfiguration, that evening in 1978,
> and for those who may have heard about it later
> and those of you coming upon it now
> for the first time, and for Kit Smart who died

in debtor's prison in 1771 at forty-nine,
and for Muriel who would die two years after that evening,
and for those witnesses who are also gone:
Paul and Etheridge and Jane and Harvey and Allen
and Allen and Grace and David and James and Joel —
and the carrier pigeon too — and for the rest of us
still standing, or sitting — and before long to topple —
let all of us rejoice and be made glad.

"Rejoice and be made glad." The sense of celebration, an instilled joyousness, pervades Kinnell's final work. He has gone through fire and come out the other side. He recognizes that we cannot escape the force field of gravity, which tethers us to the earth for good and ill. He continues to catalog sufferings and register joys. He feels the power of a great silence. Stilled wonder. An overwhelming sense of awe. For one last time he looks back at a world that is perilous and beautiful.

Edward Hirsch

EDITORS' NOTE

REVISION was a lifelong project for Galway Kinnell. He once remarked that he wished he had resisted the impulse to publish his poems until he was eighty, so that he could have brought them all out in a form that completely satisfied him. Absent that luxury, he engaged with his poems as unfinished works long after their publication, reexamining and reconsidering them at every encounter. When he was putting together a new collection, his editors at Houghton Mifflin would provide him with galleys, which he would proceed to obliterate with ink. The first sight of his poems set in type, he said, concentrated his mind like Dr. Johnson's soon-to-be-hanged man's glimpse of the gallows. His editor would then give him a clean set of galleys, vainly hoping it would represent the final version. Then would come changes in page proof, and sometimes even in blues. Alas for Houghton Mifflin, there would be revisions made in the hardcover edition for the paperback, and sometimes in subsequent paperback printings.

Galway's determined pursuit of an ever-elusive perfection meant that there were often as many as five versions of a single poem published in different books over the years. For example, some of the poems in his first book, *What a Kingdom It Was* (1960), were revised and included in his collected early poems, *The Avenue Bearing the Initial of Christ into the New World,* fourteen years later. His *Selected Poems* (1982) included more revisions to several of those same poems, some of which were again revised for *A New Selected Poems* (2000), and yet again for a reissue two years later of *The Avenue Bearing the Initial of Christ into the New World.* In *A New Selected Poems,* he acknowledged ruefully that his working over of old poems "makes me think of the digestive process of a Methuselah-ian ruminant animal, one with many many stomachs, that chews its cud for decades (though I don't want to carry this analogy to its logical alimentary end)."

In the new versions, it sometimes appeared that he was trying to revise the poet he had been at twenty-five, as well as the poems. He recognized the dangers of late revision in his elaboration of "the law of elapsed time":

> All writers know this law: revision succeeds in inverse ratio to the amount of time passed since the work was written. Revision is most likely to improve a poem when it directly follows composition, because it is, in fact, a slower, more reflective phase of the creative act. It is most likely to fail if many years have passed . . .
>
> One reason why delayed revision often fails is that the writer eventually loses track of what he or she was originally trying to do — or more likely, was doing without trying. . . . It is easy for an author to forget the reasons — if he or she ever articulated them — for those inspired leaps, those sudden decisions and shifts of direction, which were vivid and compelling during composition. . . . The poet who revises belatedly may no longer be exactly the same person who composed. [*The Essential Whitman*]

Sometimes he reckoned the cost even more bluntly, as in this note in his 1993 collection, *Three Books:*

When you substitute what seems like a splendid new passage for an old awkward one, in a poem that has been apparently finished for many years, it may seem that you have lifted it at last out of mediocrity; but when you look in on it the next day, you may find it lying in ruins. That is because there is a poetic equivalent to the organ transplant rejection syndrome. The new passage often won't cohere with the rest — in mood, in language, even in intent — and for better or worse the poem must make do with the original lines.

Indeed, sometimes he returned to his original version without regret, as he did with one of his most famous poems, "Saint Francis and the Sow." Thus in *Three Books:*

I restored a word which I had taken out a dozen years ago when I put the poem into my *Selected Poems.* At that time I thought to myself, "Can a pig really have a broken heart?" and I changed "broken" to "unbreakable." Now I think I was right in the first place, and that my earlier scruple came from the harmful and surely false idea, carefully nurtured by our kind, that there is no resonance between our emotional life and that of the other animals.

Galway also had a habit of making changes in poems while giving readings, which he described in 1973: "Standing at the podium, just about to say a line, I would feel come over me a definite reluctance to say it as written. Gradually I learned to trust this reluctance. I would either drop the line altogether . . . or else invent on the spot a revision of it." He would make these changes in his reading copy. We found many such marked copies in his shelves and considered all of his inked revisions, but did not include here any that had not eventually found their way into the next printing.

Sometimes at the end of a reading, when Galway would invite "questions or objections," a poignant complaint would issue from someone who had cut his or her teeth on a particular poem in its original book form and was outraged at Galway's tampering. At least once, a vexed reader would ask why, in "After Making Love We Hear Footsteps," he'd changed the lines about his young son Fergus's baseball pajamas:

the neck opening so small
he has to screw them on, which one day may make him wonder
about the mental capacity of baseball players —

Galway would explain that he had always had great respect for the intelligence of baseball players and for the difficulty of the game itself, and in retrospect he felt that that line was flippant, disrespectful — and incorrect.

Many objected to his late insertion of "broughamed" (an archaic word meaning "to strengthen, to gather one's strength") into the much-beloved "Blackberry Eating." Indeed, we agree that this might be an example of "organ transplant rejection syndrome," and we have returned to the original version here.

As a general rule we have chosen his final version of a poem. In those infrequent cases where we have not, we have been guided by his own editing of *The Essential Whitman*. There he chose thoughtfully from Whitman's many versions (and sometimes incorporated a preferred line from still other versions) in an attempt to present the work he loved in its strongest form. In any instance where we have used something other than his final version, we have made it clear in the textual notes.

In the course of our work, we came across early poems that he had published in literary magazines but had deliberately not included in any book, even in *First Poems* (1971), a collection of his earliest efforts. For a time, we considered appending them in this volume as his uncollected juvenilia, but it was impossible to imagine that Galway would have approved. Those early poems, archived at the Lilly Library at Indiana University and at the Milne Rare Book Room at the University of New Hampshire, may possibly be the subject of another book, another time.

We have included, however, seven new uncollected poems at the end of the book, the only poems that he felt were finished enough to publish in magazines in the last eight years of his life. No doubt, had he lived to do so, he would have revised these last poems many times over before they appeared in a book.

Finally, we offer this last word, from his note to *A New Selected Poems,* as consolation to anyone who stumbles upon something unfamiliar in a well-loved poem:

> Was it Manet whose paint box was taken from him at the door
> of the local *musée* so that he would not touch up his own paint-
> ings hanging on the walls? . . . Readers who know these poems
> from the books in which they first appeared will discover that here
> and there words, phrases, and lines have been replaced or deleted.
> I hope these faithful readers — or "unmet friends," as I think of
> them — will approve of the changes. Those who do not may al-
> ways seek out the unrevised versions which, unlike paintings, still
> exist in the original books exactly as they were.

Barbara K. Bristol and Jennifer Keller

First Poems

1946–1954

To My Mother

PART I

Two Seasons

1

The stars were wild that summer evening
As on the low lake shore stood you and I
And every time I caught your flashing eye
Or heard your voice discourse on anything
It seemed a star went burning down the sky.

I looked into your heart that dying summer
And found your silent woman's heart grown wild
Whereupon you turned to me and smiled,
Saying you felt afraid but that you were
Weary of being mute and undefiled.

2

I spoke to you that last winter morning
Watching the wind smoke snow across the ice,
Told how the beauty of your spirit, flesh,
And smile had made day break at night and spring
Burst beauty in the wasting winter's place.

You did not answer when I spoke, but stood
As if that wistful part of you, your sorrow,
Were blown about in fitful winds below:
Your eyes replied your worn heart wished it could
Again be white and silent as the snow.

A Walk in the Country

We talked all morning, she said
The day's nice, on this nice summer
Day let's walk where birds glide
At berries ripening everywhere.
And I thought, is it only me such
Beauty refuses to touch?

But I walked all the same, to please
What only an arm held close,
Through a green wood to a space
Where grass was turned over by a farmer whose
Rickety horses ploughed
While crow and robin sang out loud.

She said it was nice. It was.
But I could hear only in the close
Green around me and there in the dark
Brown ground I walked on, meadowlark
Or other thing speak sharp of shortness
That takes us all and under like that grass.

Island of Night

I saw in a dream a beautiful island
Surrounded by an abrasive river,
And soon it was all rubbed into river and
Gone forever, even the sweet millet and the clover.
Then it was night: out of dark caves

Came the thunder of horses — across the black
Desert at the touch of their hooves
Hundreds of colors kept blooming. I awoke
And touched you and your eyes opened
Into the river of darkness around us
And we were together and love happened.
I do not wonder that men should bless
The down-tearing gods, who also let us lift
These islands of night against their downward drift.

The Comfort of Darkness

Darkness swept the earth in my dream,
Cold crowded the streets with its wings,
Cold talons pursued each river and stream
Into the mountains, found out their springs
And drilled the dark world with ice.
An enormous wreck of a bird
Closed on my heart in the darkness
And sank into sleep as it shivered.

Not even the heat of your blood, nor the pure
Light falling endlessly from you, like rain,
Could stay in my memory there
Or comfort me then.
Only the comfort of darkness,
The ice-cold, unfreezable brine,
Could melt the cries into silence,
Your bright hands into mine.

Passion

At the end of a day of walking we found
A hill for our camp, and we ate
By the low fire and sat up to wait
For the stars and the embers. It was not late
When the whisper of our love was the only sound.

Then we were quiet together, like a footfall
A long time vibrant on the pine-needled ground,
Your body touching me, and in the air around
A flute of memory joining the sound
Of your breath and the noise of some small animal.

Overhead the stars stood in their right course.
Later a mourning dove stirred the night
With soft cries. I was deaf, and the light
Out of the east fell on extinguished sight.
My new eyes searched the passion of the stars.

The Feast

Juniper and cedar in the sand,
The lake beyond, here deer-flesh smoking
On the driftwood fire. And we two
Touching each other by the wash of the blue
On the warm sand together lying
As careless as the water on the land.

Now across the water the sunset blooms.
A few pebbles wearing each other
Back into sand speak in the silence;
Or else under the cliff the surf begins,
Telling of another evening, and another,
Beside lapping waters and the small, lapped stones.

The sand turns cold — or the body warms.
If love had not smiled we would never grieve.
But on every earthly place its turning crown
Flashes and fades. We will feast on love again
In the purple light, and rise again and leave
Our two shapes dying in each other's arms.

Told by Seafarers

1

It is told by seafarers
To the children who would go to sea,
When the moon lies full on the sea
It is a time when the life-bearers

Abound in the deep, and a pillar
Of water from the rocking sea
Rises, as the god sea
To the moon is an unerring sailor.

2

Fair girl — and here on the grasses
Of long afternoons, as on a sea-

Floor grasses wave in the still sea,
We lie together, in this grass oasis,

And teach you how the sea rises
Or grass teems in the sea,
When the moon lies full on the sea,
As seafarers tell, in the sea's disguises.

Night Song

I cannot think who is guilty,
One or the other, both — I remember
Only the turning of platters *leaving me*
Blue blue Jezebel — so now I hear

Outside in the raining city
The poor shiver and go on walking and the unfed
Ask alms or shelter and get pity
And I know the lonely are afraid in their beds.

A Winter Sky

Behind our back the golden woods
Hold the gold of a great season
As we lay on the shore of the woods
And watched the long afternoon
Dying in golden light in the woods.

Before us the brown marsh
Brought the dark water, dry grass,
Cattails, waste of the close-cropped marsh,
And the hunters' blinds were watching
For traffic on the blinded marsh.

It had been a long, beautiful fall
And as we sat on the shore remembering
The season behind us, the golden fall,
One of us said to the other
There may never be an end to fall.

Then two ducks flew away from winter
And a gun reached out and caught one
And dropped it like snow in winter,
And without looking back or understanding
The first flew on alone into winter.

We rose as dusky light filled the woods
And looked out over the brown marsh
Where a dog swam and where the fall
Covered the land like a winter
And winter took fall from the marsh and woods.

PART II

Walking Out Alone in Dead of Winter

Under the snow the secret
Muscles of the underearth
Grow taut
In the pain, the torn love
Of labor. The strange
Dazzled world yearning dumbly
To be born.

Spring Oak

Above the quiet valley and unrippled lake
While woodchucks burrowed new holes, and birds sang,
And radicles began downward and shoots
Committed themselves to the spring
And entered with tiny industrious earthquakes,
A dry-rooted, winter-twisted oak
Revealed itself slowly. And one morning
While the valley underneath was still sleeping
It shook itself and it was all green.

The Gallows

Turmoil finds conclusion
Somewhere. Only the years we spend
Forgetting and learning, courting illusion,
Divorcing old hopes — their promised end
Ends when the heart has formed a fusion

With the head, and the bloody foam is spanned
By reason, resignation; the dark ocean
Where the whales rove lies flat as the sand
Behind us. Turmoil owns such motion
We cannot wish, so fond
Of the torn joy, to fashion
Final peace. Dear is the bond
Binds hearts to desolation.

The cry of the wolf is longing,
Sad is the low sea-moan;
When the head's gallows are hanging
A heart, a youth's cry is pain.

A Walk in Highland Park

We came upon it suddenly — I said,
"Something red is burning in those leaves."
Leaves we would have thought, such shape they had,
The willow's leaves of fall. "That red depraves
The tree, it tells of the permanence of tears,
I think that only what is happy endures."

We turned and ran down through the yellow thorns.
But the wind about my ears played this one tune:
Upon that hill the winterberry burns,
And sorrow's coals are all that will remain.
Though quite a runner when my youth was young,
Now I cannot pace that winter song.

In the Glade at Dusk

I come back obedient:
I hear again in the leaves
My days begin, and in the grave
Light lean my body waiting — for what
If not those vanished flames to make me brave?

But the days of the suffered flame
Forsake me, and the days yet to be endured
Ring me around, and the sun puts its fire
On the trees, and wind blows in the teeth
Of days the last day only shall consume.

The glade catches fire, and where
The birds build nests they brood at evening
On burning limbs. Spirit of the wood, dream
Of all who have ever answered in the glade at dusk —
And grass, grass, blossom through my feet in flames.

The Old Moon

I sat here as a boy
On these winter rocks, watching
The moon-shapes toil through the nights —
I thought then the moon
Only wears her mortality.

Then why to these rocks
Do I keep coming back, why,

The last quarter being nearly
Wasted, does the breath
Come back dragoning the night?

Unless, perhaps,
The soul, too, is such a country,
Made of flesh and light,
And wishes to be whole
And therefore dark.

Primer for the Last Judgment

When Jesus bruised his toe on stone
Men crowned him — all of them,
The pure and the impure — punctured him
Finger and toe, and pinned him there,
And coughed less from conscience than phlegm;
Then called for traditional values, unaware
They were asking their own liquidation.
"The end is at hand," said Paul.
But it did not arrive, that looked-for day
Of devastation, except at its own slow gait.
Daily the spent heart came home to find
A space with the dimensions of home
Ambiguously empty like the three-days' tomb

And now with us: only a few
Years back, at war's close, the sun
Touching the Pacific found
Two cities crumbled. And men

World over asked, "Has the end begun?"
Maybe it has; maybe it shall come
Exploding flesh off the innocent bones,
Mechanized, official, and at once.
Or maybe it has crueler ways —
Dread of the body, the passion to subdue —
Not to be announced until it is done,
Which is each day from this day
Until the last tomb clutches the last bone.

Sunset at Timberline

I

"I watch this sonovabitch
Buy himself a fifty-cent
Cigar. Dying for the butt
I track him all over town.
When he's smoked it down
To the last inch
He tamps
The fucking thing out
On a lamp-
post and sticks it in his pocket . . ."

"Shit,
Today I see this cat
Blow his nose,
And right in front of the shoeshine
Boys he bends down

And greases his goddam shoes
With his snots . . ."

2

At timberline
A few great, skinless trees
Are clinging, blown almost
Flat,
Like pressed
Flowers. Below me the rainclouds open
To the sunset. In that
Last burst
Of light the window of, perhaps, a flophouse
Flashes.

Indian Bread

In childhood, when the ferns came up,
We would gather the roots and stew them in a pot
Letting the sprays lie broken in the grass,
Then dump the mush and bake it in loaves,
Taste it, spit it out, and leave it all for dead,
Some grey puke in the grass, our Indian bread.

Last spring I made the trip back
To the woods where we used to cook
That failed bread. It was overgrown —
Streets, curbs, hydrants, hedges, lawns,
Low-roofed houses where the people burn
Their lives out on the site of the lost fern.

I talked with the owner of a place,
Told him of the old fern-kitchen his house
Was built on. He laughed, said he reckoned
He'd cook himself a few years yet, then find
A new spot, where his kids too could take a pot,
Boil the ferns, taste them, spit them out.

On the way home I looked down
On a last woodland drifting in unbroken green,
I saw moving through it the pre-ghosts of bulldozers.
Dear God, why didn't it ever make,
This wild land where the ferns came up in spring,
For us who wasted it, Indian bread worth eating?

PART III

Conversation at Tea

1

My love had been splendid
For brilliant eyes,
Dancing bodies, star-wheels
Through the night, for flights
Of morning birds, symphonic skies
At noon, all forms of sensual delight,
All willing worlds at once. But the heart mad,
Their tinsel tore. And I declared
My war on every grain God made.

2

War, I would judge, is tragic,
But the difference between
A tragic action on the stage
And off is — one is only mimic.
If you are so insane
As to wish — how do you say? — soul-purge,
By all means go to the theater.
But never fight a war.

Come, take two seats at Cyrano
Or better, Evans doing Hamlet
(But what a shame it's cut!)
Or best, the Old Vic
Is bringing Lear here next week.
But then, the theater, it's just too —
Too something — for a man like you.

Why don't you use instead my study
And lose yourself in Chaucer.
Though my classics are a trifle dusty
For you a book is still a book I'm sure.

3

Who is it I am searching for tonight?
What disembodied voice can I surround
With flesh? Like calls of Puck there float
Into my troubled memory the sounds
Of all those voices mingling from the past —
Who is it I am seeking in this waste?

I have mourned with Troilus — not quite in jest
Known the moping madness to declare
His love; and betrayed, called the world a waste
And vanity with heart too deadly sober;
With Sampson too, and Adam, for a love misplaced
I have mourned with Troilus and the rest.

And swaggering with Cyrano, and travelling
To the moon, and sweeping with a plume
The threshold of the stars, my restless craving
Took bravado for its meat — O spume
Of glory, your vapored kind can only go
With dreams, or swagger there with Cyrano.

And on the heath shall I continue seeking?
Has the storm that lashed us then subsided
Yet, that struggled with the bitter breaking

Of a mind and heart, has it faded
For me yet, or only now begun?
And shall I through the heath continue on?

Who spoke those self-tormentings, were they yours,
Or mine, or Hamlet's own? Whose voice
Is no difference, what head invented
Doesn't matter — the Prince of all of us
Opened the pain of solitude and cursed
The tyrant stars. Do not ask who said them first.

I have been all these hearts, and more,
Heroes, criminals, frauds, and tortured fools,
I have merged my spirit with the fair
And with souls as dark as blood or bowels,
And yet I know more of providence or fate
Than who my heart is searching for tonight.

4

Yesterday I saw you
And you did not speak,
You walked as if — allow
Me to be trite —
You walked in a daze.
Do you concentrate
On things so bleak
You cannot see, for thought, your friends?
I know you saw my face
And yet as if our hands
Had never touched, you

Did not know me,
Or even seem to know
Yourself. This struck me strangely,
Your silence, since
Here we are sipping tea
And talking in present tense.
Let's agree, now we are together,
Friendship is forever.

5

I have struck gems in several friends,
Perhaps in more than most, certainly
In more than you, whose delicate tea
Tends more to water. But this is surely
Because the stars rule our destiny
Or God plots out our ends.

My drink is crude and bitter
But at least I made the stuff myself.
You might concede that nature made me better
At hunting diamond mines than you, yet if
You doubt, let me recount the story of
Two friendships now a-tatter.

Chris was one, whose fine fierce spirit spent
Its up-pent fury arguing with me
Who wandered worlds with him. One day he penned
His testament and died. If he could see
Me now, against my heart's depravity,
He could not lift, for tears, his hand.

Another friend was Gib, who did not die,
But wished to change the world, and found
It would not change. His heart fell utterly
To dust, though sometimes still he smiles around
The corners of his mouth. I saw him ruined,
He cannot therefore speak to me.

These friends were fast, for life-long working,
But as you see, a friend is not eternal.
Sometimes walking on the streets, or talking
Over tea, I drowse, conversing with an angel
Of all those days when friends went well,
And see no half-friends lurking.

6

You know, you sometimes have
A sour look — I mean
You can be affable — but I have seen
Often on your face a look of —
Not exactly pain —

But more as if
Your dreams had lain
In puddles, stained
By themselves, like cigaret butts in the rain.

You look as if you came
From some other time
And idle in this calm
Remember storms you could not tame,

And feel at twenty years quite old
— But then, our tea is getting cold.

7

What storms have blown me, and from where,
What dreams have drowned, or half-dead, here
Surround me, or whether I am old or young,
I cannot find an answer on my tongue.
Yet if you ask me to describe that dark, wild
Winter of the eyes, then I
Can speak, answer endlessly,
For that look was not on me as a child.

Each year I lived I watched the fissure
Between what was and what I wished for
Widen, until there was nothing left
But the gulf of emptiness.
Most men have not seen the world divide,
Or seen, it did not open wide,
Or wide, they clung to the safer side.
But I have felt the sundering like a blade.

8

I am old
But quite perceptive —
I could have told
You many goals you strive
To reach
Are reachless, yet in some strange way
I feel there is nothing I can teach

Or do or say, but wheel my crippled age
Away, and let you wage
Your war.

9

I have been crouching here too long, sipping
Tea, while the souls I love, wan Troilus, old King
Lear fool-guided through the world, the noble
Prince, countless more, to tell
Too endless, Gib, Chris, and all, hold hell's
Hot breath back and summon me to battle.

Now I must nurse my courage in a sling,
I dream the ancient skies are ripening,
That golden fruit shall form like summer clouds
Demanding poet-men to sing like lords
Of giant gods who pace
The mountain-tops. Then I will write my peace.

Meditation Among the Tombs

I

I am kneeling on my grave this lonely
Circle of the day or bottom half
Of night, to witness vainly
Day light candelabra on the dark horizons
Of the world. For this I tell my orisons
And char my tomb with incense for an epitaph.

The present darkness has been long,
And add, the clocks are closing down these days
Lacking a hand to push the hand ahead,
And you will hear the tick and thud
Begin to toil, as the roots of grass
Gnaw decomposition like a cud.

We who have won no issue from our dreams,
Who have never climbed the pale hills of dawn
Nor forged our fullness in the blaze of noon
Nor arched a crimson splendor down the west,
Scowl now at dark — curse God that our best
Is worse than what those grasses chew night-long.

2

Life like a coat of rose-colored paint
Is lifting from his lips. And in those eyes,
Glazed to seal their faint
Flames within, the last red coals
Sputter in his tears. "Try to raise
Your eyelids, gaze upon this cross, for souls
That burn such evil in their fires
Should quench themselves," two preachers hiss in his ears,
"With sorry vows instead of salty tears."

He flutters up those lids, but age
Has so bleared those weary
Eyes and the page
On which they register within
That the wrought and polished cross

Those phantoms hold before his chin
Seems but a pole to string its wires high
And shuttle back and forth love's perfidy.

Could such an antique hulk as this
Have ever opened eyes in wonderment of love
Or known the frenzy of a warded kiss?
It is very difficult to think.
And yet it seems he has enough
Old strings and yarns of memory to weave
A gaudy mess of dreams before he leaves.

Look, the glowing caves begin to blink:
What signals do they tell,
What dark suggestion in that skull
That life is twice, compared with death, as terrible?

3

Old Man: When youth was pounding in my veins
          And life was all a sky of light and dreams
          And none had any foresight for the pains
          A girl and I took love in summer's kiss
          Under the oak, half hidden in the grass.
  Youth: There must have been much beauty in those flames.

Old Man: Later, when our love burned not so wild
          Or brilliant, but with a steady, subtle fuse
          And she was fevered with a coming child
          They said to me, "Choose you the living wife,
          Or risking her, the babe delivered safe?"
  Youth: They might have chosen better word than choose.

Old Man: You who are young have no such memories
        Of trysting by an oak in the thick
        And shining grass, or kissing under skies
        Of singing wind. So which alternative,
        A dead creation or a dying love?
  Youth: Creation is a sorry thing to pick.

4

Born,
My child, alas, so worn
And old, as though these eyes
Could stuff your sockets with their miseries . . .
I pray
That as your father and his father
Turned the waning cycle of their day,
Bending to the midnight mother
Heaped with age
And bitter with broken rage,
You will wind your days the other
And the better way: and as you near
The end, the furrows of your age will disappear
And everything that prods you to a sudden grave
Will take a counterclockwise turn,
Strange reversal you will learn,
Until your limbs are youthful and your heart is brave.
And having said this prayer,
One word: to life's pretenders say you were
Descended from a line of vanished kings
Who sat in state upon a silver throne —
Then beat from that descent with careless wings
And of their depositions weave your crown.

5

The clock has spun while I have brooded here,
Spading up an earth of long-dead men —
Rain of memory for a rainless year —
Is this a graveyard I am digging in?

But look, the dawn is lighting up the east,
The clouds are breaking, making way — soon!
Now! — through the dusk comes sliding fast,
Alas, that sullen orange eye, the moon.

The clock's two sentinels
Are dying, and midnight has begun again.
Lord, might we witness those castles
Surrender to the fair legions of the sun.

But if the darkness finds the graves where we
Were buried under sillions of our past
Still pointing gloomy crosses at the east,
And thinks that we were niggard with our bravery,
Our ghosts, if such we have, can say at least
We were not misers in our misery.

What a Kingdom It Was

1960

To Charles and Diana Bell

PART I

First Song

Then it was dusk in Illinois, the small boy
After an afternoon of carting dung
Hung on the rail fence, a sapped thing
Weary to crying. Dark was growing tall
And he began to hear the pond frogs all
Calling on his ear with what seemed their joy.

Soon their sound was pleasant for a boy
Listening in the smoky dusk and the nightfall
Of Illinois, and from the fields two small
Boys came bearing cornstalk violins
And they rubbed the cornstalk bows with resins
And the three sat there scraping of their joy.

It was now fine music the frogs and the boys
Did in the towering Illinois twilight make
And into dark in spite of a shoulder's ache
A boy's hunched body loved out of a stalk
The first song of his happiness, and the song woke
His heart to the darkness and into the sadness of joy.

First Communion

The church is way over in the next county,
The same trip that last year we trekked
Carrying a sackful of ears to collect
The nickel-an-ear porcupine bounty.
Pictured on the wall over Jerusalem

Jesus is shining — in the dark he is a lamp.
On the tray he is a pastry wafer.
On the way home, there is regular talk
Of the fine preaching, before the regular jokes
Are allowed. The last time over
The same trail we brought two dollars homeward.
Now we carry the aftertaste of the Lord.
Soon a funny story about Uncle Abraham:
How, being liquored up, he got locked out
By his woman; how she must have gone looking for him,
For Sam says he found them, in the morning,
Asleep in each other's arms in the haybarn.

The sunlight streams through the afternoon
Another parable over the sloughs
And yellowing grass of the prairies.
Cold wind stirs, and the last green
Climbs to all the tips of the season, like
The last flame brightening on a wick.
Embers drop and break in sparks. Across the earth
Sleep is the overlapping of enough shadows.
In the wind outside a twig snaps
Like a lid clicking shut somewhere in the ear.
Jesus, a boy thinks as his room goes out,
Jesus, it is a disappointing shed
Where they hang your picture
And drink juice, and conjure
Your person into inferior bread —
I would speak of injustice,
I would not go again into that place.

To Christ Our Lord

The legs of the elk punctured the snow's crust
And wolves floated lightfooted on the land
Hunting Christmas elk living and frozen.
Inside, snow melted in a basin, and a woman basted
A bird held by feet and wings over a coal bed.

Snow had sealed the windows, candles lit
The Christmas meal. The Christmas grace chilled
The cooked bird, being long-winded and the room cold.
During the words a boy thought, is it fitting
To eat this creature killed on the wing?

He had killed it himself, climbing out
Alone on snowshoes in the Christmas dawn,
The fallen snow swirling and the snowfall gone,
Heard its throat scream when the shotgun shouted,
Watched it drop, and fished from the snow the dead.

He had not wanted to shoot. The sound
Of wings beating into the hushed air
Had stirred his love, and his fingers
Froze in his gloves, and he wondered,
Famishing, could he fire? Then he fired.

Now the grace praised his wicked act. At its end
The bird on the plate
Stared at his stricken appetite.
There had been nothing to do but surrender,
To kill and to eat; he ate as he had killed, with wonder.

At night on snowshoes on the drifting field
He wondered again, for whom had love stirred?
The stars glittered on the snow and nothing answered.
The Swan spread her wings, cross of the cold north,
The pattern and mirror of the acts of earth.

Burning

He lives, who last night flopped from a log
Into the creek, and all night by an ankle
Lay pinned to the flood, dead as a nail
But for the skin of the teeth of his dog.

I brought him boiled eggs and broth.
He coughed and waved his spoon
And sat up saying he would dine alone,
Being fatigue itself after that bath.

I sat outside in the sun with the dog.
Wearing a stocking on the ailing foot,
In monster crutches, he hobbled out,
And addressed the dog in bitter rage.

He told the yellow hound, his rescuer,
Its heart was bad, and it ought
Not wander by the creek at night;
If all his dogs got drowned he would be poor.

He stroked its head and disappeared in the shed
And came out with a stone mallet in his hands

And lifted that weight of many pounds
And let it fall on top of the dog's head.

I carted off the carcass, dug it deep.
Then he came too with what a thing to lug,
Or pour on a dog's grave, his thundermug,
And poured it out and went indoors to sleep.

I saw him sleepless in the pane of glass
Looking wild-eyed at sunset, then the glare
Blinded the glass — only a red square
Burning a house burning in the wilderness.

The Wolves

Last night knives flashed. LeChien cried
And chewed blood in his bed.
Vanni's whittling blade
Had found flesh easier than wood.

Vanni and I left camp on foot. In a glade
We came on a brown blossom
Great and shining on a thorned stem.
"That's the sensitive briar," I said.

"It shrinks at the touch," I added.
Soon we found buffalo. Picking
A bull grazing by itself, I began
The approach: while the shaggy head

Was turned I sprinted across the sod,
And when he swung around his gaze
I bellyflopped into the grass
And lay on my heartbeat and waited.

When he looked away again I made
Enough yardage before he wheeled
His head: I kneeled, leveled
My rifle, and we calmly waited.

It occurred to me as we waited
That in those last moments he was,
In fact, daydreaming about something else.
"He is too stupid to live," I said.

His legs shifted and the heart showed.
I fired. He looked, trotted off,
He simply looked and trotted off,
Stumbled, sat himself down, and became dead.

I looked for Vanni. Among the cows he stood,
Only his arms moving as he fired,
Loaded, fired, the dumb herd
Milling about him sniffing at their dead.

I called and he retreated.
We cut two choice tongues for ourselves
And left the surplus. All day wolves
Would splash blood from those great sides.

Again we saw the flower, brown-red
On a thorn-spiked stem. When Vanni
Reached out his fingers, it was funny,
It shrank away as if it had just died.

They told us in camp that LeChien was dead.
None of us cared. Nobody much
Had liked him. His tobacco pouch,
I noticed, was already missing from beside his bed.

Westport

From the hilltop we could overlook
The changes on the world. Behind us
Spread the forest, that half a continent away
Met our fathers on the Atlantic shore.
Before us lay a narrow belt of brush.
Everywhere beyond, shifting like an ocean,
Swell upon swell of emerald green,
The prairies of the west were blowing.

We mounted and set out, small craft
Into the green. The grasses brushed
The bellies of the horses, and under
The hooves the knotted centuries of sod
Slowed the way. Here and there the gray
Back of a wolf breached and fell, as in the grass
Their awkward voyages appeared and vanished.

Then rain lashed down in a savage squall.
All afternoon it drove us west. "It will be
A hard journey," the boy said, "and look,
We are blown like the weed." And indeed we were . . .
O wild indigo, O love-lies-bleeding,
You, prince's feather, pigweed, and bugseed,
Hold your ground as you can. We toss ahead
Of you in the wild rain, and we barely touch
The sad ambages compassed for yourselves.

When the storm abated, a red streak in the west
Lit up the raindrops on the land before us.
"Yes," I said, "it will be a hard journey . . ."
And the shining grasses were bowed toward the west
As if one craving had killed them. "But at last,"
I added, "the hardness is the thing you thank."
So out of forest we sailed onto plains,
And from the dark afternoon came a bright evening.

Now out of evening we discovered night
And heard the cries of the prairie and the moan
Of wind through the roots of its clinging flowers.

PART II

At the Reading of a Poet's Will

Item. A desk
Smelling of ink and turpentine
To anyone whose task
Is to sweat rain for a line.

Item. A sheaf
Of poems, a few lucid,
One or two brief,
To anyone who'll bid.

Item. Praise Jesus, who spent
His last cent
In the wilderness of himself in the try
For self-mastery.

Item. I built a desk,
I spent myself for a sheaf,
All else I committed I ask
That the Lord forgive.

I took Christ for my pattern,
Once he was kind to a slattern,
If I was led into mazes
Blame and praise Jesus. *Amen.*

Lilacs

The wind climbed with a laggard pace
Up the green hill. Meeting the sun there
It disappeared like hot wax
Into the ground. Down on the south slope
A dog stretched, and swaths of lilacs
Opened huge furnaces of scent.

A woman betook herself into the park,
Her dry legs crackling in darkness,
Past lilac, dog, the fierce and asleep.
Summer slopped at her knees,
She walked in the scent of herself breaking
Out of closets in the well-governed flesh.

She stopped. Blossoms climbed
And blazed in the air, the lawn slowly
Somersaulted under her. She turned back
To the narrow parlor, where tea and dry supper
Would be laid, and a spoon would arrange
The leaves on the bottom of her china dream.

A Toast to Tu Fu

To you, Tu Fu,
Because it didn't work out
When you lent
Yourself to government.
A poet isn't made to fix

Things up — only to celebrate
What's down, and in politics
As that Irishman found out
Is a lout.

To you, Tu Fu,
For fooling the crew
Who thought trial
Must make a man good;
And for, when the waters rose
Around the temple
You clung to in the flood,
While they prayed you'd
Let go with a prayer,
Having hung on like a bear.

And again to you, Tu Fu,
For gorging at the feast
Honoring your rescue,
For not mentioning virtue
In your short speech, nor praising rot,
And for having had the appetite and timing
To die of overeating on the spot.

Easter

To get to church you have to cross the river,
First breadwinner for the town, its wide
Mud-colored currents cleansing forever
The swill-making villages at its side.

The disinfected voice of the minister
For a moment is one of the clues,
But he is talking of nothing but Easter,
Dying so on the wood, He rose.

Some of us daydream of the morning news,
Some of us lament we rose at all,
A child beside me comforts her doll,
We are dying on the hard wood of the pews.

Death is everywhere, in the extensive
Sermon, the outcry of the inaudible
Prayer, the nickels, the dimes the poor give,
And outside, at last, in the gusts of April.

Upon the river, its Walden calm,
With wire hooks the little boats are fishing.
Those who can wait to get home
Line up, and lean on the railing, wishing.

Up through the mud can you see us
Waiting here for you, for hours,
Disappeared one, trapped or working loose,
Our hats like a row of flowers?

Then we crown you with an Easter fire,
And if you do not rise before dinner
When the flower show must retire,
Then drink if you must of the breadwinner.

Tomorrow when the brown water
Shall shove you senselessly on
Past smoking cities, works of disaster,
Kids playing ball, cows, unrealistic fishermen,

Toll bridges you slip under for free,
And you look back from the brown lorry
That floats your drenched flesh to sea,
May you, moved by goodbyes, be not altogether sorry

That the dream has ended. Turn
On all that happened an unwavering gaze.
It is as you thought. The living burn.
In the floating days may you discover grace.

For William Carlos Williams

When you came and you talked and you read with your
Private zest from the varicose marble
Of the podium, the lovers of literature
Paid you the tribute of their almost total
Inattention, although someone when you spoke of a pig
Did squirm, and it is only fair to report another gig-

gled. But you didn't even care. You seemed
Above remarking we were not your friends.
You hung around inside the rimmed
Circles of your heavy glasses and smiled and
So passed a lonely evening. In an hour
Of talking your honesty built you a tower.

When it was over and you sat down and the chair-
man got up and smiled and congratulated
You and shook your hand, I watched a professor
In neat bow tie and enormous tweeds, who patted
A faint praise of the sufficiently damned,
Drained spittle from his pipe, then scrammed.

For the Lost Generation

Oddities composed the sum of the news.
$E = mc^2$
Was another weird
Sign of the existence of the Jews.

And Paris! All afternoon in someone's attic
We lifted our glasses
And drank to the asses
Who ran the world and turned neurotic.

Ours was a wonderful party,
Everyone threw rice,
The fattest girls were nice,
The world was rich in wisecracks and confetti.

The War was a first wife, somebody's blunder.
Who was right, who lost,
Held nobody's interest,
The dog on top was as bad as the dog under.

Sometimes after whiskey, at the break of day,
There was a trace
Of puzzlement on a face,
Face of blue nights that kept bleaching away.

Look back on it all — the faraway cost,
Crash and sweet blues
(O Hiroshima, O Jews) —
No generation was so gay as the lost.

Alewives Pool

1

We lay on the grass and heard
The world burning on the pulse of April,
And were so shaken and stirred, so cut, we wondered
Which things will we forget
And which remember always? We rose like birds

And flew down the path to the Alewives Pool
Where herring driven by lust from the seas
Came swarming until the pond would spill,
And fell amazed — how they memorize
Love's never-studied maps and ritual.

2

A dying woman from her bed once told
The row of faces dimming in her glance,

Who came to her party at four years old,
What frills each wore, who laughed, who could not dance,
Who cried, whose hand she would not let hers hold.

The infant searches at his mother's breast
Looking for the night he was shipwrecked from —
But when he finds her milk he suddenly tastes
A brightness that scares him, and his days to come
Flood on his heart as if they were his past.

3

Grass lies as though beating under the wind.
In the trees even the birds are astonished
By the passion of their song. The mind
Can only know what the blood has accomplished
When love has consumed it in the burning pond.

Now by the trembling water let death and birth
Flow through our selves as through the April grass —
The sudden summer this air flames forth
Makes us again into its blossomers —
Stand on the pulse and love the burning earth.

Leaping Falls

And so it was I sheered,
Eccentric, into outer space,
And tracked with lost paces
The forgotten journey of a child,

Across the creaking snow,
Up the deer-trail,

Over the snowdrifted hill
Into the secret country
Where a boy once found,
Routing from ledge to ledge
In a tumult at sunrise,
The cascading of Leaping Falls.

Now the falls lay draped
Without motion or sound,
Icicles fastened in stories
To stillness and rock. At the bottom,
A heap of broken icicles
Lay dead blue on the snow.

Cold was through and through,
Noiseless. Nothing
But clouds at my nostrils
Moved. Then I uttered a word,
Simply a bleak word
Slid from my lips. Whereupon

A topmost icicle came loose
And fell, and struck another
With a bell-like sound, and
Another, and the falls
Leapt at their ledges, ringing
Down the rocks and on each other

Like an outbreak of bells
That rings and ceases.
The silence turned around
And became silence again.
Under the falls on the snow
A twigfire of icicles burned pale blue.

Promontory Moon

The moon: she shakes off her cloaks,
Her rings of mist and circle of blurred light,
And shines without chemistry or heat
Upon us. Milky blue in her influence
The sea dabbles at the tiers of rock.
Shadowy rabbits move feinting
Over the grass and paths. Tomorrow under the sun
Men and women will sprawl generating here;
But tonight rabbits ask nothing of the moon
And run in moonlight for delight alone.

Half rabbits, half rabbits' shadows,
They are like the night-roistering fairies
For whom as children we laid banquets
In the dusk, bits of bread and honey
That, exploring for in the dawn, we found
Untouched, the one trace of them being
The dew glistening on the moss
And grass, shed perhaps for sorrow that
Their luminous bodies have no appetite,
Being woven by the night of moonlight.

The sun makes the grass increase, feeding
The things it can corrupt. The moon
Holds her purer watches on the night,
Mirroring on this fairest time of day
Only the miracles of light;
And all within ourselves too straight to bend
In agonies of death and birth — as now
The blue-white water swirls at the moonbeams
And keeps on winding on the shining clew —
Dissolves at her touch and is made anew.

Across the Brown River

The Brown River, finger of a broken fist,
Moved sluggish through the woods and dust.
We made a bridge of the crashed oak, teetering
Across like monkeys taking up drinking,
Eschewing the deeps with our eyes,
For on the other side they said lay paradise.

It was a modern replica, built by the offspring of a rich
Dog-like dowager — some son-of-a-bitch
Who liked formal gardens of paths and shaven trees,
Hedges in a maze, and many elegant statues.
We noted "The Girl with Silk," a stone queen
With spread legs draped in the nick of time between.

In the afternoon we studied "The Last
Centaur Expiring," face folded on its breast,
All the segment that was a man pleading love

And fatal attraction for the brutal half.
A visitor beside us grew incensed
At miscegenation, and spoke out bitterly against.

We went our way at last, dancing across the oak
Into the woods. From the woods outside of Eden came a snake.
We found no principle of evil here except
Tweed packed with butter halted where it stepped,
Binoculars fixed on birds fleeing in the trees
The narrow eye bloated in the goggles of paradise.

Gothic Slide

Above the blue wash of the lake
Where the sun is a bright spectre,
And cars run, we discourse on culture;
Until the curtains close our modern talk
And faces in the slides revive
World-famous beauty, blent of light and grief.
Who can look on these stone figures,
The fatal innocence in these stone smiles,
And not sit there smitten, a credulous pupil?
Over the cloaked bodies and covered necks
The lips come alive, but they move alone;
How could we reply with tongues of stone?
The curtains open and our dazed eyes wreck
On the sunlight climbing like a dream
Into the darkness that had become our home.
Below, the waves return like breaths

On the shores of Chicago; sunlight weaves
In flashes over the curve of the Drive
Where the cars and cares of the earth crawl in a line.

One Generation

A girl of twenty walks with a gray-
haired man, her lover, a book of narrow verse
In his hand. In the sunset they sink
Down the slope together, tied
Into a knot of love, to be undone
Only by extremes and crying, and then
Never done again. An old man reads a newspaper
On the hill; not far off a little girl. The night
Comes over them. And I
Alone on the grass: what if I now should
Touch your face, child, mother, star first and faint in the sky?

Earth-Sparrow

The trees in clouds of November mist
Standing empty and the massive earth bare
I bent my head and leaned myself against
Interior gales and blizzards of unrest
Facing the squalor of November air

But stopped at last and skyward with shredded
Arms lifting ribbons of fingers and prayers

I caught in that beseeching of the cloud
A leafless lightning-splintered oak unshroud-
ing its wreckage in the waste of the year

To whose ultimate twig with a glide and
Dip a sparrow summitted and there burst-
ing as if the dead sap kept singing I leaned
Forward knowing nothing to lean on
Green as the grasslessness Lord of the earth.

Rain over a Continent

Rain over a continent, the train
From Washington to Washington plunged
In the sowing rain. He slept with
His nurse on the voyage, she was
Marked with transcontinental love,
She was his all-guessing heart when he died.
Raise the blind, he asked. Under
The rain the continent wheeled, his own land
Electric and blind, farmlights and cities'
Blazes — points, clusters, and chains —
Each light a memory, all of the darkness memory.

Reply to the Provinces

He writes from the provinces: it is
Shuttered and desolate there, will I please
Sit on a bench for him every so often

In the Luxembourg Gardens? So now
In the elegant autumn, to regard and guess —:

The sea-eyed children watching their sloops
Angling on the pond? Expectant in their books
The delicate young women? The would-be
Casters-off of expectation? The hands-in-hands?
The fellow shucking chestnuts for his girl?
The Algerians, Americans, English, Danes
Giving the Gardens their Parisian character?
Fountained light streaming on the wind?
Surely these and things of this kind —
Whatever is human. Also I marvel at the leaves
Yellow on the sky, and there on the grass
Where the leaves overlap, yellow, the yellow sun
Forcing a hidden glowing from the earth. So I sit
Peering like an ape on a branch, on a bench.

In the provinces he may have walked from town.
In a city of leaves he may have found her. Perhaps
Already they are lying in the leaves, amusing
Each other by pointing out all the faces in the leaves.

Near Barbizon

At first I thought some animal, wounded,
Thrashed in the brush, for the hunting horns
Had sounded last night and this morning.
No, it was only the woodgatherer
Out after lunch breaking twigs for his fire.

Others might have laid the stick across two rocks
And stomped in the middle. He raised it like a flail
And beat a boulder until the weapon broke.
We talked. It was election time, I asked
Who was he voting for. He screwed his eyes.
"If there came into your house by night
Thieves, to which would you offer your wife?"
Whacks he laid on the rock until the branch gave.
"I am too honest, *merde,* too poor to vote.
There's fuel on the forest floor still."
"What's your trade?" I inquired. "Gardener."
"So you make things bloom?" "Yes, and the pay's
Nothing." He flailed the rocks in savage, measured
Strokes. "The pay's nothing," he repeated,
Looking up without ceasing his labor, eyes
Flashing, this ignorant American, this fascist tool.

Duck-Chasing

I spied a very small brown duck
Riding the swells. "Little duck!"
I cried. It paddled away,
I paddled after it. When it dived,
Down I dived too: too smoky was the sea,
We were lost. It surfaced
In the west, I swam west
And when it dived I dived,
And we were lost and lost and lost
In the slant smoke of the sea.
When I came floating up on it

From the side, like a deadman,
And yelled suddenly, it took off,
It skimmed the swells as it ascended,
Brown wings burning and flashing
In the sun as the sea it rose over
Burned and flashed underneath it.
I did not see the little duck again.
Duck-chasing is a game like any game.
When it is over it is all over.

For Ruth

It was a surprise,
Seeing you. You were
More steadfast than I remember.
On the limestone shelf
You endured yourself
With grace.

The shock was only
When you laid in on tape
Some of my speech, to escape
Into or to live through
Later, when you could get blue —
But of course you would be lonely.

You of that fierce memory!
I saw you once remembering
A fisherman drunk as bait on a string
At the end of the bar —

Your chilled flesh went blue as a star.
A thing turns real eventually,

The touch is just the babytooth.
On your heap of bleached rock
You listen, wires in the mind play it back,
You hear the million sighs,
You cry for them, each cries
For ruth, for ruth.

In a Parlor Containing a Table

In a parlor containing a table
And three chairs, three men confided
Their inmost thoughts to one another.
I, said the first, am miserable.
I am miserable, the second said.
I think that for me the right word
Is miserable, said the third.
Well, they said, it's quarter to two.
Good night. Cheer up. Sleep well.
You too. You too. You too.

Guillaume de Lorris

His is the romance without a heroine —
Only the Rose in the Garden, far away,
Restless in shadows, longing to be plucked.
The intensity of his dream nourishing him

The hero walks the desert of this world
Toward, without swerving, *l'idéale Bien-Aimée.*

He comes into the Garden on broken feet
After many years: he discovers at last,
Unattended, the mysterious Rose.
Being old at this moment (he has walked
Half his life on the desert), he declines,
Out of pity, to take what he has just to take.

Suddenly, however, he remembers the quest —
The days of solitude, when everywhere,
It seemed, others were happy on the earth.
Old in his heart, now pale as the desert,
He looks for her. He sees her in the arms
Of young men, she is shedding tears for him.

Toward the Wilderness

Trekking the desert the man feels
The atmosphere weigh on him like a knapsack.
He knows the fix upon him of eyes
Hung from huge wings frayed at the edges
Floating dead and black in the sky.

And the Dead Sea, that will neither
Renew nor drown him, a glow rubbed
Into the sand, shimmers under the range
In which Nebo can be picked out
As the historic, tall, and bleak one.

He puts the bead of his will on the peak
And does not waver. His plan is
to look over the far side of the mount
On which Moses died looking this way,
And see the bitter land, and die of desire.

PART III

The Schoolhouse

    I find it now, the schoolhouse by the tree,
    And through the broken door, in brown light,
    I see the benches in rows, the floor he
    Paced across, the windows where the fruit
    Took the shapes of hearts, and the leaves windled
    In the fall, and winter snowed on his head.

    In this wreck of a house we were taught
    Everything we thought a man could know,
    All action, all passion, all ancient thought,
    What Socrates had got from Diotima,
    How Troilus laughed, in tears, in paradise,
    That crowns leapfrog through blood: casts of the dice.

    The door hangs from one hinge. Maybe the last
    Schoolboy simply forgot to lift the latch
    When he rushed out that spring, in his haste —
    Or maybe that same boy, now fat and rich,
    Snow-haired in his turn, and plagued by thought,
    Bulled his way back in, looking for the dead light.

2

    A man of letters once asked the local tramps
    To tea. No one came, and he read from Otway
    And Chatterton to the walls, and lived for months
    On the crumpets. They padlocked the gate when he died.
    Snow, sleet, rain, piss of tramps, until one year
    The lock snapped, the hinges rasped like roosters.

And now when the tramps, waking sheeted in frost,
Know it is time, they come here and sprawl
At the foot of the statue they think is of their host,
Which they call "His Better Self," which he had called
"Knowledge," sometimes "Death," whose one gesture
Seems to beckon and yet remains obscure,

And boil their tea on the floor and pick fruit
In the garden where he used to walk
Thinking of Eden and the fallen state,
And dust an apple as he had a book —
"Hey now Porky, gie's the core," one hollers;
"Wise up," says Pork, "they ain't gonna *be* a core."

3

I hear modern schoolchildren shine their pants
In buttock-soothing seats in steamy schools
Soaking up civics and vacant events
From innocents who sponge periodicals
And clop-clop the stuff out again in chalky gray
Across the blackboards of the modern day;

Yet they can guess why we fled our benches
Afternoons when we ourselves were just nice
Schoolkids too, who peered out through the branches
For one homely share of the centuries,
Fighting in Latin the wars of the Greeks,
Our green days, the apple we picked and picked

And that was never ours; though they would
Rake their skulls if they found out we returned

By free choice to this house of the dead,
And stand wondering what he could have learned,
His eyes great pupils and his fishhook teeth
Sunk in the apple of knowledge or death.

4

I recall a recitation in that house:
"*We are the school of Hellas* was the claim.
Maybe it was so. Anyway Hellas
Thought it wasn't, and put the school to flame.
They came back, though, and scavenged the ruins."
I think the first inkling of the lesson

Was when we watched him from the apple wrest
Something that put the notion in his brain
The earth was coming to its beautifulest
And would be like paradise again
The day he died from it. The flames went out
In their blue mantles; he waved us to the night —

And we are here, under the starlight. I
Remember he taught us the stars disperse
In wild flight, though constellated to the eye.
Now I can almost see the night in its course,
The slow sky uncoiling in exploding forms,
The stars that flee it riding free in its arms.

Seven Streams of Nevis

I

Jack the Blindman, whose violin
Through the harsh weathers of the street
Lifted a scraping bright and sweet,
Joked the gloomier bars of every tune;
But hardly a dime ever dropped there
And he cupped *faith* in the clankless air.

Connelly, one-eyed, half blind,
Finding the world blind, in full view
Like wind blew ropes and fences through.
Ticketless at the stiles of the mind
We ask his *hope:* down, and out,
To swear, "If scum swims to the top of the sauerkraut . . ."

They didn't sign up at the desk
Or queue at the bed, though they clapped
The night you bumped and shook and slapped
And ground for free your smart burlesque,
Peaches. We call it *mercy* when
You give and get nothing and give again.

Tossing in dreams young David Boyle
Could not evade the call of the Lord
For the meek life. He woke and poured
Over his heart the scalding oil
Of *temperance.* Now in his sleep
He yells aloud to God to let him sleep.

Justice made James Lynch Fitzstephen
Hang from a tree his guilty son;
His heart, twice guilty then,
Hanged itself in his skeleton.
Even Cicero would have known
The unjust who are just are just mad bone.

Natasha, who billowed like silk
On a pole of fire, and weeping went
To one who scrapes the burning tent
While he puffs Luckies and sips milk,
And came home like an empty cage
To find home yet emptier, tried *courage*.

Sir Henry, seeing that the dew
Gets burned each morning into mist,
Decided fire brings out the best
In things, and that anyone who
Cooks his eyes at the sunrise
Of the beautiful, and renders himself blind, is *wise*.

2

In darkness I climbed Ben Nevis, far from
Your lives. But the seven streams I came on
Were well foreknown. One sang like strings, one crashed
Through gated rocks, one vibrated, others
Went skipping like unbucketed oil across
Hot stones, or clattered like bones, or like milk
Spilled and billowed in streamers of bright silk:
Irises glimmering a visionary course,
Me grimping the dark, sniffing for the source;

And there I found it windless, lying still,
Dark, high-nested in the mountain, a pool
Whose shined waters on the blackened mountain
Held the black skies; and I rode out on the water
And the waves ringing through the dark were rings
Around the eye itself of the world, which,
Drawing down heaven like its black lid, was there
Where merely to be still was temperate,
Where to move was brave, where justice was a glide,
Knowledge the dissolving of the head-hung eyes;
And there my faith lay burning, there my hope
Was burning on the water, there charity
Burned like a sun. Oh give, O pool of heaven,
The locus of grace to seven who are whirled
Down the eddies and gutters of the world;
And Connelly and Jack and Peaches, Dave,
Lynch, Natalie, and Hank — seven who have
Bit on your hearts, and spat the gravels of
Tooth and heart, and bit again; who have wiped
The burst jellies of eyes on a sleeve
(The visions that could have been wrung from that cloth)
And sprouted sight like mushrooms — O seven
Streams of nothing backgazing after heaven,
In the heart's hell you have it, it is called God's Love.

The Descent

I

Nailed by our axes to the snow
We belayed. One by one we climbed.

Had somebody in the valley
Been looking up, it must have seemed
A crazed earthworm headed for paradise,
Or else, if he happened to rub his eyes

While we unroped, and to look back
When we had scattered in the race
For the crest, an ascension of crows.
I took the crest as the day broke,
Sure I was first. But Jan must have leapt
The crevasse for a shortcut: he lay there,

Blue lips apart, on the blue snow,
Sprawled on the shellbursts of his heart.
"It's time it went," he gasped. Four years
He had fought in the guerrilla wars.
Then he whispered, "Look — the sunrise!"
The same color and nearly the same size,

But behind his back, the sun
Was rising. When the moon he was
Staring at set in the mountains
He died. On the way back the ice
Had turned so perilous under the sun
There was no choice: we watched while he went down.

2

In Seekonk Woods, on Indian Hill,
It used to seem the branches made
A small green sky that gave off shade.
Once while I lay buried like a quail

In the grass and shadows, a shotgun
Banged, leaves burst, I blinked into the sunshine —

Two crows blown out from either hand
Went clattering away; a third
Thumped through the branches to the ground.
I scooped it up, splashed across the ford,
And lit out — I must have run half a day
Before I reached Holy Spring. (Anyway,

I thought it was holy. No one
Had told me heaven is overhead.
I only knew people look down
When they pray.) I held the dying bird
As though, should its heartbeat falter,
There wouldn't be any heartbeat anywhere.

After a while I touched the plumes
To the water. In the desert
By the tracks I dug a headstart
Taller than myself. I told him,
"Have a good journey. It can't be far.
It'll be well this side of China, for sure."

3

And had I faced Jan to the sun
Might not the sun have held him here?
Or did he know the day came on
Behind, not glancing back for fear
The full moon already was dragging from his bones
The blood as dear to them, and as alien,

As clothes to a scarecrow
Or flesh to a cross? Down snow,
Following streambeds through the trees,
We sledded him. To his valleys
Rivers have washed this adept of the sun
The moon pestled into earth again.

Heaven is in light, overhead,
I have it by heart. Yet the dead
Silting the darkness do not ask
For burials elsewhere than the dusk.
They lie where nothing but the moon can rise,
And make no claims, though they had promises.

Milkweed that grow beside the tombs
Climb from the dead as if in flight,
But a foot high they stop and bloom
In drab shapes, that neither give light
Nor bring up the true darkness of the dead;
Strange, homing lamps, that go out seed by seed.

4

I looked for Indian Hill at Easter.
It was bulldozed. A TV cross
Gleamed from the rooftop of a house
Like sticks of a scarecrow. Once more
I turned and ran: I stumbled on
Fields lying dark and savage and the sun

Reaping its own fire from the trees,
Whirling the faint panic of birds
Up turbulent light. Two white-haired
Crows cried under the wheeling rays;
And loosed as by a scythe, into the sky
A flight of jackdaws rose, earth-birds suddenly

Seized by some thaumaturgic thirst,
Shrill wings flung up the crow-clawed, burned,
Unappeasable air. And then one turned,
Dodged through the flock again, and burst
Eastward alone, sinking across the trees
On the world-curve of its wings. So it is,

Mirrored in duskfloods, the fisherbird
Stands in a desolate sky
Feeding at its own heart. In the cry
Eloi! Eloi! flesh was made word.
We hear it in wind catching in the branches.
In lost blood breaking a night through the bones.

Where the Track Vanishes

I

The snow revives in the apple trees;
The winter sun seeps from jonquils
Bright as goldmills on the slopes;
Le chemin montant dans les hautes herbes
Curves for the Alps and vanishes.

2

Pierre le Boiteux
— Yellow teeth
Gnashed into gum-level
Stumps, yellow
Eyes beaconing about,
A blackhead the size
Of a huckleberry
Making a cheek sag,
A leg gypsies
Cut the tendon of
So he could beg better as a child
Pumping under him,
Twelve goats at heel —
Mounts the track,
Limping through the wild
Grasses — toward where?

3

The track vanishes in a heap of stones
Mortared by weeds and wildflowers —
The fallen church. Nearby stand stones
Of the parish graves, dates worn away,
A handful of carved words visible:
Jacques et Geneviève, priez pour eux —
Véronique DuPrès, regrets éternels —
Sown here even to their fingertips.

Who was it wore the track through the grass?
Surely their mourners are dead, and theirs, and theirs.
Perhaps Pierre limps up every day

Training the goats where to come when it is time,
Foreseeing a terrible loneliness.
No one is lonely here: take Véronique — Jacques,
Husband of another, indifferently dissolves into her.
A skull or two, a couple of pelvises or knees.

4

My hand on the sky
Cannot shut the sky out
Any more than any March
Branch can. In the Boston Store
Once, I tried new shoes:
The shoeman put my feet
Into a machine, saying Kid
Wrig yer toes. I
Wrigged and peered:
Inside green shoes green
Twigs were wrigging by themselves
Green as the grasses
I drew from her
Hair in the springtime
While she laughed, unfoliaged
By sunlight, a little
Spray of bones I loved.

5

From villages lost in the valleys —
Moncharvet, St. Bon, La Jaura —
Thin braids of smoke waver upward
Through the clear air. A few lights
Come on, visible from the untracked snow

On the stairway to the Alps. Venus
Shines from the grave of the sun, like
The white gem churched again in its valley.

Once driving from Morristown at night,
We came over a crest: the Fish-Island
Breached shining under the strung-out stars
Of the Galaxy — a long way from Jacques
And Geneviève and Véronique in her prairie.
We stood there not thinking that for them
This would be a strange continent to be dying in,
This starry island under the continent of the stars —

Job's Coffin and the Scorpion; Jacques
And Geneviève side by side in the field of light;
Capricorn, Ophiocus; the Serpent embracing
The unhinged knees, St. Bon heaped
In its molted skin; Le Fourmier the arms
Of Hercules; the Swan sailing toward Planay;
Moncharvet, La Jaura by the singing Lyre;
Véronique rocked on the Balances; Champ Béranger —

Fields into which the Herdsman limps
Leading his flock up the trackless night, toward
A writhing of lights. Are they Notre Dame des Neiges
Where men ask their God for the daily bread —
Or the March-climbing Virgin carrying wheat?
Where the track vanishes the first land begins.
It goes out everywhere obliterating the horizons.
We may have been walking through it all our lives.

Freedom, New Hampshire

1

We came to visit the cow
Dying of fever,
Towle said it was already
Shoveled under, in a secret
Burial-place in the woods.
We prowled through the woods
Weeks, we never

Found where. Other
Children other summers
Must have found the place
And asked, Why is it
Green here? The rich
Guess a grave, maybe,
The poor think a pit

For dung, like the one
We shoveled in in the fall,
That came up a brighter green
The next year, that
Could as well have been
The grave of a cow
Or something, for all that shows.

2

We found a cowskull once; we thought it was
From one of the asses in the Bible, for the sun

Shone into the holes through which it had seen
Earth as an endless belt carrying gravel, had heard
Its truculence cursed, had learned how human sweat
Stinks, and had brayed — shone into the holes
With solemn and majestic light, as if some
Skull somewhere could be Baalbek or the Parthenon.

That night passing Towle's Barn
We saw lights. Towle had lassoed a calf
By its hind legs, and he tugged against the grip
Of the darkness. The cow stood by, chewing millet.
Derry and I took hold, too, and hauled.
It was sopping with darkness when it came free.
It was a bullcalf. The cow mopped it awhile,
And we walked around it with a lantern,

And it was sunburned, somehow, and beautiful.
It took a teat as the first business
And sneezed and drank at the milk of light.
When we got it balanced on its legs, it went wobbling
Toward the night. Walking home in darkness
We saw the July moon looking on Freedom, New Hampshire,
We smelled the fall in the air, it was the summer,
We thought, Oh this is but the summer!

3

Once I saw the moon
Drift into the sky like a bright
Pregnancy pared
From a goddess who had to
Keep slender to remain beautiful —

Cut loose, and drifting up there
To happen by itself—
And waning, in lost labor;

As we lost our labor
Too—afternoons
When we sat on the gate
By the pasture, under the Ledge,
Buzzing and skirling on toilet-
papered combs tunes
To the rumble-seated cars
Taking the Ossipee Road

On Sundays; for
Though dusk would come upon us
Where we sat, and though we had
Skirled out our hearts in the music,
Yet the not-yet dandruffed
Harps we skirled it on
Had done not much better than
Flies, which buzzed, when quick

We trapped them in our hands,
Which went silent when we
Crushed them, which we bore
Downhill to the meadowlark's
Nest full of throats, which
Derry charmed and combed
With an Arabian air, while I
Chucked crushed flies into

Innards I could not see,
For the night had fallen
And the crickets shrilled on all sides
In waves, as if the grassleaves
Shrieked by hillsides
As they grew, and the stars
Made small flashes in the sky,
Like mica flashing in rocks

On the chokecherried Ledge
Where bees I stepped on once
Hit us from behind like a shotgun,
And where we could see
Windowpanes in Freedom flash
And Loon Lake and Winnipesaukee
Flash in the sun
And the blue world flashing.

4

The fingerprints of our eyeballs would zigzag
On the sky; the clouds that came drifting up
Our fingernails would drift into the thin air;
In bed at night there was music if you listened,
Of an old surf breaking far away in the blood.

Children who come by chance on grass green for a man
Can guess cow, dung, man, anything they want,
To them it is the same. To us who knew him as he was
After the beginning and before the end, it is green
For a name called out of the confusions of the earth —

Winnipesaukee coined like a moon, a bullcalf
Dragged from the darkness where it breaks up again,
Larks which long since have crashed for good in the grass
To which we fed the flies, buzzing ourselves like flies,
While the crickets shrilled beyond us, in July.

The mind may sort it out and give it names —
When a man dies he dies trying to say without slurring
The abruptly decaying sounds. It is true
That only flesh dies, and spirit flowers without stop
For men, cows, dung, for all dead things; and it is good, yes —

But an incarnation is in particular flesh
And the dust that is swirled into a shape
And crumbles and is swirled again had but one shape
That was this man. When he is dead the grass
Heals what he suffered, but he remains dead,
And the few who loved him know this until they die.

For my brother, 1925–1957

The Supper After the Last

I

The desert moves out on half the horizon
Rimming the illusory water which, among islands,
Bears up the sky. The sea scumbles in
From its own inviolate border under the sky.
A dragon-fly floating on six legs on the sand
Lifts its green-yellow tail, declines its wings
A little, flutters them a little, and lays

On dazzled sand the shadow of its wings. Near shore
A bather wades through his shadow in the water.
He tramples and kicks it; it recomposes.

2

Outside the open door
Of the whitewashed house,
Framed in the doorway, a chair,
Vacant, waits in the sunshine.

A jug of fresh water stands
Inside the door. In the sunshine
The chair waits, less and less vacant.
The host's plan is to offer water, then stand aside.

3

They eat chicken, drink rosé. The chicken head
Has been tucked under the shelter of the wing.
Under the table a red-backed, passionate dog
Cracks chicken bones on the blood and gravel floor.

No one else but the dog and the blind
Cat watching it knows who is that bearded
Wild man guzzling overhead, the wreck of passion
Emptying his eyes, who has not yet smiled,

Who stares at the company, where he is company,
Turns them to sacks of appalled, grinning skin,
Forks the fowl-eye out from under
The large, makeshift, cooked lid, evaporates the wine,

Jellies the sunlit table and spoons, floats
The deluxe grub down the intestines of the Styx,
Devours all but the cat, to whom he slips scraps, and the dog,
The red-backed accomplice busy grinding gristle.

4

When the bones of the host
Crack in the hound's jaw
The wild man rises. Opening
His palms he announces:
I came not to astonish
But to destroy you. Your
Jug of cool water? Your
Hanker after wings? Your
Lech for transcendence?
I came to prove you are
Intricate and simple things
As you are, created
In the image of nothing,
Taught of the creator
By your images in dirt —
As mine, for which you set
A chair in the sunshine,
Mocking me with water!
As pictures of wings,
Not even iridescent,
That clasp the sand
And that cannot perish, you swear,
Having once been evoked!

5

The witnesses back off; the scene begins to float in water.
Far out in that mirage the Savior sits whispering to the world,
Becoming a mirage. The dog turns into a smear on the sand.
The cat grows taller and taller as it flees into space.

From the hot shine where he sits his whispering drifts:
You struggle from flesh into wings; the change exists.
But the wings that live gripping the contours of the dirt
Are all at once nothing, flesh and light lifted away.

You are the flesh; I am the resurrection, because I am the light.
I cut to your measure the creeping piece of darkness
That haunts you everywhere under the sun. Step into light —
I make you over. I breed the shape of your grave in the dirt.

PART IV

The Avenue Bearing the Initial of Christ into the New World

Was diese kleine Gasse doch für ein Reich an sich war . . .

I

  pcheek pcheek pcheek pcheek pcheek
  They cry. The motherbirds thieve the air
  To appease them. A tug on the East River
  Blasts the bass-note of its passage, lifted
  From the infra-bass of the sea. A broom
  Swishes over the sidewalk like feet through leaves.
  Valerio's pushcart Ice Coal Kerosene
  Moves   clack

              clack

                    clack
  On a broken wheelrim. Ringing in its chains
  The New Star Laundry horse comes down the street
  Like a roof leak whucking into a pail.
  At the redlight, where a horn blares,
  The Golden Harvest Bakery brakes on its gears,
  Squeaks, and seethes in place. A propane-
  gassed bus makes its way with big, airy sighs.

  Across the street a woman throws open
  Her window.
  She sets, terribly softly,
  Two potted plants on the windowledge
              tic   tic
  And bangs shut her window.

A man leaves a doorway tic toc tic toc tic toc tic hurrah toc splat
    on Avenue C tic etc and turns the corner.
Banking the same corner
A pigeon coasts 5th Street in shadows,
Looks for altitude, surmounts the rims of buildings,
And turns white.

The babybirds pipe down. It is day.

2

In sunlight on the Avenue
The Jew rocks along in a black fur shtraimel,
Black robe, black knickers, black knee-stockings,
Black shoes. His beard like a sod-bottom
Hides the place where he wears no tie.
A dozen children troop after him, barbels flying,
In skullcaps. They are Reuben, Simeon, Levi, Judah, Issachar,
    Zebulun, Benjamin, Dan, Naphtali, Gad, Asher.
With the help of the Lord they will one day become
Courtiers, thugs, rulers, rabbis, asses, adders, wrestlers, bakers,
    poets, cartpushers, infantrymen.

The old man is sad-faced. He is near burial
And one son is missing. The women who bore him sons
And are past bearing mourn for the son
And for the father, wondering if the man will go down
Into the grave of a son mourning, or if at the last
The son will put his hands on the eyes of his father.

The old man wades toward his last hour.
On 5th Street, between Avenues A and B,

In sunshine, in his private cloud, Bunko Certified Embalmer,
Cigar in his mouth, nose to the wind, leans
At the doorway of Bunko's Funeral Home & Parlour,
Glancing west toward the Ukrainians, eastward idly
Where the Jew rocks toward his last hour.

Sons, grandsons at his heel, the old man
Confronts the sun. He does not feel its rays
Through his beard, he does not understand
Fruits and vegetables live by the sun.
Like his children he is sallow-faced, he sees
A blinding signal in the sky, he smiles.

Bury me not Bunko damned Catholic I pray you in Egypt.

3

From the Station House
Under demolishment on Houston
To the Power Station on 14th,
Jews, blacks, Puerto Ricans
Walk in the spring sunlight.

The Downtown Talmud Torah
Blosztein's Cutrate Bakery
Areceba Panataria Hispano
Peanuts Dried Fruit Nuts & Canned Goods
Productos Tropicales
Appetizing Herring Candies Nuts
Nathan Kugler Chicken Store Fresh Killed Daily
Little Rose Restaurant

Rubinstein the Hatter Mens Boys Hats Caps Furnishings
J. Herrmann Dealer in All Kinds of Bottles
Natural Bloom Cigars
Blony Bubblegum
Mueren las Cucarachas Super Potente Garantizada de Matar las
   Cucarachas mas Resistentes
Wenig **מצבות**
G. Schnee Stairbuilder
Everyouth la Original Loción Eterna Juventud Satisfacción Dinero
   Devuelto
Happy Days Bar & Grill

Through dust-stained windows over storefronts,
Curtains drawn aside, onto the Avenue
Thronged with Puerto Ricans, blacks, Jews,
Baby carriages stuffed with groceries and babies,
The old women peer, blessed damozels
Sitting up there young forever in the cockroached rooms,
Eating fresh-killed chicken, productos tropicales,
Appetizing herring, canned goods, nuts;
They puff out smoke from Natural Bloom Cigars
And one day they puff like Blony Bubblegum.

From a rooftop a boy fishes at the sky,
Around him a flock of pigeons fountains,
Blown down and swirling up again, seeking the sky.
A red kite wriggles like a tadpole
Into the sky beyond them, crosses
The sun, lays bare its own crossed skeleton.
To fly from this place — to roll

On some bubbly blacktop in the summer,
To run under a rain of pigeon plumes, to be
Tarred, and feathered with birdshit, Icarus,

In Kugler's glass headdown dangling by yellow legs.

4

First Sun Day of the year. Tonight,
When the sun will have turned from the earth,
She will appear outside Hy's Luncheonette,
The crone who sells the *News* and the *Mirror,*
The oldest living thing on Avenue C,
Outdating much of its brick and mortar.
If you ask for the *News* she gives you the *Mirror*
And squints long at the nickel in her hand
Despising it, perhaps, for being a nickel,
And stuffs it in her apron pocket
And sucks her lips. Rain or stars, every night
She is there, squatting on the orange crate,
Issuing out only in darkness, like the cucarachas
And dread nightmares in the chambers overhead.
She can't tell one newspaper from another,
She has forgotten how Nain her dead husband looked,
She has forgotten her children's whereabouts,
Or how many there were, or what the *News*
And *Mirror* tell about that we buy them with nickels.
She is sure only of the look of the nickel
And that there is a Lord in the sky overhead.
She dwells in a flesh that is of the Lord
And drifts out, therefore, only in darkness,
Like the streetlamp outside the Luncheonette

Or the lights in the secret chamber
In the firmament, where Yahweh himself dwells.

Like Magdalene in the Battistero of Saint John
On the carved-up continent, in the land of sun,
She lives shadowed, under a feeble bulb
That lights her face, her crab's hands, her small bulk on the crate.

She is Pulchería mother of murderers and madmen,
She is also Alyona whose neck was a chicken leg.

Mother was it the insufferable wind?
She sucks her lips a little further into the mousehole.
She stares among the stars, and among the streetlamps.

The mystery is hers.

5

That violent song of the twilight!
Now, in the silence, will the motherbirds
Be dead, and the infantbirds
That were in the dawn merely transparent
Unfinished things, nothing but bellies,
Will they have been shoved out
And in the course of a morning, casually,
On scrawny wings, have taken up the life?

6

In the pushcart market, on Sunday,
A crate of lemons discharges light like a battery.
Icicle-shaped carrots that through black soil

Wove away lie like flames in the sun.
Onions with their shirts ripped seek sunlight
On green skins. The sun beats
On beets dirty as boulders in cowfields,
On turnips pinched and gibbous
From budging rocks, on embery sweets,
On Idahos, Long Islands, and Maines,
On horseradishes still growing weeds on the flat ends,
On cabbages lying about like sea-green brains
The skulls have been shucked from,
On tomatoes, undented plum-tomatoes, alligator-skinned
Cucumbers, that float pickled
In the wooden tubs of green skim milk —

Sky-flowers, dirt-flowers, underdirt-flowers,
Those that climbed for the sun in their lives
And those that wormed away — equally uprooted,
Maimed, lopped, shucked, and misaimed.

In the market in Damascus a goat
Came to a stall where twelve goatheads
Were lined up for sale. It sniffed them
One by one. Finally thirteen goats started
Smiling in their faintly sardonic way.

A crone buys a pickle from a crone,
It is wrapped in the *Mirror,*
At home she will open the wrapping, stained,
And stare and stare and stare at it.

And the cucumbers, and the melons,
And the leeks, and the onions, and the garlic.

7

Already the Avenue troughs the light of day.
Southwards, toward Houston and Pitt,
Where Avenue C begins, the eastern ranges
Of the wiped-out lives — punks, lushes,
Panhandlers, pushers, rumsoaks, all those
Who took it easy when they should have been out failing
        at something —
The pots-and-pans man pushes his cart,
Through the intersection of the light, at 3rd,
Where sunset smashes on the aluminum of it,
On the bottoms, curves, handles, metal panes,
Mirrors: of the bead curtained cave under the falls
In Freedom, Seekonk Woods leafing the light out,
Halfway to Kingston where a road branched out suddenly,
Between Pamplonne and Les Salins two meeting paths
Over a sea the green of churchsteeple copper.

Of all places on earth inhabited by men
Why is it we find ourselves on this Avenue
Where the dusk gets worse,
And the mirrorman pushing his heaped mirrors
Into the shadows between 3rd and 2nd
Pushes away a mess of old pots and pans?

The ancient black man sits as usual
Outside the Happy Days Bar & Grill. He wears

Dark glasses. Every once in a while, abruptly,
He starts to sing, chanting in a hoarse, nearly breaking
Voice —

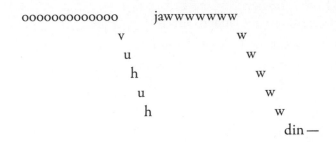

And becomes silent
       Stares into the polaroid Wilderness
Gross-Rosen, Maidanek, Flössenberg, Ravensbruck, Stutthof, Riga,
Bergen-Belsen, Mauthausen, Birkenau, Treblinka, Natzweiler,
Dachau, Buchenwald, Auschwitz —
                         Villages,
Pasture-bordered hamlets on the far side of the river.

8

The promise was broken too freely
To them and to their fathers, for them to care.
They survive like cedars on a cliff, roots
Hooked in any crevice they can find.
They walk Avenue C in shadows
Neither conciliating its Baalim
Nor whoring after landscapes of the senses,
Tarig bab el Amoud being in the blood
Fumigated by Puerto Rican cooking.

Among women girthed like cedar trees
Other, slenderer ones appear:
One yellow-haired, in August,
Under shooting stars on the lake, who
Believed in promises that broke by themselves —
In a German flower garden in the Bronx
The wedding of a child and a child, one flesh
Divided in the Adirondack spring —
One who found in the desert city of the West
The first happiness, and fled therefore —
And by a southern sea, in the pines, one loved
Until the mist rose blue in the trees
Around the spiderwebs that kept on shining,
Each day of the shortening summer.

And as rubbish burns
And the pushcarts are loaded
With fruits and vegetables and empty crates
And clank away on iron wheels over cobblestones,
And merchants infold their stores
And the carp ride motionlessly sleeplessly
In the dark tank in the fishmarket,
The figures withdraw into chambers overhead —
In the city of the mind, chambers built
Of care and necessity, where, hands lifted to the blinds,
They glimpse in mirrors backed by the blackness of the world
Awkward, cherished rooms containing the familiar selves.

9

Children set fires in ashbarrels,
Cats prowl the fires, scraps of fishes burn.

A child lay in the flames,
It was not the plan. Abraham
Stood in terror at the duplicity.
Isaac whom he loved lay in the flames.
The Lord turned away washing
His hands without soap and water
Like a common housefly.
The children laugh.
Isaac means *he laughs.*
Maybe the last instant,
The dying itself, *is* easier,
Easier anyway than the hike
From Pitt the blind gut
To the East River of Fishes,
Maybe it is as the poet said,
And the soul turns to thee
O vast and well-veiled Death
And the body gratefully nestles close to thee —

I think of Isaac reading Whitman in Chicago,
The week before he died, coming across
Such a passage and muttering, Oi!
What shit! And smiling, but not for you — I mean,

For *thee,* Sane and Sacred Death!

It was Gold's junkhouse, the one the clacking
Carts that little men pad after in harnesses
Picking up bedbugged mattresses, springs
The stubbornness has been loved out of,
Chairs felled by fat, lampshades lights have burned through,
Linolcum the geometry has been scuffed from,
Carriages a single woman's work has brought to wreck,
Would come to in the dusk and unload before,
That the whole neighborhood came out to see
Burning in the night, flames opening out like
Eyelashes from the windows, men firing the tears in,
Searchlights smashing against the brick,
The water blooming up the walls
Like pale trees, reaching into the darkness beyond.

Nobody mourned, nobody stood around in pajamas
And a borrowed coat steaming his nose in coffee
It was only Gold's junkhouse.
                                    But this evening
The neighborhood comes out again, everything
That may abide the fire was made to go through the fire
And it was made clean: a few twisted springs,
Charred mattresses (crawling still, naturally),
Perambulator skeletons, bicycles tied in knots —
In a great black pile at the junkhouse door,
Smelling of burnt rubber and hair. Rustwater
Hangs in icicles over the windows and door,
Like frozen piss aimed at trespassers,
Combed by wind, set overnight. Carriages we were babies in,
Springs that used to resist love, that gave in

And were thrown out like whores — the black
Irreducible heap, mausoleum of what we were —
It is cold suddenly, we feel chilled,
Nobody knows for sure what is left of him.

II

The fishmarket closed, the fishes gone into flesh.
The smelts draped on each other, fat with roe,
The marble cod hacked into chunks on the counter,
Butterfishes mouths still open, still trying to eat,
Porgies with receding jaws hinged apart
In a grimace of dejection, as if like cows
They had died under the sledgehammer, perches
In grass-green armor, spotted squeteagues
In the melting ice meek-faced and croaking no more,
Mud-eating mullets buried in crushed ice,
Tilefishes with scales like bits of chickenfat,
Spanish mackerels with buttercups on the flanks,
Pot-bellied pikes, two-tone flounders
After the long contortion of pushing both eyes
To the brown side that they might look up,
Lying brown side down, like a mass laying-on of hands,
Or the oath-taking of an army.

The only things alive are the carp
That drift in the black tank in the rear,
Kept living for the usual reason, that they have not died,
And perhaps because the last meal was garbage and they might
    begin smelling
On dying, before the customer got halfway home.

They nudge each other, to be netted,
The sweet flesh to be lifted thrashing into the air,
To be slugged, and then to keep on living
While they are opened on the counter.

Fishes do not die exactly, it is more
That they go out of themselves, the visible part
Remains the same, there is little pallor,
Only the cataracted eyes that have not shut ever
Must look through the mist that crazed Homer.

These are the vegetables of the deep,
The Sheol-flowers of darkness, swimmers
Of denser darknesses where the sun's rays bend for the last time
And in the sky there burns this shifty jellyfish
That degenerates and flashes and re-forms.

Fishes are nailed to the wood,
The fishmonger stands like Christ, nailing them to the wood,
He scrapes the knife up the grain, the scales fly,
He unnails them, reverses them, nails them again,
Scrapes and the scales fly. He lops off the heads,
Shakes out the guts as if they did not belong in the first place,
And they are flesh for the first time in their lives.

Dear Frau _____:
    Your husband, _____, died in the Camp Hospital on
_____. May I express my sincere sympathy on your bereavement.
_____ was admitted to the Hospital on _____ with severe
symptoms of exhaustion, complaining of difficulties in breathing

and pains in the chest. Despite competent medication and devoted medical attention, it proved impossible, unfortunately, to keep the patient alive. The deceased voiced no final requests.

Camp Commandant, _____

On 5th Street Bunko Certified Embalmer Catholic
Leans in his doorway drawing on a Natural Bloom Cigar.
He looks up the street. Even the Puerto Ricans are Jews
And the Chinese Laundry closes on Saturday.

12

Next door, outside the pink-fronted Bodega Hispano —

(A crying: you imagine
Some baby in its crib, wailing
As if it could foresee everything.
The crying subsides: you imagine
A mother or father clasping
The damned creature in their arms.
It breaks out again, this
Time in a hair-raising shriek — so,
The alleycat, in a pleasant guise,
In the darkness outside, in the alley,
Wauling slowly in its blood.

Another, loftier shrieking
Drowns it out. It begins always
On the high note, over a clang of bells:
Hook & Ladder 11 with an explosion of mufflers
Crab-walking out of 5th Street,
Accelerating up the Avenue, siren

Sliding on the rounded distances,
Returning fainter and fainter,
Like a bee looping away from where you lie in the grass.

The searchlights catch him at the topfloor window,
Trying to move, nailed in place by the shine.

The bells of Saint Brigid's
On Tompkins Square
Toll for someone who has died —
J'oïs la cloche de Serbonne,
Qui toujours à neuf heures sonne
Le Salut que l'Ange prédit . . .

Expecting the visitation
You lie back on your bed,
The sounds outside
Must be outside. Here
Are only the dead spirituals
Turning back into prayers —
You rise on an elbow
To make sure they come from outside,
You hear nothing, you lay down
Your head on the pillow
Like a pick-up arm —
    swing low
        swing low
            sweet
   lowsweet —)
— Carols of the Caribbean, plinkings of guitars.

13

The garbage-disposal truck
Like a huge hunched animal
That sucks in garbage in the place
Where other animals evacuate it
Whines, as the cylinder in the rear
Threshes up the trash and garbage,
Where two men in rubber suits
(It must be raining outside)
Heap it in. The groaning motor
Rises to a whine as it grinds in
The garbage, and between-times
Groans. It whines and groans again.
All about it as it moves down
5th Street is the clatter of trashcans,
The crashes of them as the sanitary engineers
Bounce them on the sidewalk.

If it is raining outside
You can only tell by looking
In puddles, under the lifted streetlamps.

It would be the spring rain.

14

Behind the Power Station on 14th, the held breath
Of light, as God is a held breath, withheld,
Spreads the East River, into which fishes leak:
The brown sink or dissolve,
The white float out in shoals and armadas,
Even the gulls pass them up, pale

Bloated socks of riverwater and rotted seed
That swirl on the tide, punched back
To the Hell Gate narrows, and on the ebb
Steam seaward, seeding the sea.

On the Avenue, through air tinted crimson
By neon over the bars, the rain is falling.
You stood once on Houston, among panhandlers and winos
Who weave the eastern ranges, learning to be free,
To not care, to be knocked flat and to get up clear-headed
Spitting the curses out. "Now be nice,"
The proprietor threatens; "Be nice," he cajoles.
"Fuck you," the bum shouts as he is hoisted again,
"God fuck your mother." (In the empty doorway,
Hunched on the empty crate, the crone gives no sign.)

That night a wildcat cab whined crosstown on 7th.
You knew even the traffic lights were made by God,
The red splashes growing dimmer the farther away
You looked, and away up at 14th, a few green stars;
And without sequence, and nearly all at once,
The red lights blinked into green,
And just before there was one complete Avenue of green,
The little green stars in the distance blinked.

It is night, and raining. You look down
Toward Houston in the rain, the living streets,
Where instants of transcendence
Drift in oceans of loathing and fear, like lanternfishes,
Or phosphorous flashings in the sea, or the feverish light
Skin is said to give off when the swimmer drowns at night.

From the blind gut Pitt to the East River of Fishes
The Avenue cobbles a swath through the discolored air,
A roadway of refuse from the teeming shores and ghettos
And the Caribbean Paradise, into the new ghetto and new paradise,
This God-forsaken Avenue bearing the initial of Christ
Through the haste and carelessness of the ages,
The sea standing in heaps, which keeps on collapsing,
Where the drowned suffer a C-change,
And remain the common poor.

Since Providence, for the realization of some unknown purpose, has
seen fit to leave this dangerous people on the face of the earth and
did not destroy it . . .

Listen! the swish of the blood,
The sirens down the bloodpaths of the night,
Bone tapping on the bone, nerve-nets
Singing under the breath of sleep —

We scattered over the lonely seaways,
Over the lonely deserts did we run,
In dark lanes and alleys we did hide ourselves . . .

The heart beats without windows in its night,
The lungs put out the light of the world as they
Heave and collapse, the brain turns and rattles
In its own black axlegrease —

                    In the nighttime
Of the blood they are laughing and saying,
Our little lane, what a kingdom it was!
                         oi weih, oi weih

Flower Herding on
Mount Monadnock

1964

PART I

The River That Is East

1

     Buoys begin clanging like churches
     And peter out. Sunk to the gunwales
     In their shapes, tugs push upstream.
     A carfloat booms down, sweeping past
     Illusory suns that blaze in puddles
     On the shores where it rained, past the Navy Yard,
     Under the Williamsburg Bridge
     That hangs facedown from its strings
     Over which the Jamaica Local crawls,
     Through white-winged gulls which shriek
     And flap from the water and sideslip in
     Over a chaos of illusions, dangling
     Limp red hands, and screaming as they touch.

2

     A boy swings his legs from the pier,
     His days go by. Tugs and carfloats go by,
     Each prow pushing a whitecap. On his deathbed
     Kane remembered the abrupt, missed Grail
     Called Rosebud, Gatsby may have flashed back
     To his days digging clams in Little Girl Bay
     In Minnesota, Nick fished in dreamy Michigan,
     Gant had his memories, Griffiths, those
     Who went baying after the immaterial
     And whiffed its strange dazzle in a blonde
     In a canary convertible, who died
     Thinking of the Huck Finns of themselves
     On the old afternoons, themselves like this boy

Swinging his legs, who sees the *Ile de France*
Come in, and wonders if in some stateroom
There is not a sick-hearted heiress sitting
Drink in hand, saying to herself his name.

3

A man stands on the pier.
He has long since stopped wishing his heart were full
Or his life dear to him.
He watches the snowfall hitting the dirty water.
He thinks: Beautiful. Beautiful.
If I were a gull I would be one with white wings,
I would fly out over the water, explode, and
Be beautiful snow hitting the dirty water.

4

And thou, River of Tomorrow, flowing . . .
We stand on the shore, which is mist beneath us,
And regard the onflowing river. Sometimes
It seems the river stops and the shore
Flows into the past. What is this river
But the one that drags the things we love,
Processions of debris like floating lamps
Toward the radiance in which they go out?
No, it is the River that is East, known once
From a high window in Brooklyn, in agony — river
On which a door locked to the water floats,
A window sash paned with brown water, a whisky crate,
Barrel staves, sun spokes, feathers of the birds,
A breadcrust, a rat, spittle, butts, and peels,
The immaculate stream, heavy, and swinging home again.

The Homecoming of Emma Lazarus

1

Having no father anymore, having got up
In England without hope, having sailed the strewn
Atlantic and been driven under Bedloe
In the night, where the Green Lady lifts
Over that slow, bleating, tragic harbor

Her burning hand, Emma came floating home,
To the thick, empty whistling of the tugs.
Thoreau's pocket compass had been her keepsake,
She made her way in without it, through the fog.
It was hard for her, coming in to die,

A little unfair, her father having died already.
In the attic on Union Square? Thrown out? Ah,
Somewhere in the mess of things! From Governor's Island
A bugler's loneliest notes roll slowly in
And birds rock in the fog on the slapping waves.

2

As a child she had chased a butterfly
Through Battery Park, possibly the only one
In Manhattan that afternoon, its wind-thin
Wings making cathedral windows in the sun,

While the despised grandmother
With the gleety leashes, cruddy with age,
Of her eyebeams, held on. Her doughy
Ears, too, must have been golden in the sun.

It was toward you, gilded in the day's going down,
Green Lady, that we crawled — but from what ground of nausea
Had we turned, what relinquished plot of earth
Had we reviled, which was, anyway, the earth?

3

Dark-haired, ephebic Emma, she knew
The night she floated into New York Harbor
That Atlantis had sunk while she was abroad,
She could see its rainbows shining queerly
The many thousand leagues of her life away —

Weekends on Union Square, from her father's shaving mug
She blew bubbles crawling with colors that buoyed
Into the sunshine, she made up rhymes,
She skipped rope, she sat on his knee as he put
Lilacs in her hair. Everybody loved her!

And on the last ride across 14th,
Did the English success suddenly become nothing,
Did the American childhood, including its lasting affliction,
A longing to be English, turn out to be
The paradise she died longing for?

4

Facing the Old World the Green Lady whispers, "Eden!"
Seeing her looking so trim in her American verdigris
They thought she was saying how it was here.
Seeing her gazing out to sea we read it as pure nostalgia.
Vacuumed in the wind from the Dry Cleaning Store
She may, herself, have wondered which she meant.

She crouches on the floor. She read once,
In the paper, a poem she had composed herself.
Was it just poetry, all that? It was pretty,
There is nothing she can do about it, it really was.
Her arm lies along the bench, her hand
Hangs over the edge as if she has just let something drop.

She has wept a long time now, and now poetry
Can do no more to her. Her shoulder shrugs as though
To drive away birds which probably weren't intending
To alight. In the Harbor the conscript bugler
Blows the old vow of acceptance into the night —
It fades, and the wounds of all we had accepted open.

Old Arrivals

Molded in verdigris
Shortly before she died
The Lady stands by herself,
Her electrical hand on fire.

They too in the Harbor
That chops the light to pieces
Looked up at her hand, burning,
Hair, flesh, blood, bone.

They floated in at night
On black water, cargoes
Which may not go back, waves
Breaking the rocks they break on.

Hunger unto Death

Her underarms
Clean as washbasins,
Her folds of fat resting
On layers of talcum-powdered flesh,
She proceeds towards cream-cheese-on-white,
Jelly pie, gum brownies, chocolate bars,
Rinsed down by tumblers of fresh milk,

Past the Trinity Graveyard
Filled with green, creepy plants,
Shiny-necked birds waddling about,
Monuments three-humped like children playing ghost,
Blackstone slabs racked with dates and elegies,

At which,
In the dark of the wide skirt,
First left then right,
Like a political campaigner pulling out of a station,
Her heavy rear rolls out its half-smiles of farewell,

While the face wheezes for grub,
And sweat skips and splashes from hummock down to hummock,
And inconceivable love clasps the fat of life to its pain.

Calcutta Visits

Overhead the fan wobbles on its axle.
In Delhi, on Gandhi's tomb, it said *Hai Ram* ("an old cry").
On Sudden Street they call, "Hey Johnny,
Nice girl? Chinese, Indian, European, Mixed?"
She taps a foot, finicks with phonograph needles,
Fools with buttons. "No like dance,"
She announces, collapsing on the carpet.
The bird will leave this branch at dawn
And fly away. For one full day remember her.

From this blue window? this blue, zigzagging street?
"*Five? Five* already? Ah, den, come morning . . ."
A man in white skids toward your knees,
"A morsel! A morsel!" The only city
In the world where the beggars have read Dickens,
Says the Oxford Indian of his first homecoming,
As he sits up there in the Grand Hotel,
Among bribed, sleepy bellhops, drinking himself blind,
While the fan prowls the ceiling as in a zoo.

Floodtime. Cabs practically floating through town.
The driver sizes me up in the rearview mirror
With black, mystical eyes: how exactly
To soak me . . . A Bengal poet, disciple of Tagore,
His tongue flickering through his talk like a serpent's,
Looks from his window on the city. He says
Each day he has to transcend its pain anew.
His face darkens in the light from the window.
It is his pain, by the love that asks no way out.

Doppelgänger

1

I have to bribe the policeman
To keep him from arresting the driver
For trying to make me overpay him, which I've just done.

A sailor staggers up,
All his money blown on thieves he cries,
I pay him and he goes off hunting more thieves.

The fan whips up the heat,
The ice turns to slush
Before you can throw it into your whisky.

2

I remember at daybreak,
The air on the point of cooling
Was just starting to heat up,

I heard a voice in the distance,
I looked up, far away,
There at the beginning of the world

I could make out a beggar,
Down the long street he was calling *Galway!*
I started toward him and began calling *Galway!*

To a Child in Calcutta

Dark child in my arms, eyes
The whites of them just like mine
Gazing with black, shined canniness
At mine like blue-green agates,

Whom I held as a passerby
A few stricken days down Bandook Gulli,
While they were singing, upstairs,
Everyone in Calcutta is knocking at my door,

You are my conqueror! and you were
Calmly taking in my colored eyes and
Skin burned and thin and
Browned hardly at all by your Bengal sun:

If they show you, when you reach my age,
The blown-up snapshot they took of the stranger
Holding all you once were in his arms,
What will you be able to think, then,

Of the one who came from some elsewhere
And took you in his arms
And let you know the touch of a stranger
And the old warmth in a paw from nowhere,

But that in his nowhere
He will be dying, letting go his hold

On all for which his heart tore itself
As when they snapped you in his arms like his child,

And going by the photograph
That there was this man, his hair in his eyes,
His hand bigger than your whole head,
Who held you when helplessly

You let him, that between him and you
Were this gesture and this allowance
And he is your stranger father
And he dies in a strange land, which is his own.

In Calcutta, I thought,
Every pimp, taxidriver, whore, and beggar,
Dowsed for me through the alleys day and night —
In Bandook Gulli I came upon you,

On a street crossed by fading songs
I held you in my arms
Until you slept, in these arms,
In rags, in the pain of a little flesh.

Kyoto Prints

I

In the green air
Of before the dawn
The gutturals of the prayer
Pile up in formal hiccups.

2

The lake
Every point on whose shore
Remains out of sight of some other point
Is drawn from the kokorai,
A character drawn from the heart.
In it is a flaw called the Pure Land.

3

Miko pick their way past
A phallic, thousand-year-
Old gravestone
With chalk faces, on big shoes,
Pucka pucka pucka pucka

4

After the Ceremony of Kō
The girl draws out the coals
And pokes nine vents in the clay
To let out the fire smell.

5

Tied to a few leaves
Attached loosely to the air
In the garden of moss and pine
An old eye with a spider in it
No longer troubles to look out,
A common disease of the eye.
(It has a pretty name:
I-Saw-the-Ghost-of-a-Flower.)

Koisimi Buddhist of Altitudes

He sees a skinny waterfall hanging
Like a bare root, a shape seeking water
Down which the particles of water crawl,
And climbs, crawling up the shined
Rock rubbing his fingerprints off,
And looks from the top at the land, as it was,
Clawed from within, perfectly unbroken.
In the glare, he waits, he hears
On the horizon the whine of wind
Machining its way to where he is.
The eddies begin picking up speed,
Sunlight and rock are circling
Around him, lose hold, skid
Some degrees, appear to recover,
And now skid all the way out, and vanish.
What is this wind? Koisimi challenges.
It is not I, he knows, and leans
In any direction, which is the way.

Last Spring

I

Through a dark winter
In a cold chambre de bonne
I lay still and dreamed

And as we lose our grip
On the things of the world
Settling for their glitter

It was of the things
Whose corpses outlive them,
Shellfishes, ostriches, elephants.

2

But in spring the sun's
Swath of reality started going over
The room daily, like a cleaning woman,

It sent up my keepsakes,
My inventions in dust,
It left me only my solitude

And time to walk
Head bobbing out front like a pigeon's
Knocking on the instants to let me in.

Room of Return

Room over the Hudson
Where a naked light bulb
Lights coat hangers, whisky bottles,
Umbrellas, anti-war tracts, poems,
A potted plant trimmed to a crucifixion,

From which, out the front window,
It is possible to watch
The *Vulcania* or the *France*
Or a fat *Queen*
Steaming through the buildings across the street,

To which every night
The alleycat sneaks up
To slop his saucer
Of fresh cream on the fire escape,
Washing down his rat,

Room crossed by wind from
Air conditioners' back ends,
By the clicking at all hours of invisible looms,
By cries of the night-market, hoofbeats, horns,
By bleats of lost boats on the Hudson,

Room
Where I switch the light on,
Tiny glimmer again in this city
Among all the others after an absence of years.

For Denise Levertov

Denise when you recited
With your intense unmusical voice
Poems on the objects of faith,
Buildings, rocks, birds, oranges,
A bum stood outside on Bleecker

Looking in through the glass
At you sitting in your green robe
Facing the Old World longhand
Repository of your utter, gently uttered
Solitude. Had you glanced up,
Had you seen his liquored eye,
The mowed cornfield of his gawk,
Maybe you would have paused
And seen him eye to eye,
And then gone on, in a room
Of cigarette smoke and coffee smells
And faithful friends, the hapless
Witness crying again in your breast.

Under the Williamsburg Bridge

I broke bread
At the riverbank,
I saw the black gull
Fly back black and crossed
By the decaying Paragon sign in Queens
Over ripped water, it screamed
Killing the ceremony of the dove,
Its wing muscles
Pulling apart my bones.

Tomorrow,
On the bridge,
In some riveted cranny in the sky,
The great and wondrous sun will be shining
On a spider wrapping its fly in spittle-strings.

For Robert Frost

I

Why do you talk so much
Robert Frost? One day
I drove up to Ripton to ask,

I stayed the whole day
And never got the chance
To put the question.

I drove off at dusk
Worn out and aching
In both ears. Robert Frost,

Were you shy as a boy?
Do you go on making up
For some long period of solitude?

Is it that talk
Doesn't have to be metered and rhymed?
Is talk distracting from something worse?

2

I saw you once on the TV,
Unsteady at the lectern,
The flimsy white leaf
Of hair standing straight up
In the wind, among top hats,
Old farmer and son

Of worse winters than this,
Stopped in the first dazzle

Of the District of Columbia,
Suddenly having to pay
For the cheap onionskin,
The worn-out ribbon, the eyes
Wrecked from writing poems
For us — stopped,
Lonely before millions,
The paper jumping in your grip,

And as the Presidents
Also on the platform
Began flashing nervously
Their Presidential smiles
For the harmless old guy,
And poets watching on the TV
Started thinking, Well that's
The end of *that* tradition,

And the managers of the event
Said, Boys this is it,
This sonofabitch poet
Is gonna croak,
Putting the paper aside
You drew forth
From your great faithful heart
The poem.

3

Once, walking in winter in Vermont,
In the snow, I followed a set of footprints
That aimed for the woods. At the verge
I could make out, "far in the pillared dark,"
An old creature in a huge, clumsy overcoat,
Lifting his great boots through the drifts,
Going as if to die among "those dark trees"
Of his own country. I watched him go,

Past a house, quiet, warm and light,
A farm, a countryside, a woodpile in its slow
Smokeless burning, alder swamps ghastly white,
Tumultuous snows, blanker whitenesses,
Into the pathless wood, one eye weeping,
The dark trees, for which no saying is dark enough,
Which mask the gloom and lead on into it,
The bare, the withered, the deserted.

There were no more cottages.
Soft bombs of dust falling from the boughs,
The sun shining no warmer than the moon,
He had outwalked the farthest city light,
And there, clinging to the perfect trees,
A last leaf. What was it?
What was that whiteness?   white, uncertain —
The night too dark to know.

4

He turned. *Love,*
Love of things, duty, he said,
And made his way back to the shelter
No longer sheltering him, the house
Where everything turned into words,

Where he would think on the white wave,
Folded back, that rides in place on the obscure
Pouring of this life to the sea —
And seal the broken lips
Of the darkness with the *mot juste.*

5

Poet of the country of white houses,
Of clearings going out to the dark wall of woods
Frayed along the skyline, you who nearly foreknew
The next lines of poems you suddenly left off writing,
Who dwelt in access to that which other men
Have burned all their lives to get near, who heard
The high wind, in gusts, seething
From far off, coming through the trees exactly
To this place where it must happen, who spent
Your life on the point of giving yourself away
To the dark trees, the dissolving woods,
Into which you go at last, heart in hand, deep in:

When we think of a man who was cursed
Neither with the all-lovingness of Walt Whitman
Nor with Melville's anguish to know and to suffer,
And yet cursed . . . A man, what shall I say,

Vain, not fully convinced he was dying, whose calling
Was to set up in the wilderness of his country,
At whatever cost, a man who would be his own man,
We think of you. And from the same doorway
At which you lived, between the house and the woods,
We see your old footprints going away across
The great Republic, Frost, up memorized slopes,
Down hills floating by heart on the bulldozed land.

PART II

Tillamook Journal

I have come here
From Chicago, packing
A sleeping bag, a pan
To melt snow for drinking,
Dried apricots, tea,
A great boiled beef-heart.

Two loggers drove me
As far in as they could get,
Two gunnysack loggers of the Burn,
Owning a truck and a dozer, a few cables
And saws, who drag out
The sound heartwood for money.

They said there'd
Been a prospector here a year ago,
Hunting uranium or gold,
They would run across him,
A little, swaying heap of gear,
With a Geiger counter

Lashed on like an extra heart,
They said they would find him
Mumbling about metal while
Thrashing up some avalanching gravel.
Around January he was ready
To settle for anything at all.
When spring came he vanished.

I set out walking,
Up to my ankles in gravel,
Grappling at roots and rocks.
At last I was climbing up
On my hands and knees
As though I'd come here begging.

From the top of Cedar Butte
The whole compass is visible,
To the west the Pacific
Lying out flat and shiny,
North and east, hill
After hill of white snags.

To the south, white stumps, white logs,
Washing to the valleys, bleeding scarps,
Lopped spurs, empty streambeds.
The land, split and cracked
Under the crisscross of logging roads,
Oozing down its ravines.

It is twenty-five years
Since the first blue-white puff was sighted.
Convicts have planted saplings
By the coast, schoolboys
Have planted by the highway,
So far little catches.

To the north, on the hills
Loggers can't reach,
Great virgin stands of snags

Burnt clean and bleached
In the distance keeping on
Blurring to look like smoke.

Big, immaculate snowflakes
Have been coming down, melting
On touching. All night,
As I lay trying for sleep,
I listened to Kilchis
River grinding its rocks and boulders.

The ravine is a mass of slash slippery
With rain and snow. Tree
Trunks cross and lock each other
Blocking the water,
Intricately grained
Rims for the little waterfalls.

A mule deer joined me,
Leading like a scout,
When I turned off and climbed
He stopped too, and sadly — I found myself
Sadly thinking — watched my going.
Birds wrangled and chirped.

I was sitting under
The last knoll,
Gnawing the last of the heart,
Looking back at the Burn
As it went out in the twilight,
Its crags broken, its valleys

Soaked in night, another
Plundered breast of the world.
I scrambled to my feet
And climbed, I could hear my heart
Beating in the air around me,
And came over the last summit

Into a dark wind blasting
Out of the blackness.
Behind me snow was still falling.
Before me the Pacific
Fell with long triple crashes on the shore.
It was only steps to the unburnable sea.

On Hardscrabble Mountain

1

On old slashed spruce boughs
Buoying me up off the snow
I stretched out on the slope,
Now and then a bit of snow
Would slide quietly from a branch,

Once a deerfly came by,

I could see off for about a hundred miles.

2

I waked with a start,
The sun had crawled off me,

I was shivering in thick blue shadows,
Sap was sticking me to the spruce boughs,

The wind was starting to rise.

3

On the way down, passing
The little graveyard in the woods,
I gave a thought to the human bones buried there,

I breathed something like a prayer
To a bear just shutting his eyes,
To a skunk dozing off,
To a marmot with yellow belly,
To a dog-faced hedgehog,
To a dormouse with a paunch and ears like leaves or wings.

On Frozen Fields

We walk across the snow.
The moon can be eating itself out,
Meteors can be flaring to death on earth,
The aurora borealis can be blooming and seething.
We walk arm in arm, and we are happy.

In Fields of Summer

The sun rises,
The goldenrod blooms,

My own life is adrift in me,
In my heart and hands, in my teeth,
It shines up at the old heron
Who holds out his drainpipe of a neck
And creaks along in the blue.

The goldenrod shines with its life, too,
And the great field wavers and flakes,
The rumble of the bees deepens,
A phoebe flutters up,
A lark bursts up all dew.

A Bird Comes Back

Only the head and the shoulders, only
The bust of a bird really,
Cochineal and emerald, appears,
Stinging the blossoms, there
At the open window, in the phlox,
Where there are, already,
Bees and a few white butterflies.
The timbers of the house
Shift sidewise, like stove grates,
One of the too-frequent settlings.
I think of Emily Dickinson's hummingbird.
Odd to see him now
With nothing in back of him
But New Hampshire fifty miles away and badly faded.

Cells Breathe in the Emptiness

The flowers turn to husks
And the great trees seem suddenly to die
And rocks and old weasel bones lose
The little life they had:
The air becomes so still
It gives the ears something like the bends.
Listen! That would be the sound of the teeth
Of a sloppy green cabbageworm
Eating its route through a turnip
Inside the compost heap
Now snarling like a petite chainsaw, now droning.
A butterfly battens on a buttercup,
From the junkpile jukes up a junco.

Poem of Night

I

I move my hand over
Slopes, falls, lumps of sight,
Lashes barely able to be touched,
Lips that give way so easily
It's a shock to feel under them
The hard smile of bones.

Muffled a little, barely cloaked,
Zygoma, maxillary, turbinate.

2

    I put my hand
    On the side of your face,
    You lean your head a little
    Into my hand — and so,
    I know you're a dormouse
    Taken up in winter sleep,
    A lonely, stunned weight.

3

    A cheekbone,
    A curved piece of brow,
    A pale eyelid
    Float in the dark,
    And now I make out
    An eye, dark,
    Wormed with far-off, unaccountable lights.

4

    Hardly touching, I hold
    What I can only think of
    As some deepest of memories in my arms,
    Not mine, but as if the life in me
    Were slowly remembering what it is.

    You lie here now in your physicalness,
    This beautiful degree of reality.

5

   Now the day, raft that breaks up, comes on.

   I think of a few bones
   Floating on a river at night,
   The starlight blowing in place on the water,
   The river leaning like a wave toward the emptiness.

Nightfall of the Real

   Swallows dart at one another
   Across the curve of the moon. Two
   Ravens tumble at the cliff and fall away. On the port
   The orange, white, and blue umbrellas
   Which have been turning all day to the sun
   Fold themselves. In the Bar des Guitares
   They are raking the strings.
   Mullets are leaping in the straits.

§

   On a table set by heart
   In the last sun of the day
   Olives, three fishes,
   Bread, a bottle of rosé.

   A rainbow crosses a fish,
   A glass blossoms and reblossoms,
   Flesh slides off bones which were,
   We now see, only stabbing it.

Darkness sticks itself
To empty spines. Night climbs
In glasses. A breeze. Low voices.
Paths floating on earth.

§

Olives, bread,
Fishes, pink wine:
Gradually in the dusk
A crackling across stones.

To this table one came,
Came and ate, tore actual bread,
Felt physical drink touch his soul,
Here conversed, here laughed.

§

Four faces look in
On a vanished room — the vineyard,
The olive grove, the stones,
The green sea — and themselves begin vanishing.

Out in the dark
A distant dull splash of a fish.
Yet again. Sick of weight
It leans up through its eerie life
Toward the night-flash of its emblemhood.

§

Spoon, table, mirrors,
Green portrait of vase of flowers,

Vase of flowers,
Each streaked fatally with dusk.

The light grows dim,
The richest time, which is twilight.
On the shore lies
A fern fishy and glittering.

Middle of the Way

1

I wake in the night,
An ache in the shoulder blades.
I lie amazed under the trees
That creak a little in the dark,
The giant trees of the world.

I lie on earth the way
Flames lie in the woodpile,
Or as an imprint, in sperm or egg, of what is to be.
I love the earth, and always
In its darknesses I am a stranger.

2

6 A.M. Water frozen again. Melted it and made tea. Ate a raw egg and
the last orange. Refreshed by a long sleep. The trail practically indistin-
guishable under 8" of snow. 9:30 A.M. Snow up to my knees in places.
Sweat begins freezing under my shirt when I stop to rest. The woods
are filled, anyway, with the windy noise of the first streams. 10:30 A.M.

The sun at last. The snow starts to melt off the boughs at once, falling with little ticking sounds. Mist clouds are lying in the valleys. 11:45 A.M. Slow, glittering breakers roll in on the beaches ten miles away, very blue and calm. 12 noon. An inexplicable sense of joy, as if some happy news had been transmitted to me directly, bypassing the brain. 2 P.M. From the top of Gauldy I looked back into Hebo valley. Castle Rock sticks into a cloud. A cool breeze comes up from the valley, it is a fresh, earthly wind and tastes of snow and trees. It is not like those transcendental breezes that make the heart ache. It brings happiness. 2:30 P.M. Lost the trail. A woodpecker watches me wade about through the snow trying to locate it. The sun has gone back of the trees. 3:10 P.M. Still hunting for the trail. It is getting cold. From an elevation I have an open view to the SE, a world of timberless, white hills, rolling, weirdly wrinkled. Above them a pale half moon. 3:45 P.M. Going on by map and compass. A minute ago a deer fled touching down every fifteen feet or so. 7:30 P.M. Made camp near the head of Alder Creek. Trampled a bed into the snow and filled it with boughs. Concocted a little fire in the darkness. Ate pork and beans. A slug or two of whisky burnt my throat. The night very clear. Very cold. That half moon is up there and a lot of stars have come out among the treetops. The fire has fallen to coals.

3

The coals go out,
The last smoke wavers up
Losing itself in the stars.
This is my first night to lie
In the uncreating dark.

In the human heart
There sleeps a green worm

That has spun the heart about itself,
And that shall dream itself black wings
One day to break free into the black sky.

I leave my eyes open
And lie here and forget our life.
All I see is that we float out
Into the emptiness, among the great stars,
On this little vessel without lights.

I know that I love the day,
The sun on the mountain, the Pacific
Shiny and accomplishing itself in breakers,
But I know I live half alive in the world,
Half my life belongs to the wild darkness.

Ruins under the Stars

I

All day under acrobat
Swallows I have sat, beside ruins
Of a plank house sunk up to its windows
In burdock and raspberry cane,
The roof dropped, the foundation broken in,
Nothing left perfect but axe-marks on the beams.

A paper in a cupboard talks about "Mugwumps,"
In a V-letter a farmboy has "tasted battle . . ."
The apples are pure acid on the tangle of boughs,

The pasture has gone to popple and bush.
Here on this perch of ruins
I listen for the crunch of the porcupines.

2

Overhead the skull-hill rises
Crossed on top by the stunted apple,
Infinitely beyond it, older than love or guilt,
Wait the stars ready to jump and sprinkle out of space.

Every night under those thousand lights
An owl dies, a snake sloughs his skin,
A man in a dark pasture
Feels a homesickness he does not understand.

3

Sometimes I see them,
The south-going Canada geese,
At evening, coming down
In pink light, over the pond, in great,
Loose, always-dissolving V's —
I go out into the field to hear
The cold, lonely yelping
Of their tranced bodies in the sky.

4

This morning I watched
Milton Norway's sky-blue Ford
Dragging its ass down the dirt road
On the other side of the valley.

Later, off in the woods,
A chainsaw was agonizing across the top of some stump.
A while ago the tracks of a little, snowy,
SAC bomber crawled across heaven.

What of that hairstreak
That was flopping and batting about
Deep in the goldenrod —
Did she not know, either, where she was going?

5

The bats come spelling the swallows.
In the smoking heap of old antiques
The porcupine-crackle starts up again,
The bone-saw, the ur-music of our sphere,
And up there the stars rustling and whispering.

Tree from Andalusia

This bleached tree
Dumped on the Sagaponack beach . . .

The wind has lifted and now seethes
Far up among the invisible stars.

Once on Ferry Street, at night,
Among TO LET signs and closed wholesalers.

From some loft a phrase of jazz,
y recuerdo una brisa triste por los olivos.

The wind starts fluting
In our teeth, in our ears.

It whines down the harmonica
Of the fingerbones, moans at the skull.

Blown on by their death
The things of earth whistle and cry out.

Spindrift

1

Sitting on this tree thrown up
From the sea, its tangle of roots
Letting the wind go through,
I look down the beach: at old
Horseshoe crabs, broken skates,
Sand dollars, sea horses, as though
Only primeval creatures get destroyed,
At chunks of sea-mud still quivering,
At the light glinting off the water
And the billion facets of the sand,
At their moment of shining the wind
Blows over dunes as they creep.

2

Sit down
By the clanking shore
Of this bitter, beloved sea,

Pluck
Shells from the icy surf,
Fans of gold light, sunbursts,

Lift one to the sun
As a sign you accept to go
When the time comes to the shrine of the dead.

3

This bleached root
Drifted from some other shore,
Brittle, cold, practically weightless, worn
Down to the lost grip it always essentially was.

If it has lost hold
It at least keeps
The shape of what it held,
And is the hand itself
Of that gravel, one of earth's
Wandering icons of "to have."

4

I sit listening
To the surf as it falls,
The power and inexhaustible freshness of the sea,
The suck and inner boom
As a wave tears free and crashes back
In overlapping thunders going away down the beach.

It is the most we know of time,
And it is our undermusic of eternity.

5

I think of how I
Sat by a dying woman,
Her shell of a hand
Wet and cold in both of mine,
Light, nearly out, existing as smoke.

I remember the glow of her wan, absorbed smile.

6

Under the wind
That moans in the grass
And whistles through crabs' claws
I sit holding this little lamp,
This icy fan of the sun.

Across gull tracks
And wind ripples in the sand
The wind seethes. Footprints behind me
Slogging for the absolute
Already begin vanishing.

7

What does he really love,
That old man,
His wrinkled eyes
Tortured by smoke,
Walking in the ungodly
Rasp and cackle of old flesh?

The swan dips its head
And peers at the mystic
In-life of the sea,
The gull drifts up
And eddies toward heaven,
The breeze in its arms . . .

Nobody likes to die
But an old man
Can know
A gratefulness
Toward time that kills him,
Everything he loved was made of it.

Flower Herding on Mount Monadnock

I

I can support it no longer.
Laughing ruefully at myself
For all I claim to have suffered
I get up. Damned nightmarer!

It is New Hampshire out here,
It is nearly the dawn.
The song of the whippoorwill stops
And the dimension of depth seizes everything.

2

    The whistlings of a peabody bird go overhead
    Like a needle pushed five times through the air,
    They enter the leaves, and come out little changed.

    The air is so still
    That as they go off through the trees
    The love songs of birds do not get any fainter.

3

    The last memory I have
    Is of a flower that cannot be touched,

    Through the bloom of which, all day,
    Fly crazed, missing bees.

4

    As I climb sweat gets up my nostrils,
    For an instant I think I am at the sea,

    One summer off Cap Ferrat we watched a black seagull
    Straining for the dawn, we stood in the surf,

    Grasshoppers splash up where I step,
    The mountain laurel crashes at my thighs.

5

    There is something joyous in the elegies
    Of birds. They seem
    Caught up in a formal delight,
    Though the mourning dove whistles of despair.

But at last in the thousand elegies
The dead rise in our hearts,
On the brink of our happiness we stop
Like someone on a drunk starting to weep.

6

I kneel at a pool,
I look through my face
At the bacteria I think
I see crawling through the moss.

My face sees me,
The water stirs, the face,
Looking preoccupied,
Gets knocked from its bones.

7

I weighed eleven pounds
At birth, having stayed on
Two extra weeks in the womb.
Tempted by room and fresh air
I came out big as a policeman,
Blue-faced, with narrow red eyes.
It was eight days before the doctor
Would scare my mother with me.

Turning and craning in the vines
I can make out through the leaves
The old, shimmering nothingness, the sky.

8

Green, scaly moosewoods ascend,
Tenants of the shaken paradise,

At every wind last night's rain
Comes splattering from the leaves,

It drops in flurries and lies there,
The footsteps of some running start.

9

From a rock
A waterfall,
A single trickle like a strand of wire,
Breaks into beads halfway down.

I know
The birds fly off
But the hug of the earth wraps
With moss their graves and the giant boulders.

10

In the forest I discover a flower.

The invisible life of the thing
Goes up in flames that are invisible,
Like cellophane burning in the sunlight.

It burns up. Its drift is to be nothing.

In its covertness it has a way
Of uttering itself in place of itself,
Its blossoms claim to float in the Empyrean,

A wrathful presence on the blur of the ground.

The appeal to heaven breaks off.
The petals begin to fall, in self-forgiveness.
It is a flower. On this mountainside it is dying.

Body Rags

1968

To Inés

PART I

Another Night in the Ruins

1

In the evening
haze darkening on the hills,
purple of the eternal,
a last bird crosses over,
'flop flop,' adoring
only the instant.

2

Nine years ago,
in a plane that rumbled all night
above the Atlantic,
I could see, lit up
by lightning bolts jumping out of it,
a thunderhead formed like the face
of my brother, looking down
on blue,
lightning-flashed moments of the Atlantic.

3

He used to tell me,
"What good is the day?
On some hill of despair
the bonfire
you kindle can light the great sky —
though it's true, it turns out, to make it burn
you have to throw yourself in . . ."

4

Wind tears itself hollow
in the eaves of these ruins, ghost-flute
of snowdrifts
that build out there in the dark:
upside-down ravines
into which night sweeps
our cast wings, our ink-spattered feathers.

5

I listen.
I hear nothing. Only
the cow, the cow of such
hollowness, mooing
down the bones.

6

Is that a
rooster? He
thrashes in the snow
for a grain. Finds
it. Rips
it into
flames. Flaps. Crows.
Flames
bursting out of his brow.

7

How many nights must it take
one such as me to learn
that we aren't, after all, made

from that bird that flies out of its ashes,
that for us
as we go up in flames, our one work
is
to open ourselves, to *be*
the flames?

Lost Loves

1

On ashes of old volcanoes
I lie baking
the deathward flesh in the sun.

I can hear
a door, far away,
banging in the wind:

Mole Street. Quai-aux-Fleurs. Françoise.
Greta. "After Lunch" by Po Chu-I.
"The Sunflower" by Blake.

2

And yet I can rejoice
that everything changes, that
we go from life
into life,

and enter ourselves
quaking
like the tadpole, its time come, tumbling toward the slime.

Getting the Mail

I walk back
toward the frog pond, carrying
the one letter, a few wavy lines
crossing the stamp: tongue-streaks
leaching through
from the glue and spittle beneath: my sign.

The frogs'
eyes bulge toward the visible,
an alderfly glitters past, declining
to die: her third giant step
into the world.

A name stretches over the envelope
like a blindfold.
What did *getting warm* used to mean?

I tear open the letter
to the far-off, serene
groans of a cow
a farmer milks in the August dusk
and the Kyrie of a chainsaw drifting down off Wheelock Mountain.

Vapor Trail Reflected in the Frog Pond

1

    The old watch: their
thick eyes
puff and foreclose by the moon. The young, heads
trailed by the beginnings of necks,
shiver,
in the guarantee they shall be bodies.

    In the frog pond
the vapor trail of a SAC bomber creeps,

    I hear its drone, drifting, high up
in immaculate ozone.

2

    And I hear,
coming over the hills, America singing,
her varied carols I hear:
crack of deputies' rifles practicing their aim on stray dogs at night,
sput of cattleprod,
TV going on about the smells of the human body,
curses of the soldier as he poisons, burns, grinds, and stabs
the rice of the world,
with open mouth, crying strong, hysterical curses.

3

    And by paddies in Asia
bones
wearing a few shadows

walk down a dirt road, smashed
bloodsuckers on their heel, knowing
flesh thrown down in the sunshine
dogs shall eat
and flesh flung into the air
shall be seized by birds,
shoulder blades smooth, unmarked by old feather-holes,
hands rivered
by blue, erratic wanderings of the blood,
eyes crinkled shut at almost seeing
the drifting sun that gives us our lives.

The Fossils

I

I clawed in the crushed-up
lumps half grease half dust:
atrypas came out,
lophophyllidiums still casting shadows,
corals wrapped in wrinkles,
wing-shaped allorismas,
sea-lily disks that did not molder into dust
but held.

Night rose up
in black smoke, making me
blind. My fingertips rasped
smooth on my brain, I knelt in the dark, cracking
the emptiness: poking
spirifers into flying black dust,

letting sylvan remains slither through my fingers,
whiffing the glacial roses,
palping around for the ephemera.

Will I touch at last
the ornithosuchus, whose wings
serve not to evade earth but to press closer to it?

2

While Bill Gratwick flapped, pranced
and called the dances,
light-headed
as a lizard on hind legs I sashayed
with Sylvia, of the woods, as woodwinds
flared and crackled in the leaves,
Sylph-ia, too, of that breeze
for whom even the salamander rekindles wings;
and I danced the eighteenth-century shoulder-rub
with Lucy,
my shoulder blades starting to glitter
on hers as we turned, sailbacks
in laired and changing dance,
our faces smudged with light from the fingertips of the ages.

3

Outside
in dark fields
I pressed the coiled
ribs of a fingerprint to a stone,
first light in the flesh.

Over the least fossil
day breaks in gold, frankincense, and myrrh.

The Burn

On the dirt road winding
beside the Kilchis River
down to the sea, saplings
on all the hills, I go
deep into the first forest
of Douglas firs shimmering
out of prehistory, a strange
shine up where the tops
shut out the sky, whose roots
feed in the waters of the rainbow trout.
And here, at my feet, in the grain
of a burnt log opened by a riverfall,
the swirls of the creation.
At the San Francisco airport,
Charlotte, where yesterday
my arms died around you like
old snakeskins, needletracks
on your arms marked
how the veins wander
I see you walking like a somnambulist
through a poppy field, blind
as myself on this dirt road, tiny
flowers brightening about you,
the skills of fire, of fanning

the blossoms until they flare and die,
perfected; only the power to nurture
and prolong, only this love,
impossible. The mouth of the river.
On these beaches
the sea throws itself down, in flames.

One Who Used to Beat His Way

Down the street of warehouses,
each with
its redlighted shaftway,
its Corinthian columns,
its bum crapped out on the stoop,
he staggers, among
wraiths that steam up out of manhole covers
and crimesheets skidding from the past.

He gets a backed-up
mouthful of liquor, mumbles, "Thanks God,"
and regulps it.
Behind him the continent glimmers, that wild land
crossed by the *Flying Crow*
that changes her crew at Shreveport,
the *Redball* and the *Dixie Flyer,* that go on through,
the *Big 80*
that quills her whistles to make blues on the Delta.
"Everybody's eating everybody,"
the old timer growls, poking the jungle fire . . .
"Bible-ranters, bulls, hicks, systems, scissor-bills . . ."

And he who used
to beat his way hauls himself down
into his sleeping niche, where he has cached his small possessions,
a nearly killed bottle,
a streambed of dried piss groping across the dry stone.

The Fly

The fly
I've just brushed
off my face keeps buzzing
about me, flesh-
eater
starved for the soul.

One day I may learn to suffer
his mizzling, sporadic stroll over eyelid or cheek,
even hear my own singing
in his burnt song.

The bee is the fleur-de-lys in the flesh.
She has a tuft of the sun on her back.
She brings sexual love to the narcissus flower.
She sings of fulfillment only
and stings and dies, and
everything she ever touches
is opening, opening.

And yet we say our last goodbye
to the fly last,

the flesh-fly last,
the absolute last,
the naked dirty reality of him last.

The Falls

The elemental murmur
as they plunge, *croal, croal,*
and *haish, haish,* over
the ledges,
through stepless wheels
and bare axles, down between
sawmills that have
slid sideways to their knees . . .

When I fall I would fall to my sounding . . .
the lowly,
unchanged, stillic, rainbowed sounding
of the Barton River Falls.

Mango

It opens in three: yellow-gold as dawn
on the mudwalls of Hafez' garden,
on a seagull mewing for the light,

austere,
smacking of turpentine,
stringy, like the mortal flesh.

Under the mango tree,
a few women squat by the whitening sea,
clapping, chorusing of love.

In the Anse Galet Valley

Clouds
rise by twos out of the jungle, cross
under the moon, sink
into
the peak called Font-des-Serpents.

I remember the game of angel's wings,
I remember the laid-open scallop shell,
the gowpen overspilling the milled grain,
a mole feeling its way through the daylight.

A straw torch
flickers
among the trees,
of a nightfisherman
wading upstream clubbing the fishes.

The fer-de-lances
writhe in black winding-skins.
What questions could I ask that wafer-
moon
gnawed already at its death-edge?

La Bagarède

1

    The dogs come with me
    into town, we buy chèvre and a bâtard.
    Back at La Bagarède I eat
    this little meal in the dusk
    and sit, until

    the Swan grows visible, trailing
    her indicated wings down the horizon,
    and Orion
    begins to stalk the last nights of the summer.

2

    The black
    water I gulp from the spring
    hits my brain at the root.
    The dark blooms of sunflowers
    crackle open. In the sky
    the seventh
    of the Sisters, she who hid herself
    in shame
    at having loved one who dies, is shining.

Night in the Forest

    A woman
    sleeps next to me. A strand
    of hair flows

from her cocoon sleeping bag, touching
the ground hesitantly, as if thinking
to take root.

§

A mountain brook purls,
blood winds
through its memorized labyrinths.
A few feet away
charred stick-ends surround
a bit of ashes, where flames
absently
waver, absently leap.

Going Home by Last Light

Redheaded by last light,
with high-stepped, illusionist amble
I walk toward the white room
where she will be waiting,
past
pimentos,
red cabbages,
tomatoes flickering in their bins,
past melons, past mushrooms and onions

§

Those swarms
of mayflies that used to rise
at the Vermont threshold, "imagos"

thrown up for a day,
their mouths shriveling closed,
their sexual parts newborn and perfect . . .

§

For the last few minutes
two mosquitoes have been mating
on top of this poem,
changing positions, swooning,
their legs
fragile as a baby's hairs.

§

A day!
The wings of the earth
lift and fall
to the groans, the savage thumpings of a heart.

How Many Nights

How many nights
have I lain in terror,
O Creator Spirit, maker of night and day,

only to walk out
the next morning over the frozen world,
hearing under the creaking of snow
faint, peaceful breaths . . .
snake,
bear, earthworm, ant . . .

and above me
a wild crow crying *'yaw yaw yaw'*
from a branch nothing cried from ever in my life.

Last Songs

What do they sing, the last birds
coasting down the twilight,
banking
across woods filled with darkness, their
frayed wings curved
on the world like lovers' arms
which form, night after night, in sleep,
an irremediable absence?

§

Silence. Ashes
in the grate. Whatever it is
that keeps us from heaven,
sloth, wrath, greed, fear,
could we only reinvent it on earth
as song.

In the Farmhouse

Eaves moan,
loose clapboards flap.

Behind me the potbellied
Ironside #120, rusty, cracked,
rips thick chunks of rock maple
into fire.

§

Soon it will be spring,
Soon the vanishing of the snows.

And tonight
in this flimsy jew's-harp of a farmhouse
I sit up late, mouthing
sounds that would be words
in the wind
rattling the twelve lights of blackness.

The Correspondence School Instructor Says Goodbye to His Poetry Students

Goodbye, lady in Bangor, who sent me
snapshots of yourself, after definitely hinting
you were beautiful; goodbye,
Miami Beach urologist, who enclosed plain
brown envelopes for the return of your *very*
"Clinical Sonnets"; goodbye, manufacturer
of brassieres on the Coast, whose eclogues
give the fullest treatment in literature yet
to the sagging breast motif; goodbye, you in San Quentin,
who wrote, "Being German my hero is Hitler,"

instead of "Sincerely yours," at the end of long,
neat-scripted letters extolling the Pre-Raphaelites:

I swear to you, it was just my way
of cheering myself up, as I licked
the stamped, self-addressed envelopes,
the game I had of trying to guess
which one of you, this time,
had poisoned his glue. I did care.
I did read each poem entire.
I did say everything I thought
in the mildest words I knew. And now,
in this poem, or chopped prose, no better,
I realize, than those troubled lines
I kept sending back to you,
I have to say I am relieved it is over:
at the end I could feel only pity
for that urge toward more life
your poems kept smothering in words, the smell
of which, days later, tingled in your nostrils
as new, God-given impulses
to write.

Goodbye,
you who are, for me, the postmarks again
of imaginary towns — Xenia, Burnt Cabins, Hornell —
their solitude given away in poems, only their loneliness kept.

The Poem

On this hill crossed
by the last birds, a sprinkling
of soil covers up the rocks
with green, as
the face
drifts on a skull scratched by glaciers.

The poem too
is a palimpsest, pinked
with erasures, smelling
of departure and burnt stone.

§

The full moon
slides out from the clouds, the trees'
graves all lie out at their feet:

the white-oak-leaf-
shaped tongue
of the new born and the dying
quivers, and no one interprets it.

§

Where is "The Apocalypse of Lamech"?
Where is the "Iliupersis"?
Where is the "Khavadhaynamagh"?
Where is the "Rommant du Pet au Deable"?
Where is "The Book of the Lion"?
Where is the servantose of the sixty girls of Florence?

Where are the poems Li Po folded into boats and pushed out on
    the river?
Where are the snows that fell into these graves?

§

In morning light, at the tip
of an icicle, the letter C
comes into being — trembles,
to drop, or to cling?

Suddenly a roman
carapace glitters all over it.

§

Here is a fern-leaf cementing *utter* to *illume,*
here is *unfulfilled* reflected as *mellifica* along the feather of a crow,
here is a lightning-split fir the lines down its good side becoming ever
    more whitmanesque and free,
here is a hound chasing a mate in trochaic dimeter brachycatalectic,
here are the pits where the tongue-bone is hurled at its desolate cry,
here are clothes held up by clothespins composing *emptiness* in
    khaskura,
here is a fly convulsing through the poisoned labyrinth of this hand-
    writing,
here is an armful of last-year's-snows.

§

The moment
in the late night, when baby birds
closed in dark wings almost stir, and objects
on the page grow suddenly

heavy, hugged
by an intensification of strange gravity:

the surgery of the funeral
and of the funeral oration, the absence
in the bit of speech I would leave in the world
of

§

Where are "The Onions"
heaped like swollen lachrymal sacs in a bushel basket in a grocery store
in 1948?

brong ding plang ching of a spike
driven crazy on a locust
post.

PART II

The Last River

When I cross
on the high, back-reared ferry
all burnished brass and laboring pistons
and admire the tugs and sticklighters
and the great ships from foreign lands
and wave to a deckhand gawking at the new world
of sugar cane and shanties and junked cars
and see a girl by the railing,
the shapes the breeze presses her dress against,
and the green waves lighting up . . .
the cell-block
door crawls open and they fling us a pimp.

2

The lights dim,
the dirty jokes die out.

Rumble of trailertrucks
on Louisiana 1 . . . I think
of the rides
back from the courthouse in Amite,
down the canyon between
faces smiling from the billboards,
the car filled
with men and women who tried to register to vote
crawling down the canyon made
of billboards of huge, smiling, white faces . . .
Tickfaw . . . Independence . . . Albany . . .

Moan of
a riverboat creeping
upstream . . . yap and screech
of police dogs
attacking the police in their dreams.

3

Under the blue flasher
and the siren's wail, a man in handcuffs
gazes out at anything,
anything at all of the world . . .
surreal spittoon . . .
glow of EAT . . .
fresh-hit carcass . . . cat . . . coon . . .
polecat . . .

Suddenly lightning flashes,
path strung out across the storm,
bolt even made of hellfire
between any strange life and any strange life,
blazed
for those who shudder in their beds
hearing a siren's wail fading down
a dead-ridden highway at night . . .
thump . . . armadillo . . . thump . . . dog . . .

4

Somebody wakes,
he's got himself a "nightcrawler" — one of those
jokes you come to in your sleep —
about girls who have "cross-bones"

and can't, some say,
be entered . . . An argument now develops
on whether it is or is not possible
to circumvent the cross-bone.
"Sheee-it! Sheee-it!" the copbeater cries,
and the carthief says, "Jeee-ziz! Jeee-ziz!"
"All right boys," the pimp puts in from time to time.
"What say? Let's get a little fucking sleep."

5

One day in Ponchatoula,
watching the IC from Chicago creep
into the weeds of the Deep South, and stop,
I thought I saw three
of my kinsmen from the North
in the drinking car, boozing their way
down to New Orleans,
putting themselves across,
selling themselves,
dishing up soft soap,
plump, manicured, shit-eating, opulent, razor-sharp . . .

Then the train
lurched and pushed on, carrying them off,
Yankee . . . egalitarian . . . grease
in the palm of their golden aspirations.

6

When I get to feeling America consists
only of billboards that smile,
I think of my friends

out there,
from Plaquemine or Point Coupee,
going from shanty to shanty
in the dust,
keeping empty
a space within them,
trudging through dust become
pollen of sunflowers under their feet.

7

The carthief's face,
oddly childish as he sleeps,
reminds me now of Jesus — a Jesus
I saw on a black funeral parlor's calendar,
blue-eyed, rosy-cheeked, milky and soft . . .

I remember his beautiful speech of the old days . . .
those prayers, funeral orations, anthems,
war songs, and — actual poems! some of them
as true as,
for example, "Wall Kill," "Terre Haute,"
"Stillwater," "Alcatraz" . . .
each more escapeproof,
more supersecure,
more insane than the last,
liberty, said Shelley, being
"brightest in dungeons."

The carthief moans in his sleep, his face
now like a cat's.

8

Beyond the crisscross
of bars at the tiny window
swallows dart in last light,
late-flying creatures that surpass us in plain view,
bits of blurred flesh,
wavy lines . . .

Nothing's there now but a few stars
brightening
under the ice-winds of the emptiness.

Isn't it strange
that all love, all granting of respect,
has no face for its passing expressions but yours, Death?

9

I hear now
the faintest of songs, the humming
the dew makes
evaporating from the garlic leaf.

A new night
and the dew will come back,
for so many men and women
the chance to live under justice
does not ever come.

10

I remember
the ancient ex-convict who lives

in a shanty under the levee, standing
in sunlight on the dirt road.

In the green, blistered sewer,
among beer cans, weeds, plastic flowers,
a few lumps of excrement, winged
with green flies.

The dust on the road
swirls up into wing-shapes, that blow off,
the road made of dust goes down.

The air brightens as though ashes
of lightning bolts had been scattered through it.

What is it that can make a human face,
bit of secret,
lighted flesh, open the earth?

II

A girl lies with me
on the grass of the levee. Two
birds whirr overhead. We lie close, surprised
to have waked a bit early
in bodies of glory.

In its skin of light, the river
bends into view, rising
between the levees, flooding for the sky,
a hundred feet down pressing its long weight
silently into the world.

We wander slowly homeward, lost
in the history of every step.

12

I am lying face-down
by the Ten Mile River, half mud
half piss, that runs
between the Seekonk Woods
and the red mills of Pawtucket
with their thousand windows and one smokestack,
breathing the burnt air,
watching a bug break itself up,
holding to my eye a bleached catfish
skull that turned up in the grass,
inside it, in the pit of light, a cross,
hearing hornpout sounding
their horns mournfully deep inside the river.

13

Across
the dreamlit waters pushes
the flag-topped Plaquemine ferry,
midway between shore and shore
it sounds its horn, catfishes
of the Mississippi caterwaul and nose over,
heavy-skulled, into the flinty, night-smelling depths.

14

All my life, of rivers
I have heard
the longing cries, the rut-roar

of shifted wind
on gongs of beaten water:

the Ten Mile of Hornpout,
the Drac hissing in its bed of sand,
the Ruknabad scribbled over by nightingales,
the Passumpsic breaking up all down its length in spring,
the East River of Fishes, the more haunting for not having a
        past either,
the Mississippi coursing into the Gulf through the silt of all its days,
the snake-cracked Tangipahoa, lifting with a little rush from the hills
        and dwindling in the undernourished greenery.

15

Was there some last
fling at grace in those eddies, a swirl
of sweet scraping, out there
where an Illinois cornstalk
drifts, turning the hours,
and the grinned skull of a boy?

The burning fodder dowses down,
seeking the snagged
bodies of the water-buried,
bits
of sainfoin sopped in fire, snuffed from below

by the flesh-dark Tallahatchie,
the bone-colored Pearl.

16

I wrench a tassel of moss from a bough
to be my lightning-besom, and sweep
the mists from the way.

Ahead of me a boy is singing,

    didn't I ramble
    I rambled
    I rambled all around
    in and out the town
    I rambled
    I rambled till the butcher cut me down

He steps out of the mist,
he says his name is Henry David,
he takes my hand and leads me over the plain of crushed asphodels.

17

Who's this
at water's edge,
oar in hand, kneeling beside
his pirogue of blue stern . . .
no nose left,
no hair,
no teeth,
little points of flame for eyes,
limbs tied on with knots and rags?

"Let's go," I say, a big
salty wafer of spit in my mouth.

We step in
to the threshold groan, the pressurized
bayou water squirts in
at the seams, we oar out
on water brown-green
in the patches free of scum, nothing on all sides
but a quiet, curious diet of green,
alligatorwood,
swamp gum, tupelo, liquid amber,
live oak chrisomed in air-eating moss,
cypress risen among all her failed roots.

18

Down here the air's
so thick with American radio-waves,
almost with our bare ears we can pick up
the groggy, backcountry announcers
drawling their pitches and hardsells
at old men forgotten under armies of roaches,
at babies with houseflies walking on their lips,
at men without future puking up present and past,
at recidivists sentenced deep into the hereafter,
at wineheads with only self-loathing for self-defense,
at hillbilly boys scratching their heads at the anti-sweat ads,
at . . .
            "Listen!" says Henry David.
"Sheee-it! Sheee-it!" a cupreous-
throated copbeater is chattering far off in the trees.

19

On the shore four shades
cry out in pain: one lashed
by red suspenders to an
ever-revolving wheel, one with
red patches on the seat of his pants
shrieking while paunchy vultures
stab at his bourbon-squirting liver,
one pushing uphill
a belly puffed up with blood money
that crashes back and crushes him,
another stuck up to his neck
in the guck he caused others to upchuck.
"Southern politicians," Henry David says.
"Yonder, in Junkie's Hollow,
you'll find Northern ones . . ." I see one,
formerly mayor of a great city, withdrawing
a huge needle from his arm,
blood spurts, bits
of testicle press out through the puncture.

20

A man comes lurching
toward me with big mirrors for eyes,
"Sammich!" he cries and doubles up in laughter.
I remember him at once, from ten years ago,
in Chicago, on a Sunday
in a park on the death-scented South Side,
in the days almost before my own life had begun,

when full of strut and happiness
he came up and cried, "Sammich!"
and now he says, "A fight,
I was makin' the scene and the fuzz
did blast my fuckin' ass off." He laughs.
He is also crying. He shrinks back. "Hey,"
he calls, "thanks for that sammich
that day . . . fat white bastard."

21

We come to a crowd, hornets
in their hair, worms in their feet.
"They weren't for anything or against anything,"
Henry David says, "they looked out
for themselves."
Three men trot beside us,
peddling bits of their flesh,
dishing up soft screams,
plump, manicured, shit-eating, opulent . . .

Underfoot a man
with stars on his shoulders
grapples in the slime with a large McCarthyite.
I drag the man off him and he gets up.
"In life I stood above all partisan squabbles,"
he howls,
flashes the grin
that so loved itself it sold itself to the whole world,
and at once is pulled back into the slime by a racist.

22

We come to robed
figures bunched on their knees,
meek eyes rolled up. By twitches
in their throats we gather they're alive.
"Rafel mai ameck zabi almi," they intone.

Down on all fours, like a cat
at his saucer of fresh cream, their leader,
blue-eyed, rosy-cheeked, milky and soft, laps
with big tongue at a mirror.

23

Off to one side there's a man
signing restrictive covenants with a fingernail
on a blackboard. "That one,"
says my guide, "was
well-meaning; he believed
in equality and supported good causes;
he was surprised to find out
this place is run by logicians . . ."
Hearing us talk, the man half turns . . .
"Come on," I tell my guide, for I know him.

24

We pass
victims of the taste for blood
who were hanged by the mob
just as the law was about to hang them,
we pass victims of justice

hanged by the mob for having obtained
stays of execution, executive pardons, fair trials,
we pass victims of prohibitions against glancing at a white woman,
who cover, as we approach, the scabs at their crotches.

Here and there stray
"unknown persons"
killed for "unknown reasons"
at the hands of "persons unknown," including
those who "just took off and caught a freight (they say)."

25

We come to a river
where thousands kneel, sucking up
its cloudy water.

"The Mystic River," Henry David says,
"the Healing Stream free to all
that flows from Calvary's Mountain . . . the liquor
that makes you forget."

"And on the far shore?" "That?"
he says. "That's Camp Ground."

Behind us the police are whipping
a child who refuses to be born,
who shrieks
and scrambles for the riverbank
and stands
singing in a gospel wail,
"Oh Death, he is a little man . . ."

"What's it like in Camp Ground?"

But in the mist I only hear,

> I rambled
> in and out the town
> didn't I ramble.

26

My brain rids itself of light,
at last it goes black,
slowly
slowly
a tiny cell far within it
lights up:

a man of noble face
sits on the iron bunk, wiping
a pile of knifeblades clean
in the rags of his body.
My old hero. Should I be surprised?

"Hard to wash off . . .
buffalo blood . . . Indian blood . . ." he mutters,
at each swipe singing, *"mein herz! mein herz!"*

"Why you," I ask him,
"you who, in your life, loathed our crimes?"

"Seeking love . . . love
without human blood in it,
that leaps above
men and women, flesh and erections,
which was revealed to me
in a Massachusetts gravel bank in spring,
seeking love,
unable to know I only loved
mein herz! mein fucking *herz!*"

"Hey," somebody
from another cellblock shouts, "What say?
Sleep . . . sleep . . ."

The light goes out. In the darkness
a letter for the blind
gets put in my stunned hands.

Did I come all this way only for this, only
to feel out the world-braille of my complicity,
only to choke down this last poison wafer?

For Galway alone.
I send you my mortality.
Which leans out from itself, to spit on itself.
Which you would not touch.
All you have known.

27

On one bank
of the last river stands
a black man, on the other
a white man, on the water between
a man of no color,
body of beryl,
face of lightning,
eyes lamps of wildfire,
arms and feet polished brass.

There will come an agony upon you
beyond any
this nation has known;
and at that time thy people,
given intelligence, given imagination, given love, given . . .

Here his voice falters, he drops
to his knees, he is
falling to pieces,
no nose left,
no hair,
no teeth,
limbs dangling from prayer-knots and rags,

he sits down and waits by the grief-tree
of the last river.

PART III

Testament of the Thief

1

Under the forked
thief-shadow swinging on the breeze,
a coolie sits, resting,
shirt open,
legs spread,
head lolled to one side,
sweat-trickles,
plants,
tiny animals,
stylized all over him.

2

On good terms
with the claustrophobic pewk-worm,
the louse,
the nerve-wracked flea,

a beggar has sprawled here
all day
whether from laziness or love, while the waters

rustle in their blue grooves, and birds
ask,
       'koja? koja?'

3

"This fellow is a colonel,
the degenerate next to him is a cop,

the scarecrow in the coma is a highschool principal,
the one dyed yellow
is chief of the narcotics squad,
that meatsack smokes to bring his weight down,
the squat one
puffing tragically is a poet
broken by failure to become Minister of Finance.

"Me? I just fix
their pipes, and otherwise stab
my poor portion of the world
with skinny assbones and wait for my favorite to come,
a mean little boy
who is my most glorious punishment yet.

"Oh once
I regretted my life,
the only regret I have left,
is how much these days
they soak you for opium.

"I may be washed up,
but if you ever think of me, mull over
this proverb, will you? *If
the cat had wings
he would gobble up every bird in the sky*"

4

The wild rose dies,
the hollyhock falls before finishing its blossoming,
the poppy does not come back,

the moth preens herself by stages
for her carnal moment.

And yet a rose
has tossed the corpse its perfume.
That that bloated snout can catch it proves
the body, too,
has its origins in paradise.

5

A breeze from the bazaar,
lotus,
wild olive,
gum tragacanth,
indigo, musk,
burnt seed of wild rue,
gillyflower . . .

The poor huddle at
pushcarts of fire, eating
boiled beets,
gut,
tongue,
testicle,
cheeks, forehead, little feet.

Down this street the thief
would pick his way, in his pajamas.
After a meal he would sprawl
on just this spot, letting earth
draw down his bones upon her.

Stop a moment on his bones' dents,
stand without moving, listen
to the ordinary people
as they pass. They do not sing
of what is gone or to come, they sing
of the old testaments of their lives,
the little meals,
the airs,
the streets of our time.

6

"*Item,* to the opium master
dying from too much paradise: this round nose,
in working disorder,
that tracks down
the fumes of the real.

"*Item,* to the beggar
dumped on blue stone, gasping
as, one after one, the friends
of his youth hallucinate his sleep:
this set of bones, their
iron faithfulness to loss.

"*Item,* to the navvy
who trudges over the earth
bearing earth on his backbones,
whose skeleton at the last will howl
for its dust just like any other:
this ultimate ruckus on the groan-meat."

7

Item, to the pewk-worm
who lives all his life inside flesh,
sleaching along through fat or lean,
skinny or soft, gnawing himself
a peephole when lost, in buttock or cheek,
whom you can drag out of you
only by winding him up on a matchstick
a quarter turn a day for the rest of your days:
these crawl-maps of my innards.

The Porcupine

1

Fatted
on herbs, swollen on crabapples,
puffed up on bast and phloem, ballooned
on willow flowers, poplar catkins, first
leafs of aspen and larch,
the porcupine
drags and bounces his last meal through ice,
mud, roses and goldenrod, into the stubbly high fields.

2

In character
he resembles us in seven ways:
he puts his mark on outhouses,
he alchemizes by moonlight,
he shits on the run,
he uses his tail for climbing,

he chuckles softly to himself when scared,
he's overcrowded if there's more than one of him per five acres,
his eyes have their own inner redness.

3

Digger of
goings across floors, of hesitations
at thresholds, of
handprints of dread
at doorpost or window jamb, he would
gouge the world
empty of us, hack and crater
it
until it is nothing, if that
could rid it of all our sweat and pathos.

Adorer of ax
handles aflow with grain, of arms
of Morris chairs, of hand
crafted objects
steeped in the juice of fingertips,
of surfaces wetted down
with fist grease or elbow oil,
of clothespins that have
grabbed our body rags by underarm and crotch . . .

Unimpressed — bored —
by the whirl of the stars, by *these*
he's astonished, ultra-
Rilkean angel!

for whom the true
portion of the sweetness of earth
is one of those bottom-heavy, glittering, saccadic
bits
of salt water that splash down
the haunted ravines of a human face.

4

A farmer shot a porcupine three times
as it dozed on a tree limb. On
the way down it tore open its belly
on a broken
branch, hooked its gut,
and went on falling. On the ground
it sprang to its feet
and paying out gut heaved
and spartled through a hundred feet of goldenrod
before
the abrupt emptiness.

5

The Avesta
puts porcupine killers
into hell for nine generations, sentencing them
to gnaw out
each other's hearts for the
salts of desire.

I roll
this way and that in the great bed, under

the quilt
that mimics this country of broken farms and woods,
the fatty sheath of the man
melting off,
the self-stabbing coil
of bristles reversing, blossoming outward —
a red-eyed, hard-toothed, arrow-stuck urchin
tossing up mattress feathers,
pricking the
woman beside me until she cries.

6

In my time I have
crouched, quills erected,
Saint
Sebastian of the
scared heart, and been
beat dead with a locust club
on the bare snout.
And fallen from high places
I have fled, have
jogged
over fields of goldenrod,
terrified, seeking home,
and among flowers
I have come to myself empty, the rope
strung out behind me
in the fall sun
suddenly glorified with all my blood.

7

And tonight I think I prowl broken
skulled or vacant as a
sucked egg in the wintry meadow, softly chuckling, blank
template of myself, dragging
a starved belly through the lichflowered acres,
where burdock looses its arks of seed
and thistle holds up its lost blooms
and rosebushes in the wind scrape their dead limbs
for the forced-fire
of roses.

The Bear

1

In late winter
I sometimes glimpse bits of steam
coming up from
some fault in the old snow
and bend close and see it is lung-colored
and put down my nose
and know
the chilly, enduring odor of bear.

2

I take a wolf's rib and whittle
it sharp at both ends
and coil it up
and freeze it in blubber and place it out
on the fairway of the bears.

And when it has vanished
I move out on the bear tracks,
roaming in circles
until I come to the first, tentative, dark
splash on the earth.

And I set out
running, following the splashes
of blood wandering over the world.
At the cut, gashed resting places
I stop and rest,
at the crawl-marks
where he lay out on his belly
to overpass some stretch of bauchy ice
I lie out
dragging myself forward with bear-knives in my fists.

3

On the third day I begin to starve,
at nightfall I bend down as I knew I would
at a turd sopped in blood,
and hesitate, and pick it up,
and thrust it in my mouth, and gnash it down,
and rise
and go on running.

4

On the seventh day,
living by now on bear blood alone,
I can see his upturned carcass far out ahead, a scraggled,

steamy hulk,
the heavy fur riffling in the wind.

I come up to him
and stare at the narrow-spaced, petty eyes,
the dismayed
face laid back on the shoulder, the nostrils
flared, catching
perhaps the first taint of me as he
died.

I hack
a ravine in his thigh, and eat and drink,
and tear him down his whole length
and open him and climb in
and close him up after me, against the wind,
and sleep.

5

And dream
of lumbering flatfooted
over the tundra,
stabbed twice from within,
splattering a trail behind me,
splattering it out no matter which way I lurch,
no matter which parabola of bear-transcendence,
which dance of solitude I attempt,
which gravity-clutched leap,
which trudge, which groan.

6

Until one day I totter and fall —
fall on this
stomach that has tried so hard to keep up,
to digest the blood as it leaked in,
to break up
and digest the bone itself: and now the breeze
blows over me, blows off
the hideous belches of ill-digested bear blood
and rotted stomach
and the ordinary, wretched odor of bear,

blows across
my sore, lolled tongue a song
or screech, until I think I must rise up
and dance. And I lie still.

7

I awaken I think. Marshlights
reappear, geese
come trailing again up the flyway.
In her ravine under old snow the dam-bear
lies, licking
lumps of smeared fur
and drizzly eyes into shapes
with her tongue. And one
hairy-soled trudge stuck out before me,
the next groaned out,
the next,
the next,
the rest of my days I spend

wandering: wondering
what, anyway,
was that sticky infusion, that rank flavor of blood, that poetry,
    by which I lived?

The Book of Nightmares

1971

To Maud and Fergus

But this, though: death,
the whole of death, — even before life's begun,
to hold it all so gently, and be good:
this is beyond description!

— Rilke

I

Under the Maud Moon

On the path,
by this wet site
of old fires —
black ashes, black stones, where tramps
must have squatted down,
gnawing on stream water,
unhouseling themselves on cursed bread,
failing to get warm at a twigfire —

I stop,
gather wet wood,
cut dry shavings, and for her,
whose face
I held in my hands
a few hours, whom I gave back
only to keep holding the space where she was,

I light
a small fire in the rain.

The black
wood reddens, the deathwatches inside
begin running out of time, I can see
the dead, crossed limbs
longing again for the universe, I can hear
in the wet wood the snap
and re-snap of the same embrace being torn.

The raindrops trying
to put the fire out
fall into it and are
changed: the oath broken,
the oath sworn between earth and water, flesh and spirit, broken,
to be sworn again,
over and over, in the clouds, and broken again,
over and over, on earth.

2

I sit awhile
by the fire, in the rain, speak
a few words into its warmth —
stone saint smooth stone — and murmur
one of the songs I used to croak
for my daughter, in her nightmares.

Somewhere out ahead of me
a black bear sits alone
on his hillside, nodding from side
to side. He sniffs
the blossom-smells, the rained earth,
finally he gets up,
eats a few flowers, trudges away,
all his fur glistening
in the rain.

The singed grease streams
out of the words, the one
held note
remains — a love-note

twisting under my tongue, like the coyote's bark,
curving off, into a
howl.

3

A round-
cheeked girlchild comes awake
in her crib. The green
swaddlings tear open,
a filament or vestment
tears, the blue
flower opens.

And she who is born,
she who sings and cries,
she who begins the passage, her hair
sprouting out,
her gums budding for her first spring on earth,
the mist still clinging about
her face, puts
her hand
into her father's mouth, to take hold of
his song.

4

It is all over,
little one, the flipping
and overleaping, the watery
somersaulting alone in the oneness
under the hill, under
the old, lonely bellybutton

pushing forth again
in remembrance,
the drifting there furled in the dark,
pressing a knee or elbow
along a slippery wall, sculpting
the world with each thrash — the stream
of omphalos blood humming all about you.

5

Her head
enters the headhold
that starts sucking her forth: existence
closes down all over her, draws her
into the shuddering
grip of departure, the slow,
agonized clenches making
the last molds of her life in the dark.

6

The black eye
opens, the pupil
droozed with black hairs
stops, the chakra
on top of the brain throbs a long moment in world light,

and she skids out on her face into light,
this peck
of stunned flesh
clotted with celestial cheesiness, glowing
with the astral violet
of the underlife. As they cut

her tie to the darkness
she dies
a moment, turns blue as a coal,
the limbs shaking
as the memories rush out of them. When

they hang her up
by the feet, she sucks
air, screams
her first song — and turns rose,
the slow,
beating, featherless arms
already clutching at the emptiness.

7

When it was cold
on our hillside, and you cried
in the crib rocking
through the darkness, on wood
knifed down to the curve of the smile, a sadness
stranger than ours, all of it
turned back toward the other world,

I used to come to you
and sit by you
and sing to you. You did not know,
and yet you will remember,
in the silent zones
of the brain, a specter, descendant
of the ghostly forefathers, singing

to you in the nighttime —
not the songs
of light said to wave
through the bright hair of angels,
but a blacker
rasping flowering on that tongue.

For when the Maud moon
glimmered in those first nights,
and the Archer lay
sucking the icy biestings of the cosmos
in his crib of stars,

I had crept down
to riverbanks, their long rustle
of being and perishing, down to marshes
where the earth oozes up
in cold streaks, touching the world
with the underglimmer
of the beginning,
and there learned my only song.

And in the days
when you find yourself orphaned,
emptied
of wind-singing, of light,
the pieces of cursed bread on your tongue,

may there come back to you
a voice,

spectral, calling you
sister!
from everything that dies.

And then
you shall open
this book, even if it is the book of nightmares.

II

The Hen Flower

    Sprawled
on our faces in the spring
nights, teeth
biting down on hen feathers, bits of the hen
still stuck in the crevices — if only
we could let ourselves go
like her, throw ourselves
on the mercy of darkness, like the hen,

tuck our head
under a wing, hold ourselves still
a few moments, as she
falls out into her little trance in the witchgrass,
or turn over
and be stroked with a finger
down the throat feathers,
down the throat knuckles,
down over the hum
of the wishbone tuning its high D in thin blood,
down over
the breastbone risen up
out of breast flesh, until the fatted thing
woozes off, head
thrown back
on the chopping block, longing only
to die.

2

When the axe-
scented breeze flourishes
about her, her cheeks crush in,
her comb
grays, the gizzard
that turns the thousand acidic millstones of her fate
convulses: ready or not
the next egg, bobbling
its globe of golden earth,
skids forth, ridding her even
of the life to come.

3

Almost high
on subsided gravity, I remain afoot,
a hen flower
dangling from a hand,
wing
of my wing,
of my bones and veins,
of my flesh
hairs lifting all over me in the first ghostly breeze
after death,

wing
made only to fly — unable
to write out the sorrows of being unable
to hold another in one's arms — and unable
to fly,

and waiting, therefore,
for the sweet, eventual blaze in the genes,
that one day, according to gospel, shall carry it back
into pink skies, where geese
cross at twilight, honking
in tongues.

4

I have glimpsed
by corpse-light, in the opened cadaver
of hen, the mass of tiny,
unborn eggs, each getting
tinier and yellower as it reaches back toward
the icy pulp
of what is, I have felt the zero
freeze itself around the finger dipped slowly in.

5

When the Northern Lights
were opening across the black sky and vanishing,
lighting themselves up
so completely they were vanishing,
I put to my eye the lucent
section of the spealbone of a ram —

I thought suddenly
I could read the cosmos spelling itself,
the huge broken letters
shuddering across the black sky and vanishing,

and in a moment,
in the twinkling of an eye, it came to me
the mockingbird would sing all her nights the cry of the rifle,
the tree would hold the bones of the sniper who dared not
    climb down,
the rose would bloom no one would see it,
the chameleon longing to be changed would remain the color
    of blood.

And I went up
to the henhouse, and took up
the hen killed by weasels, and lugged
the sucked
carcass into first light. And when I hoisted
her up among the young pines, a last
rubbery egg slipping out as I flung her high, didn't it happen
the dead
wings creaked open as she soared
across the arms of the Bear?

6

Sprawled face down, waiting
for the rooster to groan out
it is the empty morning, as he groaned out thrice
for the disciple
of stone,
he who crushed with his heel the brain out of the snake,

I remember long ago I sowed
my own first milk
tooth under hen feathers, I planted under hen feathers

the hook
of the wishbone,
which had broken itself toward me.

For the future.

It has come to this.

7

Listen, Kinnell,
dumped alive
and dying into the old sway bed,
a layer of crushed feathers all that there is
between you
and the long shaft of darkness shaped as you,
let go.

Even this haunted room
all its materials photographed with tragedy,
even the tiny crucifix drifting face down at the center of the earth,
even these feathers freed from their wings forever
are afraid.

III

The Shoes of Wandering

I

    Squatting at the rack
    in the Store of the Salvation
    Army, putting on, one after one,
    these shoes strangers have died from, I discover
    the eldershoes of my feet,
    that take my feet
    as their first feet, clinging
    down to the least knuckle and corn.

    And I walk out now,
    in dead shoes, in the new light,
    on the steppingstones
    of someone else's wandering,
    a twinge
    in this foot or that saying
    turn or *stay* or *take*
    forty-three giant steps
    backwards, frightened
    I may already have lost
    the way: *the first step,* the Crone
    who scried the crystal said, *shall be*
    to lose the way.

2

    Back at the Xvarna Hotel, I leave
    unlocked the door jimmied over and over,
    I draw the one,
    lightning-tracked blind

in the narrow room under the freeway, I put off
the shoes, set them
side by side
by the bedside, curl
up on bedclothes gone stiff
from love-acid, night-sweat, gnash-dust
of tooth, and lapse back
into darkness.

3

A faint,
creaking noise
starts up in the room,
low-passing wing-
beats, or great, labored breath-takings
of somebody lungsore or old.

And the old
footsmells in the shoes, touched
back to life by my footsweats, as by
a child's kisses, rise,
drift up where I lie
self-hugged on the bedclothes, slide
down the flues
of dozed, beating hairs, and I can groan

or wheeze, it will be
the groan or wheeze of another — the elderfoot
of these shoes, the drunk
who died in this room, whose dream-child
might have got a laugh

out of those clenched, corned feet, putting
huge, comical kisses on them
through the socks, or a brother
shipped back burned
from the burning of Asians, sweating
his nightmare out to the end
in some whitewashed warehouse
for dying — the groan
or wheeze of one
who lays bare his errors by a harsher light,
his self-mutterings worse
than the farts, grunts, and belches
of an Oklahoma men's room,
as I shudder down to his nightmare.

4

The witness trees
blaze themselves a last time: the road
trembles as it starts across
swampland streaked with shined water, a lethe-
wind of chill air touches
me all over my body,
certain brain cells crackle like softwood in a great fire
or die,
each step a shock,
a shattering underfoot of mirrors sick of the itch
of our face-bones under their skins,
as memory reaches out
and lays bloody hands on the future, the haunted
shoes rising and falling

through the dust, wings of dust
lifting around them, as they flap
down the brainwaves of the temporal road.

5

Is it the foot,
which rubs the cobblestones
and snakestones all its days, this lowliest
of tongues, whose lick-tracks tell
our history of errors to the dust behind,
which is the last trace in us
of wings?

And is it
the hen's nightmare, or her secret dream,
to scratch the ground forever
eating the minutes out of the grains of sand?

6

On this road
on which I do not know how to ask for bread,
on which I do not know how to ask for water,
this path
inventing itself
through jungles of burnt flesh, ground of ground
bones, crossing itself
at the odor of blood, and stumbling on,

I long for the mantle
of the great wanderers, who lighted

their steps by the lamp
of pure hunger and pure thirst,

and whichever way they lurched was the way.

7

But when the Crone
held up my crystal skull to the moon,
when she passed my shoulder bones
across the Aquarian stars, she said:

You live
under the Sign
of the Bear, who flounders through chaos
in his starry blubber:
poor fool,
poor forked branch
of applewood, you will feel all your bones
break
over the holy waters you will never drink.

IV

Dear Stranger
Extant in Memory by the Blue Juniata

1

Having given up
on the deskman passed out
under his clock, who was to have banged
it is morning
on the police-locked, sheetmetal door,

I can hear the chime
of the Old Tower, tinny sacring-bell drifting out
over the city — chyme
of our loves
the peristalsis of the will to love forever
drives down, grain
after grain, into the last,
coldest room, which is memory —

and listen for the maggots
inhabiting beds old men have died in
to crawl out,
to break into the brain and cut
the nerves which keep the book of solitude.

2

Dear Galway,
      It began late one April night when I couldn't sleep. It was the
dark of the moon. My hand felt numb, the pencil went over the

page drawn on its way by I don't know what. It drew circles and figure-eights and mandalas. I cried. I had to drop the pencil. I was shaking. I went to bed and tried to pray. At last I relaxed. Then I felt my mouth open. My tongue moved, my breath wasn't my own. The whisper which forced itself through my teeth said, *Virginia, your eyes shine back to me from my own world.* O God, I thought. My breath came short, my heart opened. O God I thought, now I have a demon lover.

Yours, faithless to this life,

Virginia

3

At dusk, by the blue Juniata —
"a rural America," the magazine said,
"now vanished, but extant in memory,
a primal garden lost forever . . ."
("You see," I told Mama, "we just *think* we're here . . .") —
the root-hunters
go out into the woods, pull up
love-roots from the virginal glades, bend
the stalks over shovel-handles
and lever them up, the huge,
bass, final
thrump
as each root unclutches from its spot.

4

Take kettle
of blue water.
Boil over twigfire

of ash wood. Grind root.
Throw in. Let macerate. Reheat
over ash ashes. Bottle.
Stopper with thumb
of dead man. Ripen
forty days in horse dung
in the wilderness. Drink.
Sleep.

And when you rise —
if you do rise — it will be in the sothic year
made of the raised salvages
of the fragments all unaccomplished
of years past, scraps
and jettisons of time mortality
could not grind down into his meal of blood and laughter.

And if there is one more love
to be known, one more poem
to be opened into life,
you will find it here
or nowhere. Your hand will move
on its own
down the curving path, drawn
down by the terror and terrible lure
of vacuum:

a face materializes into your hands,
on the absolute whiteness of pages

a poem writes itself out: its title — the dream
of all poems and the text
of all loves — "Tenderness toward Existence."

5

On this bank — our bank —
of the blue, vanished water, you lie,
crying in your bed, hearing those
small,
fearsome thrumps
of leave-taking trespassing the virginal woods at dusk.

I, too, have eaten
the meals of the dark shore. In time's
own mattress, where a sag shaped as a body
lies next to a sag — graves
tossed into it
by those who came before,
lovers,
or loving friends,
or strangers,
who loved here,
or ground their nightmared teeth here,
or talked away their one-night stands,
the sanctus-bell
going out each hour to die against the sheerglass city —

I lie without sleeping, remembering
the ripped body

of hen, the warmth of hen flesh
frightening my hand,
all her desires,
all her deathsmells,
blooming again in the starlight. And then the wait —

not long, I grant, but all my life —
for the small, soft
thud of her return among the stones.

Can it ever be true —
all bodies, one body, one light
made of everyone's darkness together?

6

Dear Galway,

    I have no one to turn to because God is my enemy. He gave me
lust and joy and cut off my hands. My brain is smothered with his
blood. I asked why should I love this body I fear. He said, *It is so
lordly, it can never be shaped again — dear, shining casket. Have you
never been so proud of a thing you wanted it for your prey?* His voice
chokes my throat. Soul of asps, master and taker: he wants to kill
me. Forgive my blindness.

Yours, in the darkness,

Virginia

7

Dear stranger
extant in memory by the blue Juniata,
these letters

across space I guess
will be all we will know of one another.

So little of what one is threads itself through the eye
of empty space.

Never mind.
The self is the least of it.
Let our scars fall in love.

V

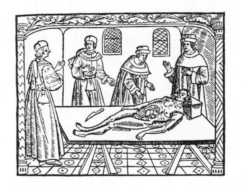

In the Hotel of Lost Light

1

In the left-
hand sag the drunk smelling of autopsies
died in, my body slumped out
into the shape of his, I watch, as he
must have watched, a fly
tangled in mouth-glue, whining his wings,
concentrated wholly on
time, time, losing his way worse
down the downward-winding stairs, his wings
whining for life as he shrivels
in the gaze
from the spider's clasped forebrains, the abstracted stare
in which even the nightmare spatters out its horrors
and dies.

Now the fly
ceases to struggle, his wings
flutter out the music blooming with failure
of one who gets ready to die, as Roland's horn, winding down
from the Pyrenees, saved its dark, full flourishes
for last.

2

In the light
left behind by the little
spiders of blood who garbled
their memoirs across his shoulders

and chest, the room
echoes with the tiny thrumps
of crotch hairs plucking themselves
from their spots; on the stripped skin
the love-sick crab lice
struggle to unstick themselves and sprint from the doomed position —

and stop,
heads buried
for one last taste of the love-flesh.

3

Flesh
of his excavated flesh,
fill of his emptiness,
after-amanuensis of his after-life,
I write out
for him in this languished alphabet
of worms, these last words
of himself, post for him
his final postcards to posterity.

4

"I sat out by twigfires flaring in grease strewn from the pimpled
        limbs of hen,
I blacked out into oblivion by that crack in the curb where the forget-
        me blooms,
I saw the ferris wheel writing its huge, desolate zeroes in neon on
        the evening skies,
I painted my footsoles purple for the day when the beautiful color
        would show,

I staggered death-sentences down empty streets, the cobblestones
     assured me, *it shall be so,*
I heard my own cries already howled inside bottles the waves washed
     up on beaches,
I ghostwrote my prayers myself in the body-Arabic of these night-
     mares.

"If the deskman knocks, griping again
about the sweet, excremental
odor of opened cadaver creeping out
from under the door, tell him, 'Friend, *To Live*
has a poor cousin,
who calls tonight, who pronounces the family name
To Leave, she
changes each visit the flesh-rags on her bones.'"

5

Violet bruises come out
all over his flesh, as invisible
fists start beating him a last time; the whine
of omphalos blood starts up again, the puffed
bellybutton explodes, the carnal
nightmare soars back to the beginning.

6

As for the bones to be tossed
into the aceldama back of the potting shop, among
shards and lumps
which caught vertigo and sagged away
into mud, or crawled out of fire
crazed or exploded, they shall re-arise

in the pear tree, in spring, to shine down
on two clasping what they dream is one another.

As for these words scattered into the future —
posterity
is one invented too deep in its past
to hear them.

7

The foregoing scribed down
in March, of the year Seventy,
on my sixteen-thousandth night of war and madness,
in the Hotel of Lost Light, under the freeway
which roams out into the dark
of the moon, in the absolute spell
of departure, and by the light
from the joined hemispheres of the spider's eyes.

VI

The Dead Shall
Be Raised Incorruptible

I

A piece of flesh gives off
smoke in the field —

caput mortuum,
orts,
pelf,
nast,
fenks,
sordes,
gurry dumped from hospital trashcans.

Lieutenant!
This corpse will not stop burning!

2

"That you Captain? Sure,
sure I remember — I still hear you
lecturing at me on the intercom, *Keep your guns up, Burnsie!*
and then screaming, *Stop shooting, for crissake, Burnsie,*
those are friendlies! But crissake, Captain,
I'd already started, burst
after burst, little black pajamas jumping
and falling . . . and remember that pilot
who'd bailed out over the North,
how I shredded him down to a bunch of guts on his strings?
one of his slant eyes, a piece

of his smile, sail past me
every night right after the sleeping pill . . .

"It was only
that I loved the *sound*
of them, I guess I just loved
the *feel* of them sparkin' off my hands . . ."

3

On the television screen:

Do you have a body that sweats?
Sweat that has odor?
False teeth dropping into your breakfast?
Case of the dread?
Headache so steady it may outlive you?
Armpits sprouting hair?
Piles so huge you hardly need a chair to sit at a table?

We shall not all sleep, but we shall be changed . . .

4

In the Twentieth Century of my trespass on earth,
having exterminated all I could of heathens,
heretics, Jews, Moslems, witches, mystical seekers,
Asians, black men, and white Christian brothers,
every one of them for his own good,

a continent of red men for living in community
and having spiritual relations with the land,

one billion species of animals for being sub-human,
and ready to take on the bloodthirsty creatures from the other planets,
I, white Christian man, groan out this testament of my last will.

I give my blood fifty parts polystyrene,
twenty-five parts benzene, twenty-five parts good old gasoline,
to the last bomber pilot aloft, that there shall be one acre
in the dull world where the kissing flower may bloom,
which kisses you so long your bones explode under its lips.

My tongue goes to the Secretary of the Dead
to tell the corpses, "I'm sorry, fellows,
the killing was just one of those things
difficult to pre-visualize — like a cow,
say, getting blown up by lightning."

My stomach, which has digested
four hundred treaties giving the Indians
eternal right to their land, I give to the Indians,
I throw in my lungs which have spent four hundred years
sucking in good faith on peace pipes.

My soul I leave to the bee
that he may sting it and die, my brain
to the fly, his back the hysterical color of slime,
that he may eat it and die, my flesh to the advertising man,
the anti-prostitute, who loathes human flesh for money.

I assign my crooked backbone
to the dice maker, to chop up into dice,
for casting lots as to who shall see his own blood

on his shirt front and who his brother's,
for the race isn't to the swift but to the crooked.

To the last person surviving on earth
I give my eyelids worn out by fear, to wear
in the long nights of radiation and silence,
so that the eyes can't close, for regret
is like tears seeping through closed eyelids.

I give the emptiness my hand: the pinkie picks no more noses,
slag clings to the black stick of the ring finger,
a bit of flame jets from the tip of the fuck-you finger,
the first finger accuses the heart, which has vanished,
on the thumb stump wisps of smoke ask a ride into the emptiness.

In the Twentieth Century of my nightmare
on earth, I swear on my chromium testicles
to this testament
and last will
of my iron will, my fear of love, my itch for money, and my madness.

5

In the ditch
snakes crawl cool paths
over the rotted thigh, the toe bones
twitch in the smell of burnt rubber,
the belly
opens like a deadly nightflower,
the tongue has evaporated,
the nostril
hairs sprinkle themselves with yellowish-white dust,

the five flames at the end
of each hand go out, a mosquito
sips a last meal from this plate of serenity.

And the fly,
the last nightmare, hatches himself.

6

I ran
my neck broken I ran
holding my head up with both hands I ran
thinking the flames
the flames may burn the oboe
but listen buddy boy they can't touch the notes.

7

A few bones
lie about in the smoke of bones.

Effigies pressed into grass,
mummy windings,
desquamations,
union suits on racks in thrift shops
sags incinerated mattresses gave back to the world,
memories left in mirrors on whorehouse ceilings,
angel's wings
flagged down into the snows of yesteryear,

kneel
on the scorched earth
in the shapes of men and animals:

do not let this last hour pass,
do not remove this last, poisoned cup from our lips.

And a wind holding
the cries of love-making from our nights and days
moves among the stones, hunting
for two twined skeletons to blow its last cry across.

Lieutenant!
This corpse will not stop burning!

VII

Little Sleep's-Head
Sprouting Hair in the Moonlight

I

You cry, waking from a nightmare.

When I sleepwalk
into your room, and pick you up,
and hold you up in the moonlight, you cling to me
hard,
as if clinging could save us. I think
you think
I will never die, I think I exude
to you the permanence of smoke or stars,
even as
my broken arms heal themselves around you.

2

I have heard you tell
the sun, *don't go down,* I have stood by
as you told the flower, *don't grow old,*
don't die. Little Maud,

I would blow the flame out of your silver cup,
I would suck the rot from your fingernail,
I would brush your sprouting hair of the dying light,
I would scrape the rust off your ivory bones,
I would help death escape through the little ribs of your body,
I would alchemize the ashes of your cradle back into wood,
I would let nothing of you go, ever,

until washerwomen
feel the clothes fall asleep in their hands,
and hens scratch their spell across hatchet blades,
and rats walk away from the cultures of the plague,
and iron twists weapons toward the true north,
and grease refuses to slide in the machinery of progress,
and men feel as free on earth as fleas on the bodies of men,
and lovers no longer whisper to the presence beside them in the
    dark, *O corpse-to-be* . . .

And yet perhaps this is the reason you cry,
this the nightmare you wake crying from:
being forever
in the pre-trembling of a house that falls.

3

In a restaurant once, everyone
quietly eating, you clambered up
on my lap: to all
the mouthfuls rising toward
all the mouths, at the top of your voice
you cried
your one word, *caca! caca! caca!*
and each spoonful
stopped, a moment, in midair, in its withering
steam.

Yes,
you cling because
I, like you, only sooner
than you, will go down

the path of vanished alphabets,
the roadlessness
to the other side of the darkness,
your arms
like the shoes left behind,
like the adjectives
in the halting speech of old men,
which once could call up the lost nouns.

4

And you yourself,
some impossible Tuesday
in the year Two Thousand and Nine, will walk out
among the black stones
of the field, in the rain,

and the stones saying
over their one word, *ci-gît, ci-gît, ci-gît,*

and the raindrops
hitting you on the fontanel
over and over, and you standing there
unable to let them in.

5

If one day it happens
you find yourself with someone you love
in a café at one end
of the Pont Mirabeau, at the zinc bar
where wine finds its shapes in upward opening glasses,

and if you commit then, as we did, the error
of thinking,
one day all this will only be memory,

learn to reach deeper
into the sorrows
to come — to touch
the almost imaginary bones
under the face, to hear under the laughter
the wind crying across the black stones. Kiss
the mouth
that tells you, *here,*
here is the world. This mouth. This laughter. These temple bones.

The still undanced cadence of vanishing.

6

In the light the moon
sends back, I can see in your eyes

the hand that waved once
in my father's eyes, a tiny kite
wobbling far up in the twilight of his last look:

and the angel
of all mortal things lets go the string.

7

Back you go, into your crib.

The last blackbird lights up his gold wings: *farewell.*
Your eyes close inside your head,
in sleep. Already
in your dreams the hours begin to sing.

Little sleep's-head sprouting hair in the moonlight,
when I come back
we will go out together,
we will walk out together among
the ten thousand things,
each scratched in time with such knowledge, *the wages
of dying is love.*

VIII

The Call Across
the Valley of Not-Knowing

1

In the red house sinking down
into ground rot, a lamp
at one window, the smarled ashes letting
a single flame go free,
a shoe of dreaming iron nailed to the wall,
two mismatched halfnesses lying side by side in the darkness,
I can feel with my hand
the foetus rouse himself
with a huge, fishy thrash, and re-settle in his darkness.

Her hair glowing in the firelight,
her breasts full,
her belly swollen,
a sunset of firelight
wavering all down one side, my wife sleeps on,
happy,
far away, in some other,
newly opened room of the world.

2

Sweat breaking from his temples,
Aristophanes ran off
at the mouth — made it all up, nightmared it all up
on the spur
of that moment which has stabbed us ever since:
that each of us
is a torn half

whose lost other we keep seeking across time
until we die, or give up —
or actually find her:

as I myself, in an Ozark
Airlines DC-6 droning over
towns made of crossroads, headed down
into Waterloo, Iowa, actually found her,
held her face a few hours
in my hands; and for reasons — cowardice,
loyalties, all which goes by the name "necessity"—
left her . . .

3

And yet I think
it must be the wound, the wound itself,
which lets us know and love,
which forces us to reach out to our misfit
and by a kind
of poetry of the soul, accomplish,
for a moment, the wholeness the drunk Greek
extrapolated from his high
or flagellated out of an empty heart,

that purest,
most tragic concumbence, strangers
clasped into one, a moment, of their moment on earth.

4

She who lies halved
beside me — she and I once

watched the bees, dreamers not yet
dipped into the acids
of the craving for anything, not yet burned down into flies, sucking
the blossom-dust
from the pear-tree in spring,

we two
lay out together
under the tree, on earth, beside our empty clothes,
our bodies opened to the sky,
and the blossoms glittering in the sky
floated down
and the bees glittered in the blossoms
and the bodies of our hearts
opened
under the knowledge
of tree, on the grass of the knowledge
of graves, and among the flowers of the flowers.

And the brain kept blossoming
all through the body, until the bones themselves could think,
and the genitals sent out wave after wave of holy desire
until even the dead brain cells
surged and fell in god-like, androgynous fantasies —
and I understood
the unicorn's phallus could have risen, after all,
directly out of thought itself.

5

Of that time in a Southern jail,
when the sheriff, as he cursed me

and spat, took my hand in his hand, rocked
from the pulps the whorls
and tented archways into the tabooed realm, that underlife
where the canaries of the blood are singing, pressed
the flesh-flowers
into the dirty book of the
police-blotter, afterwards what I remembered most
was the care, the almost loving,
animal gentleness of his hand on my hand.

Better than the rest of us, he knows
the harshness of that cubicle
in hell where they put you
with all your desires undiminished, and with no body to
    appease them.

And when he himself floats out
on a sea he almost begins to remember,
floats out into a darkness he has known already;
when the moan of wind
and the gasp of lungs call to each other among the waves
and the wish to float
comes to matter not at all as he sinks under,

is it so impossible to think
he will dream back to all the hands black and white
he took in his hands
as the creation
touches him a last time all over his body?

6

Suppose I had stayed
with that woman of Waterloo, suppose
we had met on a hill called Safa, in our own country,
that we had lain out on the grass
and looked into each other's blindness, under leaf-shadows
wavering across our bodies in the drifts of sun,
our faces
inclined toward each other, as hens
incline their faces
when the heat flows from the warmed egg
back into the whole being, and the silver moon
had stood still for us in the middle of heaven —

I think I might have closed my eyes, and moved
from then on like the born blind,
their faces
gone into heaven already.

7

We who live out our plain lives, who put
our hand into the hand of whatever we love
as it vanishes,
as we vanish,
and stumble toward what will be, simply by arriving,
a kind of fate,

some field, maybe, of flaked stone
scattered in starlight
where the flesh

swaddles its skeleton a last time
before the bones go their way without us,

might we not hear, even then,
the bear call
from his hillside — a call, like ours, needing
to be answered — and the dam-bear
call back across the darkness
of the valley of not-knowing
the only word tongues shape without intercession,

yes . . . yes . . . ?

IX

The Path Among the Stones

1

On the path winding
upward, toward the high valley
of waterfalls and flooded, hoof-shattered
meadows of spring,
where fish-roots boil
in the last grails of light on the water,
and vipers pimpled with urges to fly
drape the black stones hissing *pheet! pheet!* — land
of quills
and inkwells of skulls filled with black water —

I come to a field
glittering with the thousand sloughed skins
of arrowheads, stones
which shuddered and leapt forth
to give themselves into the broken hearts
of the living,
who gave themselves back, broken, to the stone.

2

I close my eyes:
on the heat-rippled beaches
where the hills came down to the sea,
the luminous
beach dust pounded out of funeral shells,
I can see

them living without me, dying
without me, the wing
and egg
shaped stones, broken
war-shells of slain fighting conches,
dog-eared immortality shells
in which huge constellations of slime, by the full moon,
writhed one more
coat of invisibility on a speck of sand,

and the agates knocked
from circles scratched into the dust
with the click
of a wishbone breaking, inward-swirling
globes biopsied out of sunsets never to open again,

and that wafer-stone
which skipped ten times across
the water, suddenly starting to run as it went under,
and the zeroes it left,
that met
and passed into each other, they themselves
smoothing themselves from the water . . .

3

I walk out from myself,
among the stones of the field,
each sending up its ghost-bloom
into the starlight, to float out
over the trees, seeking to be one
with the unearthly fires kindling and dying

in space — and falling back, knowing
the sadness of the wish
to alight
back among the glitter of bruised ground,
the stones holding between pasture and field,
the great, granite nuclei,
glimmering, even they, with ancient inklings of madness and war.

4

A way opens
at my feet. I go down
the night-lighted mule-steps into the earth,
the footprints behind me
filling already with pre-sacrificial trills
of canaries, go down
into the unbreathable goaf
of everything I ever craved and lost.

An old man, a stone
lamp at his forehead, squats
by his hell-flames, stirs into
his pot
chopped head
of crow, strings of white light,
opened tail of peacock, dressed
body of canary, robin breast
dragged through the mud of battlefields, wrung-out
blossom of caput mortuum flower — salts
it all down with sand
stolen from the upper bells of hourglasses . . .

Nothing.
Always nothing. Ordinary blood
boiling away in the glare of the brow lamp.

5

And yet, no,
perhaps not nothing. Perhaps
not ever nothing. In clothes
woven out of the blue spittle
of snakes, I crawl up: I find myself alive
in the whorled
archway of the fingerprint of all things,
skeleton groaning,
blood-strings wailing the wail of all things.

6

The witness trees heal
their scars at the flesh fire,
the flame
rises off the bones,
the hunger
to be new lifts off
my soul, an eerie blue light blooms
on all the ridges of the world. Somewhere
in the legends of blood sacrifice
the fatted calf
takes the bonfire into his arms, and *he*
burns *it*.

7

As above: the last scattered stars
kneel down in the star-form of the Aquarian age:
a splash
on the top of the head,
on the grass of this earth even the stars love, splashes of the
    sacred waters . . .

So below: in the graveyard
the lamps start lighting up, one for each of us,
in all the windows
of stone.

X

Lastness

The skinny waterfalls, footpaths
wandering out of heaven, strike
the cliffside, leap, and shudder off.

Somewhere behind me
a small fire goes on flaring in the rain, in the desolate ashes.
No matter, now, whom it was built for,
it keeps its flames,
it warms
everyone who might stray into its radiance,
a tree, a lost animal, the stones,

because in the dying world it was set burning.

2

A black bear sits alone
in the twilight, nodding from side
to side, turning slowly around and around
on himself, scuffing the four-footed
circle into the earth. He sniffs the sweat
in the breeze, he understands
a creature, a death-creature,
watches from the fringe of the trees,
finally he understands
I am no longer here, he himself
from the fringe of the trees watches
a black bear

get up, eat a few flowers, trudge away,
all his fur glistening
in the rain.

And what glistening! Sancho Fergus,
my boychild, had such great shoulders,
when he was born his head
came out, the rest of him stuck. And he opened
his eyes: his head out there all alone
in the room, he squinted with pained,
barely unglued eyes at the ninth-month's
blood splashing beneath him
on the floor. And almost
smiled, I thought, almost forgave it all in advance.

When he came wholly forth
I took him up in my hands and bent
over and smelled
the black, glistening fur
of his head, as empty space
must have bent
over the newborn planet
and smelled the grasslands and the ferns.

3

Walking toward the cliff overhanging
the river, I call out to the stone,
and the stone
calls back, its voice searching among the rubble
for my ears.

Stop.
As you approach an echoing
cliffside, you sense the line
where the voice calling from stone
no longer answers,
turns into stone, and nothing comes back.

Here, between answer
and nothing, I stand, in the old shoes
flowed over by rainbows of hen-oil,
each shoe holding the bones
that ripple together in the communion
of the step
and that open out
in front into toes, the whole foot trying
to dissolve into the future.

A clatter of elk hooves.
Has the top sphere
emptied itself? Is it true
the earth is all there is, and the earth does not last?

On the river the world floats by holding one corpse.

Stop.
Stop here.
Living brings you to death, there is no other road.

4

This is the tenth poem
and it is the last. It is right
at the last, that one
and zero
walk off together,
walk off the end of these pages together,
one creature
walking away side by side with the emptiness.

Lastness
is brightness. It is the brightness
gathered up of all that went before. It lasts.
And when it does end
there is nothing, nothing
left,

in the rust of old cars,
in the hole torn open in the body of the Archer,
in river-mist smelling of the weariness of stones,
the dead lie,
empty, filled, at the beginning,

and the first
voice comes craving again out of their mouths.

5

That Bach concert I went to so long ago —
the chandeliered room
of ladies and gentlemen who would never die . . .

the voices go out,
the room becomes hushed,
the violinist
puts the irreversible sorrow of his face
into the opened palm
of the wood, the music begins:

a shower of rosin,
the bow-hairs listening down all their length
to the wail,
the sexual wail
of the back-alleys and blood strings we have lived
still crying,
still singing, from the sliced intestine
of cat.

6

This poem
if we shall call it that,
or concert of one
divided among himself,
this earthward gesture
of the sky-diver, the worms
on his back still spinning forth
and already gnawing away
the silks of his loves, who could have saved him,
this free floating of one
opening his arms into the attitude
of flight, as he obeys the necessity and falls . . .

7

Sancho Fergus! Don't cry!

Or else, cry.

On the body,
on the yellowed flesh, when it is
laid out, see if you can find
the one flea that is laughing.

Mortal Acts, Mortal Words

1980

to Demetrio Delgado de Torres
tu valiente alegría

. . . mortal beauty, acts, and words have put
all their burden on my soul.

— Petrarch

PART I

Fergus Falling

He climbed to the top
of one of those million white pines
set out across the emptying pastures
of the fifties — some program to enrich the rich
and rebuke the forefathers
who cleared it all once with ox and axe —
climbed to the top, probably to get out
of the shadow
not of those forefathers but of this father,
and saw for the first time,
down in its valley, Bruce Pond, giving off
its little steam in the afternoon,

pond where Clarence Akley came on Sunday mornings to cut down
 the cedars around the shore, I'd sometimes hear the slow spondees
 of his work, he's gone,
where Milton Norway came up behind me while I was fishing and
 stood awhile before I knew he was there, he's the one who put the
 cedar shingles on the house, some have curled or split, a few have
 blown off, he's gone,
where Gus Newland logged in the cold snap of '58, the only man will-
 ing to go into those woods that never got warmer than ten below,
 he's gone,
pond where two wards of the state wandered on Halloween, the Na-
 tional Guard searched for them in November, in vain, the next fall
 a hunter found their skeletons huddled together, in vain, they're
 gone,
pond where an old fisherman in a rowboat sits, drowning hooked
 worms, when he goes he's replaced and he's never gone,

and when Fergus
saw the pond for the first time
in the clear evening, saw its oldness down there
in its old place in the valley, he became heavier suddenly
in his bones
the way fledglings do just before they fly,
and the soft pine cracked . . .

I would not have heard his cry
if my electric saw had been working,
its carbide teeth speeding through the bland spruce of our time,
    or scorching
black arcs into some scavenged hemlock plank,
like dark circles under eyes
when the brain thinks too close to the skin,
but I was sawing by hand, and I heard that cry
as though he were attacked; we ran out,
when we bent over him he said, "Galway, Inés, I saw a pond!"
His face went gray, his eyes fluttered closed a frightening moment.

Yes — a pond
that lets off its mist
on clear afternoons of August, in that valley
to which many have come, for their reasons,
from which many have gone, a few for their reasons, most not,
where even now an old fisherman only the pinetops can see
sits in the dry gray wood of his rowboat, waiting for pickerel.

After Making Love We Hear Footsteps

For I can snore like a bullhorn
or play loud music
or sit up talking with any reasonably sober Irishman
and Fergus will only sink deeper
into his dreamless sleep, which goes by all in one flash,
but let there be that heavy breathing
or a stifled come-cry anywhere in the house
and he will wrench himself awake
and make for it on the run — as now, we lie together,
after making love, quiet, touching along the length of our bodies,
familiar touch of the long-married,
and he appears — in his baseball pajamas, it happens,
the neck opening so small he has to screw them on —
and flops down between us and hugs us and snuggles himself to sleep,
his face gleaming with satisfaction at being this very child.

In the half darkness we look at each other
and smile
and touch arms across this little, startlingly muscled body —
this one whom habit of memory propels to the ground of his making,
sleeper only the mortal sounds can sing awake,
this blessing love gives again into our arms.

Angling, a Day

Though day is just breaking
when we fling two nightcrawlers
bunched on a hook as far out

as we can into Crystal Lake so leaden
no living thing could possibly swim through it
and let them lie on the bottom, under
the layer of water and, on top of it,
the layer of mist in which the doubled sun
soon appears and before long the doubled
mountains; though we drag Lake Parker
with fishing apparatus of several sorts,
catching a few yellow perch which we keep
just to have caught *something;* though
we comb with fine, and also coarse,
toothed hooks Shirley's Pond stocked
with trout famous for swallowing
any sharpened wire no matter
how inexpertly disguised as a worm;
though we fish the pools thick with fish
Bill Allen has divined by dip of bamboo
during all those misspent days trout witching
Miller Run; though we cast some hours
away at the Lamoille, at the bend
behind Eastern Magnesia Talc Company's
Mill No. 4, which Hayden Carruth
says his friend John Engels says
is the best fishing around ("hernia bend,"
Engels calls it, I believe on account of the weight
of fish you haul out of there); and though we
fish the Salmon Hole of the Winooski
in which twenty-inch walleyes moil,
we and a dozen others who keep faith
with earth by the thinness of that string
tying each person to the river at twilight,

casting and, as we reel in, twitching the rod,
our bodies curvetting in that curious motion
by which people giving fish motions to lures
wiggle themselves like fish, until Fergus' jig,
catching a rock as he reels in,
houdinies out of its knot, and the man
fishing next to us, Ralph, reeling
somewhat himself due to an afternoon of much ale,
lends us one of his, and with shaking hands
ties a stout knot between line and jig,
while a fellow from downcountry
goes on about how to free a snagged line
by sliding a spark plug down it —
"Well," Ralph says a couple of times,
"I sure never heard of that one,"
though sure enough, a few minutes later,
when Ralph's own line gets snagged,
he takes the fellow up on the idea,
borrows the man's spark plug, taps
the gap closed over the line as directed,
and lets her slide, wiggling
vigorously as the plug disappears
into the water, and instantly loses it
and the jig both, and says, "Nope,
I sure never heard of that one" —
though, in brief, we have crossed the entire state
up at its thick end, and fished with hope
all the above-mentioned fishing spots
from before first light to after nightfall
and now will just be able to make it
to Essex Junction in time

to wait the several hours that must pass
before the train arrives in reality,
we have caught nothing — not counting,
of course, the three yellow perch Fergus
gave away earlier in the day to Bill and Anne
Allen's cat Monsoon, who is mostly dead
along her left side though OK on her right,
the side she was no doubt lying on the night
last winter when, literally, she half froze to death —
and wondering if Fergus, who's so tired
he now gets to his feet only to cast
and at once sits back down, might be thoroughly
defeated, and his noble passion for fishing
broken, I ask him how he feels:
"I'm disappointed," he says, "but not discouraged.
I'm not saying I'm a fisherman, but fishermen know
there are days when you don't catch anything."

Saint Francis and the Sow

The bud
stands for all things,
even for those things that don't flower,
for everything flowers, from within, of self-blessing;
though sometimes it is necessary
to reteach a thing its loveliness,
to put a hand on its brow
of the flower
and retell it in words and in touch
it is lovely

until it flowers again from within, of self-blessing;
as Saint Francis
put his hand on the creased forehead
of the sow, and told her in words and in touch
blessings of earth on the sow, and the sow
began remembering all down her thick length,
from the earthen snout all the way
through the fodder and slops to the spiritual curl of the tail,
from the hard spininess spiked out from the spine
down through the great broken heart
to the sheer blue milken dreaminess spurting and shuddering
from the fourteen teats into the fourteen mouths sucking and
    blowing beneath them:
the long, perfect loveliness of sow.

The Choir

Little beings with hair blooming
so differently on skulls of odd sizes
and eyes serious and jaws
firm from singing in Gilead,
and mouths gaping, "Ah!" for God
and "O!" for alphabets short on O's,
they stand in rows, each suspended
from that fishing line
hooked at the breastbone, ready to be hauled upward.

Everyone while singing is beautiful.
Even the gloomiest music

requires utter happiness to sing:
eyes, nostrils, mouth must delight each other in quintal harmony
to sing Joy or Death well.

Two Set Out on Their Journey

We sit side by side,
brother and sister, and read
the book of what will be, while a breeze
blows the pages over —
desolate odd, cheerful even,
and otherwise. When we come
to our own story, the happy beginning,
the ending we don't know yet,
the ten thousand acts
encumbering the days between,
we will read every page of it.
If an ancestor has pressed
a love-flower for us, it will lie hidden
between pages of the slow going,
where only those who adore the story
ever read. When the time comes
to shut the book and set out,
we will take childhood's laughter
as far as we can into the days to come,
until another laughter sounds back
from the place where our next bodies
will have risen and will be telling
tales of what seemed deadly serious once,

offering to us oldening wayfarers
the light heart, now made of time
and sorrow, that we started with.

Brother of My Heart

for Etheridge Knight

Brother of my heart,
isn't it true there's only one
walking into the light, one,
before the light
flashes out and this bravest knight
crashes his black bones into the earth?

You may not return
with your cried-out face
laughing; those who
die by the desire to die
may love their way back,
but maybe as grubs who latch
on to the first sorrow and lie there.

And so just as you are,
sing, even if you cry; the bravery
of the singing turns it into the true song; soul brother
in heaven, on earth
broken heart brother, sing
in this place that loses its brothers,
this emptiness the singing sometimes almost fills.

Fisherman

for Allen Planz

Solitary man, standing
on the Atlantic, high up on the floodtide
under the moon, hauling at nets
that shudder sideways under the mutilated darkness:
the one you hugged and slept with so often,
who hugged you and slept with you so often,
who has gone away now
into the imaginary moonlight of the greater world,
perhaps looks back at where you stand abandoned
on the floodtide, hauling at nets
and dragging from the darkness
anything, and reaches back
as if to touch you
and speak to you
from that other relation to which she suddenly acquiesced
    dumbfounded,
but finds she can only sing to you
in the sea-birds and breeze you truly hear but imagine you're
    remembering.

I don't know how you loved
or what marriage was and wasn't between you —
not even close friends understand very much of that —
but I know ordinary life was hard
and worry joined your brains' faces in pure, baffled lines,
and therefore some part of you will have gone
with her, imprinted now

into that world that she alone doesn't fear
and that now you have to that degree also ceased fearing,
and waits there to recognize you into it
after you've lived, lived past the sorrows,
if that happens, after all the time in the world.

Wait

Wait, for now.
Distrust everything if you have to.
But trust the hours. Haven't they
carried you everywhere, up to now?
Personal events will become interesting again.
Hair will become interesting.
Pain will become interesting.
Buds that open out of season will become interesting.
Second-hand gloves will become lovely again;
their memories are what give them
the need for other hands. The desolation
of lovers is the same: that enormous emptiness
carved out of such tiny beings as we are
asks to be filled; the need
for the new love *is* faithfulness to the old.

Wait.
Don't go too early.
You're tired. But everyone's tired.
But no one is tired enough.

Only wait a little and listen:
music of hair,
music of pain,
music of looms weaving our loves again.
Be there to hear it, it will be the only time.

PART II

Daybreak

On the tidal mud, just before sunset,
dozens of starfishes
were creeping. It was
as though the mud were a sky
and enormous, imperfect stars
moved across it as slowly
as the actual stars cross heaven.
All at once they stopped,
and as if they had simply
increased their receptivity
to gravity, they sank down
into the mud, faded down
into it and lay still, and by the time
pink of sunset broke across them
they were as invisible
as the true stars at daybreak.

The Gray Heron

It held its head still
while its body and green
legs wobbled in wide arcs
from side to side. When
it stalked out of sight,
I went after it, but all
I could find where I was
expecting to see the bird

was a three-foot-long lizard
in ill-fitting skin
and with linear mouth
expressive of the even temper
of the mineral kingdom.
It stopped and tilted its head,
which was much like
a fieldstone with an eye
in it, which was watching me
to see if I would go
or change into something else.

In the Bamboo Hut

The washerwomen would throw dresses,
shirts, pants, into the green water,
beat them, wring them out,
arrange them empty in our shapes
on stones, murmuring, laughing,
sometimes a voice more forlorn
would rise above the others, a singing
like the aftersinging, those nights
when we would wail as one under
the sign of the salamander, motionless,
attentive, on the wall above our bed.

Lava

(The Hawaiian words — *pahoehoe*, *aa*, and *heiau* — are
pronounced pä•hō•ā•hō•ā; ä•ä; and hā•ē•ow.)

I want to be pahoehoe,
swirled, gracefully lined,
folded, frozen where it flowed,
a clear brazened surface
one can cross barefooted,
it's true; but even more,
I want to be aa,
a mass of rubble still
tumbling after it has stopped —
which a person without shoes
has to do deep knee-bends across,
groaning "aaaah! aaaah!" —
and be heaped into a heiau
in sea-spray on an empty coast,
and know in all my joints
the soft, velcroish clasp
of aa hanging on to aa.

When I approach the dismal shore
made I know of pahoehoe,
which is just hoi polloi of the slopes,
I don't want to call "ahoy! ahoy!"
and sail meekly in. No,
I want to turn and look back
at that glittering, black aa
where we loved in the moon,

and all our atoms broke and lived,
where even now two kneecaps gasp
"ah! ah!" to a heiau's stone floor,
to which the floor replies
"aaaaaah, aaaaaah," in commiseration
with bones that find the way very long.

Blackberry Eating

I love to go out in late September
among the fat, overripe, icy, black blackberries
to eat blackberries for breakfast,
the stalks very prickly, a penalty
they earn for knowing the black art
of blackberry making; and as I stand among them
lifting the stalks to my mouth, the ripest berries
fall almost unbidden to my tongue,
as words sometimes do, certain peculiar words
like *strengths* or *squinched,*
many-lettered, one-syllabled lumps,
which I squeeze, squinch open, and splurge well
in the silent, startled, icy, black language
of blackberry eating in late September.

Kissing the Toad

Somewhere this dusk
a girl puckers her mouth

and considers kissing
the toad a boy has plucked
from the cornfield and hands
her with both hands,
rough and lichenous
but for the immense ivory belly,
like those old fat cats
sprawled on Mediterranean beaches,
with popped eyes, it watches
the girl who might kiss it,
pisses, quakes, tries
to make its smile wider:
to love on, oh yes, to love on.

Crying

Crying only a little bit
is no use. You must cry
until your pillow is soaked.
Then you can get up and laugh.
Then you can jump in the shower
and splash-splash-splash!
Then you can throw open your window
and, "Ha ha! ha ha!"
And if people say, "Hey,
what's going on up there?"
"Ha ha!" sing back, "Happiness
was hiding in the last tear!
I wept it! Ha ha!"

Les Invalides

At dusk by Les Invalides
a few old men play at boules,
holding the crouch
long after the toss, listening for the clack
of steel on steel, strolling over and studying the ground.

At boules, it is the creaking grace, the slow amble, the stillness,
the dusk deepening,
a plane tree casting loose a few leaves,
shadows lying behind the undistracted eyes.

It is empty cots lined up
in the darkness of rooms where the last true men
listen each dusk
for the high, thin clack
sounding from the home village very far away.

On the Tennis Court at Night

We step out on the green rectangle
in moonlight. The lines glow,
which for many have been the only lines
of justice. We remember
the thousand erased trajectories
of that close-contested last set —
blur of volleys, soft arcs of drop shots,
huge ingrown loops of lobs with topspin
that went running away, crosscourts recrossing

down to each sweet (and in exact proportion, bitter)
✪ in Talbert and Old's *The Game of Doubles in Tennis.*
The breeze has carried them off but we still hear
the mutters, the doublefaulter's groans,
cries of "Deuce!" or "Love two!,"
squeak of tennis shoes, grunt of overreaching,
all dozen extant tennis quips — "Just out!"
or, "About right for you?" or, "Want to change partners?" —
and *baaah* of sheep translated very occasionally
into *thonk* of well-hit ball, among the pure
right angles and unhesitating lines
of this arena where every man grows old
pursuing that repertoire of perfect shots,
darkness already in his strokes,
even in death cramps squeezing a tennis ball
for forearm strength, to the disgust of the night nurse,
and smiling; and a few hours later found dead —
the smile still in place but the ice bag
that had been left cooling the brow now
icing the right elbow — causing
all the bright trophies to slip permanently out of reach,
except for the thick-bottomed young man
about to doublefault in soft metal on the windowsill:
"Runner-Up Men's Class B Consolation Doubles
St. Johnsbury Kiwanis Tennis Tournament 1969."

Clouds come over the moon;
the lines go out. November last year
in Lyndonville: it is getting dark,
snow starts falling, Zander Rubin wobble-twists
his worst serve out of the black woods behind him,

Tommy Glines lobs into a gust of snow,
Don Bredes smashes at where in theory the ball
could be coming down, the snow blows
and swirls about our legs, darkness flows
across a disappearing patch of green-painted asphalt
in the north country, where four souls,
half-volleying, poaching, missing, grunting,
begging mercy of their bones, hold their ground,
as winter comes on, all the winters to come.

PART III

The Sadness of Brothers

He comes to me like a mouth
speaking from under several inches of water.
I can no longer understand what he is saying.
He has become one
who never belonged among us, someone
it is useless to think about or remember.

But this morning, I don't know why,
twenty-one years too late,
I imagine him back: his beauty
of feature somewhat wastreled down
to wattles and thick chin, his eyes
ratty, liver-lighted, he stands
in the doorway and we face each other,
each of us knowing the lost brother.

2

There was a photograph
of a tractor ploughing a field, the ploughman
twisted in his iron seat
looking behind him at the turned-up earth, among
the photographs and drawings he had hoarded up
of all the aircraft in the sky, Heinkel HE70s, Dewoitine D333
    "Antares," Loire-et-Olivier H24-2,
especially the fighting aircraft, Gloster Gauntlet, Fairey Battle I,
    Vickers Vildebeest Mark VII,
each shown crookedly
climbing an empty sky

the killer's blue of his eyes,
into which all his youth he knew
he would fly. Twelve years after
the war and the end of flying
he raced his big car
through the desert night, under
the Dipper that moved
like a great windshield wiper
squeegee-ing existence
clean of its damaged dream life
leaving only old goods, few possessions,
matter which ceased to matter, among the detritus,
these photographs of airplanes, and showing off
its gravitational allegiance
the tractor, and in its iron
seat the farmer, half-turned, watching
the earth flattening away
behind him into nowhere.

3

In this brother
I remember back is the father
I had so often seen in him: the serene-
seeming, sea-going gait which took him
down Oswald Street in dark of each morning
and up Oswald Street in dark of each night,
that small, well-wandered Scotsman
who appears now in memory's memory,
in light of last days, jiggling
his knees as he used to do —
get out of here, I knew

they were telling him, *get out of here, Scotty* —
control he couldn't control
thwarting his desires down
into knees which could only jiggle
the one bit of perhaps useful advice
this man stuck in his ending-earth
of Pawtucket, Rhode Island, ever received.

4

I think he's going to ask
for beer for breakfast, sooner
or later he'll start making obnoxious
remarks about race or sex
or criticize our loose ways
of raising children, while his eyes
grow more slick, his heart more pure,
this boy who at sixteen
would slip out at night, blackjack
in pocket, .22 pistol in armpit holster,
to make out with rich men's wives
at the Narragansett Track, now vanished
from its site on the even more vanished
What Cheer Airport, where a Waco biplane
flew up for a joyride in 1931
with him waving from the rear cockpit.

5

But no, that's fear's reading. In the doorway,
in the frailty of large,
fifty-odd-year-old bodies

of brothers, we stand —
in this vision that came to me today
of a man twenty-one years strange to me,
tired, vulnerable, half the world old,
with sore, well or badly spent, but spent,
hearts — facing each other, friends with reality,
knowing the ordinary sadness of brothers.

Goodbye

1

My mother, poor woman, lies tonight
in her last bed. It's snowing, for her, in her darkness.
I swallow down the goodbyes I won't ever get to use,
tasteless, with wretched mouth-water;
whatever we are, she and I, we're nearly cured.

The night years ago when I walked away
from that final class of junior high school students
in Pittsburgh, the youngest of them chased
after me down the dark street. "Goodbye!" she called,
snow swirling across her face, tears shining.

2

Tears have a history of falling. Gravity
has taught them a topographical understanding
of the human face. At each last embrace
the snow brings down its ragged curtain.
The mind shreds the present, once the past is over.

In the Derry graveyard where only her longings sleep
and armfuls of flowers go out in the drizzle,
the bodies not yet risen must lie nearly forever.
"Sprouting good Irish grass," the graveskeeper blarneys,
he can't help it, "a sprig of shamrock, if they were young."

3

In Pittsburgh tonight, those who were young
will be less young, those who were old, more old, or likely
no more; and the street where Syllest,
fleetest of my darlings, caught up with me
and hugged me and said goodbye will be empty. Well,

one day the streets all over the world will be empty —
already in heaven the golden cobblestones have fallen still —
everyone's arms will be empty, everyone's mouth, the Derry earth.
It is written in our hearts, the emptiness is all.
That is how we have learned, the embrace is all.

Looking at Your Face

Looking at your face
now you have become ready to die
is like kneeling at an old gravestone
on an afternoon without sun, trying to read
the white chiselings of the poem
in the white stone.

The Last Hiding Places of Snow

I

The burnt tongue
fluttered, "I'm dying..."
and then, "Why did...? Why...?"
What earthly knowledge did she need
just then, when
the tongue failed
or began speaking in another direction?

Only the struggle for breath
remained: groans made
of all the goodbyes ever spoken
all turned meaningless; surplus world sucked back
into a body laboring to live
as far as it could into death; and past it, if it must.

There is a place in the woods
where one can hear
such sounds: sighs, groans
seeming to come
from the purplish murk of spruce boughs at dusk,
from the glimmer-at-night of white birches,
from the last hiding places of snow,

wind,
that's all, blowing
across obstructions: every stump
speaks,

spruce needles play out of it
the sorrows cried into it somewhere else.

Passing the place, I've
imagined I heard
my old mother thinking out loud her
feelings toward me, over those many miles
from where her bones lie,
five years
in earth now, with my father's thirty-years' bones.

I used to feel
anointed by what I thought was her love, its light
seeming then like sunlight
falling through broken panes
onto the floor
of a deserted house: we may go, it remains,
telling of goodness of being, of permanence.

So lighted I imagined
I could wander anywhere,
among any foulnesses, any contagions,
I could climb through the entire empty world
and find my way back and learn again to be happy.

But when I stopped and listened,
all that may once have been speech
or groans had been shredded down to a hiss
from being blown through this valley of needles.

2

I was not at her bedside
that final day, I did not grant her ancient,
huge-knuckled hand
its last wish, I did not let it
let go of the son's hand gradually — and so
hand her, with some steadiness, into the future.

Instead, old age took her
by force, though with the aid
of her old, broken attachments
which had broken
only on this side of death
but kept intact on the other.

I would know myself lucky if my own children
could be at my deathbed, to take
my hand in theirs and with theirs
bless me momentarily back into the world,
with smoothness pressed into roughness,
with folding-light fresh runner hands to runner of wasted breath,
with mortal touch whose mercy two bundled-up figures greeting on a
    freezing morning, each extending the ribboned end of an arm and
    entwining these, squeeze back and forth before walking on,
with memories these hands keep, of strolling down Bethune Street
    in spring, a little creature hanging from each arm by a hand that
    can do no more than press its tiny thumb into the soft beneath my
    thumb.

But for my own mother I was not there . . .
and at the gates of the world, between

holy ground
and ground of almost all its holiness gone, I loiter
in stupid fantasies I can live that day again.

Why did you come so late?
Why will you go too early?

I know there are regrets
we can never be rid of,
that fade but never leave:
permanent remorse. Knowing this, I know also
I am to draw from that surplus stored up
of tenderness that was hers by right,
which possibly no one ever gave her,
and give it away, freely.

3

A child, a little girl,
in violet hat, blue scarf, green sweater, yellow skirt, orange socks,
    red boots,
on a rope swings, swings
in sunlight
over a garden in Ireland, backfalls,
backrises,
forthsinks,
forthsoars, her charmed life holding its breath
innocent of groans, beyond any
future, far past the past: into a pure present.

Now she wears rhythmically into the air of morning
the rainbow's curve, but upside down
so that the angels might see
beloved dross promising heaven:
no matter what fire we invent to destroy us
ours will have been the brightest world ever existing.

Every so often, when I look
at the dark sky, I know she remains
among the old endless blue lightedness
of stars; or finding myself out in a field
in November, when a strange
starry perhaps first snowfall blows
down across the darkening air, lightly,
I know she is there, where snow
falls   flakes   down   fragile   softly
falling until I can't see the earth
any longer, only its shrouded shapes.

Even now, when I wake
in some room far from everyone,
sometimes the darkness lightens a little,
and then, because of nothing,
in spite of nothing,
in an imaginary daybreak, I see her,
and for that moment I am still her son
and in the holy land, and twice in the holy land,
remembered within her, and remembered in the memory
her old body slowly executes into the earth.

52 Oswald Street

for my sisters Wendy and Jill

Then, when the full moonlight
would touch our blanketed bodies,
we liked to think it filled
us with actual bright matter
drifted down from the regions
of the moon, so that when we woke
we would be changed. Now,
wherever we are on earth,
in loneliness, or loneliness-
easing arms, we three
who have survived the lives
and deaths in the old house
on Oswald Street can almost
feel that full moonlight again,
as someone might hear the slow-
given sighs of post-coital bliss
the lover who took off could be
breathing this minute in someone
else's arms, and taste
the lost fullness and know how
far our hearts have fallen, how
our feelings too long attuned
to having don't bear up,
and how for us it turns out
three gravesides were too many
to stand at, or turn from,
that most mired of pivotings,
and our mouths fill with three

names that can't find their meanings,
theirs, and before we know it, also
ours, and we pull up more tightly
around us the coverings of
full moonlight that fall down
now from unrepeatable life
on bodies of mother and father
and three children, and a fourth,
sleeping, quite long ago.

PART IV

The Rainbow

The rainbow appears above us
for its minute, then vanishes, as though
we had wished it, making us
turn more carefully to what we can
touch, things and creatures
we know we haven't dreamed: flutings
on a match stick, the blurry
warmth a match gives back
to thumb and forefinger
when we hold it to the spewing
gas, for instance, or
the pelvic bones of a woman
lying on her back, which rise
on either side of the crater
we floated in, in the first life,
that last time we knew
more of happiness than of time,
before the world-ending inkling
of what pain would be for all
of our natural going — a blow
so well-struck space
simply breaks — befell us.
Then we fell, scanning about,
the cleverest of us, for a lover
to cling to, and howling
howls of the damned so fierce
they put terrified grooves
permanently into the throat,

until the day the carcass
has swirled its defeated desire
toward those invisible fires,
the other, unfulfilled galaxies,
to win them over, too, into time and ruin.

The Apple

The brain
cringes around the worst
that it knows; just as the apple
must have done, around the poison
said to have poisoned those two
into the joy
that watches itself go away.

No one easily
survives love; neither the love
one has, nor the love
one has not; they break down
in the red smoke blown up
of the day when all love will have gone on.

A little sadness,
a little more self-cruelty,
a little more uselessness
added to our world.
These won't last.
What will last is that
no one will know

to let go, everyone will need
the one he or she doesn't know
all the way to the day we become
moonstones, broken open
under the moon, only an
icy brightness remembering inside us.

Memory of Wilmington

Thirty-some years ago, hitchhiking
north on Route 1, I stopped for the night
at Wilmington, Delaware, one of those American cities
that start falling apart before they ever get finished.
I met, I remember, an ancient hobo — I almost remember
his name — at the ferry — now dead,
of course, him,
and also the ferry —
in great-brimmed hat, coat to his knees,
pants dragging the ground, semi-zootish rig
plucked off various clotheslines.

He taught me how to grab a hen
so the dogs won't hear: come up on it
from behind, swoop down and seize it
and whirl it up, all in one motion
breaking the neck, and also twisting
silent any cry
of alarm it might start to utter.

It doesn't matter.

It doesn't matter
that we ill-roasted our hen over brushwood
or that with the squeamishness
of the young I dismouthed the rawest of it
into the black waters of Delaware Bay.

After he ate, the old hobo
— *Amos!* yes, that's it! — old Amos
rasped out a song or two, his voice
creaking more and more slowly,
like a music box when time slows itself down inside it.
I sat in the last light and listened, among rocks,
tin cans, feathers, ashes, old stars.

The next day when I sailed north
on the ferry the sun was shining.
From the decaying landing Amos waved.
I was fifteen, I think. Wilmington then
was far along on its way to becoming a city
and equally advanced on its way back to dust.

The Still Time

I know there is still time —
time for the hands
to open,
to be filled
by those failed harvests,
the imagined bread of the days of not having.

I remember those summer nights
when I was young and empty,
when I lay through the darkness
wanting, wanting,
knowing
I would have nothing of anything I wanted —
that total craving
that can hollow a heart out irreversibly.

So it surprises me now to hear
the steps of my life following me —
so much of it gone
it returns, everything that drove me crazy
comes back, as if to modify the misery
of each step it took me into the world;
as though a prayer had ended
and the changed
air between the palms went free
to become that inexplicable
glittering we see on ordinary things.

And the voices,
which once made broken-off, parrot-incoherences,
speak again, this time
speaking on the palatum cordis,
saying there is time, still time
for those who can groan to sing,
for those who can sing to be healed.

There Are Things I Tell to No One

1

There are things I tell to no one.
Those close to me might think
I was depressed, and try to comfort me.
At such times I go off alone, in silence, as if listening for God.

2

I say "God"; I believe,
rather, in a music of grace
that we hear, sometimes, playing
from the other side of happiness.
When we hear it and it flows
through our bodies, it lets us live
these days intensified by their vanity
worshipping, as the other animals do,
who live and die in the spirit
of the end, that backward-spreading
brightness. It speaks in notes struck
or caressed or blown or plucked
off our own bodies: *remember*
existence already remembers
the flush upon it you will have been,
you who have reached out ahead
and touched the dust we become.

3

Just as the supreme cry
of joy also has a ghastliness to it,
as though it touched forward

into the chaos where we break apart,
so the death-groan, though sounding
from another direction, carries us back
to our first world, where we see
a grandmother sitting only yesterday
oddly fearless on the tidy porch, her little boned body drowsing
    almost unobserved into the agreement to die.

4

Brothers and sisters;
lovers and children;
great mothers and grand fathers
whose love-times have been chiseled
by now into stone; great
grand fœtuses spelling
the past into the flesh's waters:
can you bless, or not curse,
everything that struggles to stay alive
on this planet of struggles?

Then the last cry in the throat
or only imagined into it
by its threads too wasted to make sound,
will disappear into the music
that carries our time on earth
away, on the catafalque
of bones marrowed with god's-flesh,
thighs bruised by the blue flower,
pelvis that makes angels shiver to know down here we make love
    with our bones,
I want to live forever. But when I hear

through the walls grace-notes blown
out of the wormed-out bones,
music that their memory of blood
plucks from the straitened arteries,
music that lovers caressed from each other
in the holy days of their vanity,
that the two hearts drummed
out of their ribs together,
the hearts that know everything (and even
the little knowledge they can leave
stays, to be the light of this house),
then it is not so difficult
to go out and turn and face
the spaces that gather into one
sound the waves of spent existence
that flow toward, and toward, and on which we flow
and grow drowsy and become fearless again.

Pont Neuf at Nightfall

Just now a sprinkling
of rain begins. It brings with it
an impression of more lasting existence —
brings it by removal, by the swiftness
of each drop's drying from the stone.
When stone becomes wet, that's
when desolation comes into the world.
We can't grasp our full debt to those
who heaped up stones into palaces,
arches, spires, into a grace

which, being behind us, is beyond us.
But we pay them some envy, we imagine
a reality filled almost completely
with what is, without room
for longing backward; and also
the knowledge that happiness exists
even if sometimes out of reach.
A girl walks by, a presence
in someone's anticipation, she is
clasping flowers, trailing
their odor and their memory
of her into a past so brief
it follows close behind.
A light comes on very dim in a hotel
window, a glint of what once was
the light of the world. In a tiny room
overlooking a bridge and a dark river,
that is where such a light could come on:
above a narrow bed where a girl and a boy
take themselves perhaps for the first time out of time.

The Apple Tree

I remember this tree,
its white flowers all unfallen.
It's the fall, the unfallen apples
hold their brightness
a little longer into the blue air, hold the idea
that they can be brighter.

We create without turning,
without looking back, without ever
really knowing we create.
Having tasted
the first flower of the first spring
we go on,
we don't turn again
until we touch the last flower of the last spring.

And that day, fondling
each grain one more time, like the neck of the hourglass,
we die
of the return-streaming of everything we have lived.

When the fallen apple rolls
into the grass, the apple worm
stops, then goes
all the way through and looks out
at the creation unopposed, the world
made entirely of lovers.

Or else there is no such thing as memory,
or else there are only the empty branches,
only the blossoms upon them,
only the apples,
that still grow full,
that still fail into brightness,
that still invent past their own decay the hope
they can be brighter,
that still
that still

The one who holds still and looks out,
alone
of all of us, may die mostly of happiness.

A Milk Bottle

A tiny creature slides
through the tide pool, holding up
its little fortress foretelling
our tragedies; another clamps
itself down to the stone. A sea anemone
sucks at my finger, mildly, I can just
feel it, though it may mean to kill — no,
it might say, to use me to receive
more life. All these creatures
even half made of stone thrill
to altered existences. As we do ourselves,
who advance so far, then stop, then creep
a little, stop, then gasp — breath
is the bright shell
of the life-wish encasing us — gasp
it all in again, on seeing that
any time would be OK
to disappear back into all things — as when
lovers wake up at night and see
the other is tearful and think, *Yes,*
but it doesn't matter, already
we will have lived forever. Yes,
if we could do that: separate
time from happiness, skim off

the molecules scattered
throughout our flesh that remember,
fling them at non-conscious things,
who may always have craved them . . . It's funny,
I seem actually to remember a certain
quart of milk that has just finished
clinking against one of its brethren
in the milkman's great hand and stands
freeing itself from itself on the rotting
doorstep in Pawtucket in 1932; and is then
picked up and taken indoors
by one in whom time hasn't yet
woven its tangles. The bottle
will of course have shattered by now
in the decay of its music,
the sea eagle have rung
its glass voice back down into the sea
the sea's creatures transfigure over and over.
Look, around us the meantime has begun overflowing.
In every direction its own almost-invisibility
streams and sparkles over everything.

Flying Home

I

Flying home, looking about
in this swollen airplane, every seat
of it squashed full with one of us,
it occurs to me I might be one of the lucky ones
in this planeload of the species;

for earlier,
in the airport men's room, seeing
the middleaged men my age,
as they washed their hands after touching
their penises — when it might have been more in accord
with the lost order to wash first, then touch —
peer into the mirror
and then stand back, as if asking, who is this?

Looking around, I could only think
that one looks relieved to be getting away,
that one dreads going where he goes.
As for me, at the very same moment
I feel regret at leaving
and happiness to be flying home.

2

Very likely she has always understood
what I have slowly learned
and which only now, after being about as far away
as one can get on this globe, almost
as far as thoughts can carry — yet still in her presence,
still surrounded not so much by reminders of her
as by things she had already reminded me of,
cast forward and waiting — can I try to express:

that while many good things are easy, love is hard,
because it is first of all a power,
its own power,
and must keep making its way forward, from night
into day, from transcending union forward into difficult day.

3

And as the plane starts its descent, it comes to me,
that once the lover
recognizes the other, knows for the first time
what is most to be valued in another,
from then on, love is very much like courage,
perhaps it *is* courage, and even
perhaps
only courage. Squashed
out of old selves, smearing the darkness
of expectation across experience, all of us little
thinkers it brings home having similar thoughts
of landing to the imponderable world,
the transcontinental airliner,
resisting its huge weight down, comes in almost lightly,
to where
with sudden, tiny, white puffs and long, black, rubberish smears
all its tires know the home ground.

The Past

1985

---

for Inés

PART I

The Road Between Here and There

Here I heard the snorting of hogs trying to re-enter the underearth.

Here I came into the curve too fast, on ice, touched the brake pedal
and sailed into the pasture.

Here I stopped the car and snoozed while two small children crawled
all over me.

Here I reread *Moby Dick,* skipping big chunks, skimming others, in a
single day, while Maud and Fergus fished.

Here I abandoned the car because of a clonk in the motor and hitch-
hiked (which in those days in Vermont meant walking the whole
way with a limp) all the way to a garage, where I passed the after-
noon with ex-loggers who had stopped by to oil the joints of their
artificial limbs and talk.

Here a barn burned down to the snow. "Friction," one of the ex-loggers
said. "Friction?" "Yup, the mortgage, rubbin' against the insurance
policy."

Here I went eighty but was in no danger of arrest, for I was blessed-
speeding, trying to get home to see my children before they slept.

Here I bought speckled brown eggs with bits of straw shitted to them.

Here I brought home in the back seat two piglets who rummaged
around inside the burlap sack like pregnancy itself.

Here I heard again on the car radio a Handel concerto transcribed for
harp and lute, which Inés played to me the first time, making me
want to drive after it and hear it forever.

Here I sat on a boulder by the winter-steaming river and put my head
in my hands and considered time — which is next to nothing,
merely what vanishes, and yet can make one's elbows nearly pierce
one's thighs.

Here I forgot how to sing in the old way and listened to the frogs
at dusk.

Here the local fortune teller took my hand and said, "What is still
    possible is inspired work, faithfulness to a few, and a last love,
    which, being last, will be like looking up and seeing the parachute
    turning into a shower of gold."
Here is the chimney standing up by itself and falling down, which
    tells you you approach the end of the road between here and there.
Here I arrive there.
Here I must turn around and go back and on the way back look care-
    fully to left and to right.
For when the spaces along the road between here and there are all
    used up, that's it.

The Angel

This angel, who mediates between us
and the world underneath us, trots ahead
so cheerfully. Now and then she bends
her spine down hard, like a dowser's branch,
over some, to her, well-known splashing spot
of holy water, of which she herself in turn
carefully besoms out a thrifty sprinkle.
Trotting ahead again, she scribbles her spine's
continuation into immaterial et cetera,
thus signaling that it is safe for us now
to go vertically wagging our legs
across the ups and downs under which
lie ancestors dog-toothed millennia ago into oblivion.
Tonight she will crouch at the hearth,
where demons' breaths flutter up among the logs,
gnawing a freshly unearthed bone — of a dog,

it could be — making logs and bone
cry through the room, *crack splinter groan.*

Middle of the Night

A telephone rings through the wall.
Nobody answers. Exactly how
the mouth shapes itself inside
when saying the word "gold" is what sleep
would be like if one were happy.
So Kenny Hardman and George Sykes
called "Gaw-way-ay!" at the back
of the house. If I didn't come out
they would call until nightfall,
like summer insects. Or like
the pay phone at the abandoned
filling station, which sometimes
rang, off and on, an entire day.
The final yawn before one sleeps sounds
like the word "yes" said too many times,
too rapidly. On the landing
she turned and looked back. Something
in her of the sea turtle heavy with eggs,
looking back at the sea. The shocking dark
of her eyes awakened in me
an affirmative fire. It would have hurt
to walk away, just as it would bewilder
a mouth at certain moments in life to say "no."

Conception

Having crowed the seed
of the child of his heart
into the egg of the child
of her heart, in the dark
middle of the night, as cocks
sometimes cry out to a light
not yet visible to the rest,
and lying there with cock
shrugging its way out of her,
and rising back through phases
of identity, he hears her
say, "Yes, I am two now,
and with you, three."

The Sow Piglet's Escapes

When the little sow piglet squirmed free,
Gus and I ran her all the way down to the swamp
and lunged and floundered and fell full-length
on our bellies stretching for her, and got her,
and lay there, all three shining with swamp slime,
she yelping, I laughing, Gus gasping and gasping.
It was then I knew he would die soon.
She made her second escape on the one day
when she was big enough to dig an escape hole
and still small enough to squeeze through it.
Every day I took a bucket of meal up to her plot
of rooted-up ground in the woods, until

one day there she stood, waiting for me,
the wild beast evidently all mealed out of her.
She trotted over and let me stroke her back
and, dribbling corn down her chin, put up her little worried face
as if to remind me not to forget to recapture her,
though, really, a pig's special alertness to death
ought to have told her: in Sheffield the *dolce vita*
leads to the Lyndonville butcher. When I seized her
she wriggled hard and cried *oui oui oui* all the way home.

The Olive Wood Fire

When Fergus woke crying at night,
I would carry him from his crib
to the rocking chair and sit holding him
before the fire of thousand-year-old olive wood.
Sometimes, for reasons I never knew
and he has forgotten, even after his bottle the big tears
would keep on rolling down his big cheeks
— the left cheek always more brilliant than the right —
and we would sit, some nights for hours, rocking
in the light eking itself out of the ancient wood,
and hold each other against the darkness,
his close behind and far away in the future,
mine I imagined all around.
One such time, fallen half-asleep myself,
I thought I heard a scream
— a flier crying out in horror
as he dropped fire on he didn't know what or whom,

or else a child thus set aflame —
and sat up alert. The olive wood fire
had burned low. In my arms lay Fergus,
fast asleep, left cheek glowing, God.

Milk

When he pulls back on the oars
slightly too large for him, the boat
surges forward, toward the island
where he picks up the milk bottle
the old man he's never seen
puts out each morning at the end of the dock;
toward the shore by the highway
where he sets down four empty
milk bottles and picks up four full
left by the milkman he's never seen;
toward the dock where he leaves
a full bottle for the old man;
and then homeward across water
around which the trees stand
right side up in the world
and upside down in the world under it
into which utterly still moments
are the doors childhood almost opens.

Lake Memphremagog

We loaf in our gray boat in the sunshine.
The Canadian Pacific freight following the shoreline sends a racket
  of iron over Lake Memphremagog.
The children cast, the fishes do not bite.
They leap into the water and splash, the Memphremagog monster
  does not bite.
In the center of Newport, the train blows, one after one, all its five
  horns.
I think I astonished my cheeks with the amount of tears one child
  can cry.
Those nights now lie almost farther away than memory goes.
All the elsewheres, as the train's cries fade, fade.
Our boat lies very still in the Memphremagog water, and it's still.
Here everybody is OK.
I am fifty. The children are just little ones.

The Man Splitting Wood in the Daybreak

The man splitting wood in the daybreak
looks strong, as though, if one weakened,
one could turn to him and he would help.
Gus Newland was strong. When he split wood
he struck hard, flashing the bright steel
through the air so hard the hard maple
leapt apart, as it's feared marriages will do
in countries reluctant to permit divorce,
and even willow, which, though stacked
to dry a full year, on being split

actually weeps — totem wood, therefore,
to the married-until-death — sunders
with many little lip-wetting gasp-noises.
But Gus is dead. We could turn to our fathers,
but they help us only by the unperplexed
looking-back of the numerals cut into headstones.
Or to our mothers, whose love, so devastated,
can't, even in spring, break through the hard earth.
Our spouses weaken at the same rate we do.
We have to hold our children up to lean on them.
Everyone who could help goes or hasn't arrived.
What about the man splitting wood in the daybreak,
who looked strong? That was years ago. That was me.

The Frog Pond

In those first years I came down
often to the frog pond — once called,
before the earthen dam eroded,
the farm pond — to bathe, wading out
and standing on a rock up to my knees
in pond water, which I sauce-panned over me —
and doing it quickly because of the leeches,
who need but minutes to know you're there —
or to read the mail or to scribble
or to loaf and think, sometimes
of the future, while the one deerfly
that torments whoever walks out in Vermont
in July — smack it dead as often
as one will — orbited about my head.

Then the beavers arrived, the waters rose,
and the frog pond became the beaver pond.
A year later a sunken rowboat surfaced,
with sheet metal nailed all around it
to hold the hull boards in place
while they rotted. The four
of us would oar, pole, and bail
a few feet above the underwater green bank
where a man used to sit and think
and look up and seem to see four people
up here oaring and poling and bailing
above him: the man *seems* happy,
the two children laugh and splash,
a slight shadow crosses the woman's face.
Then one spring the beavers disappeared —
trapped off, or else because of gnawing down
all the edible trees — and soon this pond,
and the next, and the one after that,
will flow off, leaving behind its print
in the woods, a sudden green meadow
with gleams of sky meandering through it.
The man who lies propped up
on an elbow, scribbling, will be older
and will remember the pond as it was then,
writhing with leeches and overflown
by the straight blue bodies of dragonflies,
and will think of small children
grown up and of true love broken
and will sit up abruptly and swat
the hard-biting deerfly on his head,
crushing it into his hair, as he has done before.

The Old Life

The waves collapsed into themselves
with heavy rumbles in the darkness
and the soprano shingle whistled
gravely its way back into the sea.
When the moon came from behind clouds
its white full-moon's light
lightly oiled the little beach stones
back into silence. We stood
among shatterings, glitterings,
the brilliance. And now it happens
another lifetime is up for us,
another life is upon us.
What's left is what is left
of the whole absolutely love-time.

PART II

Prayer

Whatever happens. Whatever
what is is is what
I want. Only that. But that.

The Ferry Stopping at MacMahon's Point

It comes vigorously in,
nudges the jetty and ties up,
the usually ill-tossed line tossed twice,
presses by engine pressure against
the pilings for a half-minute,
backs out, turns, and prow lifted
like the head of a swimming dog,
makes for the Lavender Bay jetty.

Mount Fuji at Daybreak

From the Fuji-view stand made of cinder block
a crow watches Fuji rise into daybreak.
Trash smoke light-blues the exhausted valley.
Hot-spring steam blows up out of steam holes.
Up the road leaving town a tanker truck groans.
An electric bullhorn starts crackling messages
to workers coming early out of their doors.
From the cinder block Fuji-view stand the crow
flies off repeating the round vowel "ah!"
to the mountain now risen bright into daybreak,
or else, in another mood, "ha! ha! ha!"

Break of Day

He turns the light on, lights
the cigarette, goes out on the porch,
chainsaws a block of green wood down the grain,
chucks the pieces into the box stove,
pours in kerosene, tosses in the match
he has set fire to the next cigarette with,
stands back while the creosote-lined, sheet-
metal rust-lengths shudder but just barely
manage to direct the *cawhoosh* in the stove —
which sucks in ash motes through gaps
at the bottom and glares out fire blaze
through overburn-cracks at the top —
all the way to the roof and up out through into
the still starry sky starting to lighten,
sits down to a bowl of crackers and bluish milk
in which reflections of a 40-watt ceiling bulb
appear and disappear, eats, contemplates
an atmosphere containing kerosene stink,
chainsaw smoke, chainsmoke, wood smoke, wood heat,
gleams of the 40-watt ceiling bulb bobbing in blue milk.

Farm Picture

Black earth
turned up, clods
shining on their
western sides, grass
sprouting on top

of bales of spoiled
hay, an old
farmer bent far
over, like *Australopithecus*
robustus, carrying two dented
pails of water out
to the hen yard.

Some Song

On a stoop
the old man
is drinking him
some beer,
the boy in
his yellow shirt
is playing
him some banjo tune,
the old fellow
hasn't any
teeth, the boy
sings him then
some song.

Coinaliste

She can drink from a beer bottle.
She can light a cigar and sneeze out the match.
She can drag on it so hard the end blazes.

She can inhale without coughing.
She can blow a smoke ring or two.
She can withdraw and introspect.

She can play the nose flute: f# with lower hole unstopped; a with both
   holes unstopped; c# with both stopped: the tonic, the mediant,
   the dominant of the chord of F# major.
She can suck the whole instrument inside, where it continues to sing
   and cry.
She can speak a pouting, pidgin blabber.

She can clench on the ictus and moan on the arsis but cannot come on
   the thesis.
She can wink and throw French kisses.
She can motherly-kiss the fuzzy cheeks of young sailors.
She can pick up the money they toss, including the dollar bills.
She can count but not give change.
She can smile.

Driftwood from a Ship

It is the white of faces from which the sunburn has been scared away.
It has the rounded shoulders of one who fears he will pass the rest of
   his days alone.
The black residue inside the line of nine nail holes — three close to-
   gether, three far apart, three close together — is the memory ham-
   mered just in case of shipwreck into those vanishing places.
A carpenter's plane's long, misericording *shhhhhhhhh*'s long ago
   soothed away the halo-segments that a circular saw longer ago tor-
   mented across it.

The pebbles it rubs itself across fuzz up all over it a first beard, white
from the start.
The grain cherishes the predicament of the Norway spruce, which has
a trunk that rises and boughs that droop.
Its destiny, which is to disappear, could be accomplished when a
beachcomber extracts its heat, leaving the smoke and ashes; or
in the normal way, through a combination of irritation and
evanescence.

Fire in Luna Park

The screaming produced by the great fright machines —
one like a dough beater that lifts, whirls, plunges the victims strapped
in its arms,
one a huge fluted pan that tries to fling its passengers off the earth,
one that holds its riders upside down and pummels them until they
pour out their screams freely,
and above them the roller coaster, creeping seemingly lost among its
struts and braces,
and under them the Ghost Train that jerks through dark tunnels here
and there suddenly lighted by fluorescent bones —
has fallen still today.

To us who live on Lavender Bay,
once Hulk Bay, before that probably few if any now know what,
it seemed the same easily frightened, big-lunged screamer cried out in
mock terror each night across the water, and we hardly heard or
took notice.
But last night shrieks of true terror pierced through our laughter, and
kept at it, until we sat up startled.

The Ghost Train, now carrying seven souls and the baffled grief of
    families,
has no special destination,
but, looking for forgetfulness, must thrust forward, twist, backtrack
    through the natural world,
where all are born, all suffer, and many scream,
and no one is healed but gathered and used again.

The Geese

As soon as they come over the peak
into the Connecticut Valley and espy the river
that they will follow until nightfall,
bodies, or cells, begin to tumble
between the streamers of their formation,
thinning the left, thickening the right,
until like a snowplowing skier the flock shifts weight
and shaking up its inner equipoise
turns, and yahonks and spirit-cries
toward the flow of light spelled
into the river's windings eons ago,
each body flashing white against
the white sky when the wings lift,
and black when they fall, the invisible
continuously perforating the visible —
and trembles away, to vanish, but before that
to semi-vanish, as a mirage or deepest
desire does when it gets the right
distance from us and becomes rhythmic.

The Shroud

Lifted by its tuft
of angel hairs, a milkweed
seed rises and dips
across a meadow, chalking
in outline the rhythms
wavering through air all along.
Spinus tristis, who expends
his days transfiguring gold
back into sod, sinks and soars,
following the same undulations.
What immense coat or shroud
that can wrap the whole earth
are these golden needles
stitching at so restlessly?
When will it ever be finished?

PART III

Chamberlain's Porch

On three sides of the stretcher bed
where I half sleep, rainwater runs down
boughs all broken out in buds out there
in the world that the porch screen crisscrosses
into tiny, very perishable rectangles.
Rain putters down on wood shingles,
now smattering, becoming a language,
now slackening, making kissing sounds
which some would memorize into the grave.
It seems the mechanism driving the inner
pluckings of things, which lives by crescendo,
here stops and tries out low-key backward variations
on a cedar-shingled porch roof in Connecticut.

Cemetery Angels

On these cold days
they stand over
our dead, who will
erupt into flower as soon
as memory and human shape
rot out of them, each bent
forward and with wings
partly opened as though
warming itself at a fire.

December Day in Honolulu

This day, twice as long as the same day in Sheffield, Vermont, where
    by five the stars come out,
gives the postman opportunity to boggle the bell thrice.
First, a letter from Providence lamenting the "siege against poets" —
    Wright, Rukeyser, Hayden.
Next, Richard Hugo's memoir of James Wright.
Last, around the time of stars in Sheffield, a package holding four
    glass doorknobs packed in a *New York Times* of a year ago, which
    Muriel Rukeyser had sea-mailed to me, in explanation of those
    somewhat alarming words she would whisper whenever we met:
    "Galway, I have your doorknobs."
The wail of a cat in heat breaks in, the voice of propagation itself:
This one or that one dies but never the singer: whether in Honolulu in its
    humid mornings or New York in its unbreathable dusk or Sheffield
    now dark but for chimney sparks dying into the crowded heaven, one
    singer falls and the next steps into the empty place and sings . . .
The cat's next wail comes more heavily, as if from a longer inner
    distance.
It could be it's just a very old cat, singing its last appearance in the
    magic circle of a trash can lid, perhaps from its final life trying to
    cry back the first life's first, irreplaceable lover, before turning to-
    tally faithful forever.

On the Oregon Coast

In memoriam Richard Hugo

Six or seven rows of waves struggle landward.
The wind batters a pewtery sheen on the valleys between them.

Much of each wave making its way in gets blown back out to sea.
The bass rumble of sea stones audible under their outrush itself blows
out to sea.
A log maybe thirty feet long and six across at the fat end gets up and
trundles down the beach, using its two ends like feet.
Like a dog fetching a stick, it flops unhesitatingly into the water.
An enormous wave at once sends it wallowing back up the beach.
It comes to rest among other lost logs, almost panting.
Sure enough, in a few minutes it trundles down the beach again.
The last time I was on this coast I had dinner with Richard Hugo
north of here, in a restaurant over the sea.
The conversation came around to personification.
We agreed that eighteenth- and nineteenth-century poets almost
had to personify, it was like mouth-to-mouth resuscitation, the
only way they could think up to keep the world from becoming
dead matter.
And that as post-Darwinians it was up to us to anthropomorphize
the world less and animalize, vegetablize, and mineralize ourselves
more.
We didn't know if pre-Darwinian language would let us.
Our talk turned to James Wright, how his confabulations with rep-
tiles, spiders, and insects drifted him back through the evolution-
ary stages.
When a group of people get up from a table, the table doesn't know
which way any of them will go.
James Wright went back to the end. So did Richard Hugo.
The waves swaffing in burst up through their crests and fly very bril-
liant back out to sea.
The log gets up once again, rolls and bounces down the beach,
plunges as though for good into the water.

Last Holy Fragrance

In memoriam James Wright

When by first light I went out
from the last house on the chemin de Riou
to start up the cistern pump, I saw him,
mumbling into his notebook
while the valley awakened: a cock
called full force, a car's gears
mis-shifted, a dog made feeble yaps.
The next winter in Mt. Sinai,
tufted with the stubble that sticks out
of chins on skid row in St. Paul,
Minnesota, he handed me the poem
of that Vence morning. Many times since,
I have said it and each time I have heard
his voice saying it under mine,
and in fact in those auditoriums
that don't let you hear yourself, sometimes
I have heard *only* his voice, surprising language
a little with the mourning
that goes on inside it, for what it names.
And in the droning mutter I remember
sometimes his eyes would pop,
as he read, showing the whites
when his own poems startled him.

"How am I ever going to be able to say this?
The truth is there is something terrible,
almost unspeakably terrible in our lives,
and it demands respect, and, for some reason

that seems to me quite insane, it doesn't hate us.
There, you see? Every time I try
to write it down it comes out gibberish."

He lies back fast asleep in the airplane seat.
Under his eyelids consciousness flickers.
A computation: the difference, figured
in a flash, between what has been lived
and what remains to be. He dreams perhaps
of whittling a root, transfiguring it
by subtraction — of whatever it is in roots
that makes them cling — perhaps into
a curled up, oriental death's body
mummified into the memories of last visitors.
Even asleep his face sweats. SS
torturers start working Cagney over.
He knows he will crack and spill
the invasion plans. When he hears
the rumbling of B-29s
come to shut his mouth, he cracks
a grin. When the bombs explode
he madly laughs. Sitting up,
he peers out the small, round window
to see if we might be coming in too low,
ready himself to laugh among the screams.

For this poet, the blessed moment
was not only at the end, in Fano, in spring,
where, with his beloved Annie,
just before returning home to die,
he got well, but also at first,

forty years earlier, by the Ohio,
where he sat and watched it
flow, and flowed himself inside it,
humming and lulling first beginnings
of poems that would heal himself
but also everybody, including those
who lie on sidewalks, like dropped
flowers waiting to be lady slippered
into first perfume or last stink.

The computation darkens.
Again and again it used to show
plenty of time. Now, even on
the abacus of the rosary, or the petals,
hushed to the tabletop, of roses,
which we mortal augurers figure
and refigure things out on our
incredulous infinity of times,
it comes out: a negative number.
Fear, the potion of death, is yet
a love derivative, and some terrible
pinch of it must be added one
way or another to bring back
our will to cling.

Near where it first forms,
the Ohio stops in its bed
and baptizes under ice
its creatures, as well as the boy sitting soon
in nobody's memory some days downriver.
He went away, three-quarters

whittled root of silenus wood, taking
a path that, had it vanished,
we could imagine keeps going, toward a place
where he waits to rise again
into the religion of the idolatry
of the things of earth graven
their moment into being-born-and-dying.

The path ends where a white rose
lies on top of its shadow in Martin's Ferry,
Ohio, let drop by a child too stunned
by dead bells pounding through sunlight
to hold it, or anything, or anyone, tight
that day, giving up its last holy fragrance
into this ending-time, when the earth
lets itself be shoveled open to take in a body.
It will be a long time before anyone comes
who can lull the words he will now not again use
— words which, now he has gone, turn this way and that —
hum and inveigle them to press up against, shape
themselves by, know, true-love, and idolize.

The Past

A chair under one arm,
a desktop under the other,
the same Smith-Corona
on my back I even now batter
words into visibility with,
I would walk miles,

assemble my writing stall,
type all day, many sheets
of prose and verse later
to blow away, while gulls,
sometimes a sightseeing plane,
turned overhead. The lean-
to of driftwood that thirty-
three-and-a-third years back
I put up on this spot
leans down all the way.
Its driftwood re-drifts.
Spray jumps and blows.
A few gulls fly that way,
a few this. One duck
whettles out to sea
in straight flight.
As for the Quonset hut
I broke into without breaking it
when the storms came, it too
has gone, swept out to sea, burned up,
buried under, torn down.
Too bad. But for me not all
that bad. For of the four
possibilities — from *me-and-it-
still-here* to *it-and-me-
both-gone* — this one, *me-here-
it-gone,* is second best,
and will do, for me, for now.
But I wanted to sit at the table again
and look up and see the sea spray
and beach grass happy together.

I wanted to remember
the dingy, sprouted potatoes,
the Portuguese bread, the Bokar coffee,
the dyed oranges far from home,
the water tasting of eroded aluminum,
the kerosene stench. The front
steps where I watched
the elation in the poverty grass,
when the wind blew. In a letter
that cast itself down in General
Delivery, Provincetown, my friend
and mentor warned, "Don't lose
all touch with humankind." One day
while all around gulls gave
exhausted screams, the wind
put a sudden sheen or flatness
like spiritual quietness across the water.
Now two waves of the North Atlantic
roll landward side by side,
converge, ripple into one,
rush up the beach, making me
jump back, and sink away under
white bubbles all suddenly
popping away at once. Here
waves slap not in time but in
evanescence, a rhythmless medium.
Mere comings, mere goings. Though now
there's somewhat less coming
in the comings and more
going in the goings. Between
the two straggles a wandering

thread of sea litter
along the beach. So you see,
to reach the past is a snap. A snap
of the sea and a third of a century's
gone. All nothing. Or all all,
if that sounds more faithful. But anyway
vanished. The work of
whoziwhatzit — Zeit . . . Zman . . . Chas . . .
whatever . . . Whichever
you strike with the desperate tongue coughs up
a deadened sound, as though
the thing itself were fake; or unutterable.

First Day of the Future

They always seem to come up
on the future, these cold, earthly dawns;
the whiteness and the blackness
make the flesh shiver as though starting to break.
But so far it's just another day they illuminate
of the permanent present. Except for today.
A motorboat sets out across the bay,
a transfiguring spirit, its little puffy gasps
of disintegration collected
and hymned out in a pure purr of dominion.
In the stillness again the shore lights remember
the dimensions of the black water.
I don't know about this new life.
Even though I burned the ashes of its flag

and ate the ticket that would have conscripted me into its ranks
    forever
and squandered my talents composing my emigration papers,
I think I want to go back now and live again in the present time,
    back there
where someone milks a cow and jets of intensest nourishment go
    squawking into a pail,
where someone is hammering, a bit of steel at the end of a stick hitting
    a bit of steel, in the archaic stillness of an afternoon,
or somebody else saws a board, back and forth, like hard labor
in the lungs of one who refuses to come to the very end.
But I guess I'm here. So I must take care. For here
one has to keep facing the right way, or one sees one dies, and one dies.

The Fundamental Project of Technology

"A flash! A white flash sparkled!"
                — Tatsuichiro Akizuki, *Concentric Circles of Death*

Under glass: glass dishes that changed
in color; pieces of transformed beer bottles;
a household iron; bundles of wire become solid
lumps of iron; a pair of pliers; a ring of skull-
bone fused to the inside of a helmet; eyeglasses
taken off the eyes of an eyewitness, without glass,
which vanished, when a white flash sparkled.

An old man, possibly a soldier back then,
now simply somebody who will die soon,

sucks at the cigarette dangling from his lip, peers
at the uniform, scorched, of some tiniest schoolboy,
sighs out bluish mists of his own ashes over
a pressed tin lunch box well crushed back then when
the word future first learned, in a white flash, to jerk tears.

On the bridge outside, in navy black, a group
of schoolchildren line up, hold it, grin at a flash-pop,
scatter like pigeons across grass, see a stranger, cry
hello! hello! hello! and soon *bye-bye! bye-bye! bye-bye!*
having pecked up the greetings that fell half unspoken
and the going-sayings that those who went the day
it happened a white flash sparkled did not get to say.

If all a city's faces were to shrink back all at once
from their skulls, would a new sound come into existence,
audible above moans eaves extract from wind that smooths
the grass on graves, or raspings heart's-blood greases still,
or wails infants trill born already skillful at the grandpa's rattle,
or infra-screams bitter-knowledge's speechlessness
memorized, at that white flash, inside closed-forever mouths?

To de-animalize human mentality, and at the same time to purge it
of unfavorable evolutionary characteristics, in particular
the foreknowledge of death, which terrorizes the contents
of skulls, is the fundamental project of technology;
however, *pseudologica fantastica*'s mechanisms require
to establish deathlessness it is necessary to eliminate
those who die; a task become conceivable, when a white flash sparkled.

Unlike the trees of home, which continuously evaporate
along the skyline, these trees have been enticed down
into eternity here. No one can say which gods they enshrine.
Does it matter? Awareness of ignorance is as devout
as knowledge of knowledge. Or more so. Even though not knowing,
sometimes we weep, from surplus of gratitude, even though knowing,
twice already on earth sparkled a flash, a white flash.

The children go away. By nature they do. And by memory,
in scorched uniforms, holding tiny crushed lunch tins.
All the ecstasy-groans of each night call them back, satori
their ghostliness back into the ashes, in the momentary shrines,
the thankfulness of arms, from which they will go
again and again, until the day flashes and no one lives
to look back and say, a flash, a white flash sparkled.

The Waking

What has just happened between the lovers,
who lie now in love-sleep under the owls' calls,
call, answer, back and forth, and so on,
until one, calling faster, overtakes the other
and the two whoo together in a single
shimmering harmonic, is called "lovemaking."
Lovers who come exalted to their trysts,
who approach from opposite directions
through the pines, along a path by the sea,
meet, embrace, go up from the sea,
lie crushed into each other under
the sky half-golden, half deep-blueing

its moon and stars into shining, know
they don't "make" love, but are earth-creatures
who live and — here maybe no other word will do —
fuck one another forever if possible across the stars.
An ancient word, formed perhaps before
sacred and profane had split apart
when the tongue, like a flame
in the mouth, lighted each word
as it was spoken, to remind it
to remember; as when flamingos
change feeding places on a marsh,
and there is a moment, after the first to fly
puts its head into the water in the new place
and before in the old place the last
lifts up its head to see the rest have flown,
when, scattered with pink bodies, the sky
is one vast remembering. They still hear,
in sleep, the steady crushing and uncrushing
of bedsprings; they imagine a sonata in which
violins' lines draw the writhings and shiftings.
They lie with heads touching, thinking
themselves back across the blackness.
When dawn comes their bodies re-form
into two heaps of golden matter sieved
out of the night. The bed, caressed threadbare,
worn almost away, is now more than ever
the place where such light as humans
shine with seeps up into us. The eyelids,
which love the eyes and lie on them to sleep,
open. *This is a bed. That is a fireplace.*
That is last morning's breakfast tray

which nobody has yet bothered to take away.
This face, too alive with feeling to survive past
the world in which it is said, "Ni vous
sans moi, ni moi sans vous," so unguarded
that this day might be breaking in the Middle Ages,
is the illusion fate's randomness chooses
to beam into existence, now, on this pillow.
In a ray of sun the lovers see motes cross,
mingle, collide, lose their way, in this puff
of ecstatic dust. Tears overfill their eyes,
wet their faces, then drain quickly away
into their smiles. One leg hangs off the bed.
He is still inside her. His big toe
sticks into the pot of strawberry jam. "Oh migod!"
They kiss while laughing and hit teeth
and remember they are bones and laugh
naturally again. The feeling, perhaps
it is only a feeling, perhaps mostly due
to living only in the overlapping lifetimes
of dying things, that time starts up again,
comes over them. They put on clothes,
go out. For a few moments longer
are still in their elsewhere, beside a river,
their arms around each other, in the aura
earth has when it remembers its former beauty.
An ambulance sirens a bandage-stiffened
body toward St. Vincent's; a police car
running the red lights parodies
in high pitch the owls of paradise. So the lovers
enter the ordinary day the ordinary world
providentially provides. Their pockets ring.

Good. For now askers and beggarmen
come up to them needing change for breakfast.

That Silent Evening

I will go back to that silent evening
when we lay together and talked in low, silent voices,
while outside slow lumps of soft snow
fell, hushing as they got near the ground,
with a fire in the room, in which centuries
of tree went up in continuous ghost-giving-up,
without a crackle, into morning light.
When we got home we turned and looked back
at our tracks twining out of the woods,
where the branches we brushed against let fall
puffs of sparkling snow, quickly, in silence,
like stolen kisses, and where the *scritch scritch scritch*
among the trees, which is the sound that dies
inside the sparks from the wedge when a sledge
hits it off center telling everything inside
it is fire, jumped to a black branch, puffed up
but without arms and so to our eyes lonesome,
and yet also — how can we know this? — *happy!*
in shape of chickadee. Lying still in snow,
not iron-willed, like railroad tracks, willing
not to meet until heaven, but here and there
treading slubby kissing stops, our tracks wobble
across the snow their long, interrupted scratch.
So many things that happen here are little more,
if even that, than a scratch. Words in our mouths

are almost ready, already, to bandage the one
whom the *scritch scritch scritch,* meaning *if how when*
we might lose each other, scratches scratches scratches
from this moment to that. Then I will go back
to that silent evening, when the past just managed
to overlap the future, if only by a trace,
and the light doubled and cast
through the dark the sparkling that heavened the earth.

The Seekonk Woods

When first I walked here I hobbled
along ties set too close together
for a boy to step easily on each.
I thought my stride one day
would reach every other and from then on
I would walk in time with the way
toward that Lobachevskian haze
up ahead where the two rails meet.
Here we put down our pennies, dark,
on shined steel; they trembled, fell still;
then the locomotive out of Attleboro
rattling its berserk wheel-rods into perfect circles,
brightened them into wafers, the way a fork
mashes into view the inner light of a carrot
in a stew. In this late March sunshine,
crossing the trees at the angle of a bow
when it effleurages out of the chanterelle
the C three octaves above middle C,
the vertical birthwood remembers

its ascent lines, shrunken by half, exactly
back down, each tree on its fallen summer.
Back then, these rocks often asked
blood offerings — but this one, once, asked bone,
the time Billy Wallace tripped and broke out
his front teeth. Fitted with gold replicas,
he asked, speaking more brightly, "What good
are golden teeth, given what we've got
to eat?" Nebuchadnezzar
spent seven years down on all fours
eating vetch and alfalfa, ruminating
the mouth-feel of "bloom" and "wither,"
until he was whole. If you
held a grass blade between both thumbs
and blew hard you could blurt a shriek
out of it — like that beseeching leaves oaks
didn't drop last winter just now scratch
on a breeze. Maybe Billy, lured
by bones' memory, comes back
sometimes, too, to the Seekonk Woods,
to stand in the past and just look at it.
Here he might kneel, studying this clump of grass,
as a god might inspect the strands of a human sneeze
that percusses through. Or he might stray
into the now untrafficked whistling-lanes
of the mourning doves, who used to call and call
into the future, and give a start, as though,
this very minute, by awful coincidence,
they reach it. And at last traipse off
down the tracks, with arrhythmic gait,
as wanderers must do once they realize:

the over-the-unknown route, too, ends up
where time wants. On this spot
I skinned the muskrat. The musk breezed away.
I buried the rat. Of the fur
I made a hat, which as soon as put on
began to rot off, causing my scalp to crawl.
In circles, of course, keeping to the skull.
One day could this scrap of damp skin
crawl all the way off, and the whole organism
follow? To do what? Effuse with musk,
or rot with rat? When, a quarter-
turn after the sun, the half-moon,
too, goes down and we find ourselves
in the night's night, then somewhere
hereabouts in the dark must be death.
Knowledge of it beforehand is surely among
existence's most spectacular feats — and yet right here,
on this ordinary afternoon, in these woods,
with a name meaning "black goose" in Wampanoag,
or in modern Seekonkese, "slob blowing fat nose,"
this unlikely event happens — a creature
walking the tracks knows it will come.
Then too long to touch every tie, his stride
is now just too short to reach every other,
and so he is to be still the wanderer, the hirple
of too much replaced by the common limp
of too little. But he almost got there.
Almost stepped in consonance with the liturgical,
sleeping gods' snores you can hear humming up
from former times inside the ties. He almost
set foot in that border zone where what follows

blows back, shimmering everything, making
walking like sleepwalking, railroad tracks
a country lane on a spring morning,
on which a man, limping but blissful,
makes his way homeward, his lips, suppled
by kissing to bunch up like that, blowing
these short strands of hollowed-out air,
haunted by future, into a tune on the tracks.
I think I'm about to be shocked awake.
As I was in childhood, when I battered myself
back to my senses against a closed door,
or woke up hanging out of an upstairs window.
Somnambulism was my attempt to slip
under cover of nightmare across no father's land
and embrace a phantasm. If only
I had found a way to enter his hard time
served at labor by day, by night in solitary,
and put my arms around him in reality,
I might not now be remaking him
in memory still; anti-alchemizing bass kettle's
golden reverberations back down
to hair, flesh, blood, bone, the base metals.
I want to crawl face down in the fields
and graze on the wild strawberries, my clothes
stained pink, even for seven years
if I must, if they exist. I want to lie out
on my back under the thousand stars and think
my way up among them, through them,
and a little distance past them, and attain
a moment of absolute ignorance,
if I can, if human mentality lets us.

I have always intended to live forever;
but not until now, to live now. The moment
I have done one or the other, I here swear,
no one will have to drag me, I'll come
but never will I agree to burn my words.
The poplar logs creosoted asleep under the tracks
have stopped snoring. Maybe they've
already waked up. The bow saws at G.
An oak leaf rattles on its tree. The rails
may never meet, O fellow Euclideans,
for you, for me. So what if we groan.
That's our noise. Laughter is our stuttering
in a language we can't speak yet. Behind,
the world made of wishes goes dark. Ahead,
if not now then never, shines what is.

When One Has Lived a Long Time Alone

1990

To Sharon Olds

PART I

The Tragedy of Bricks

1

The twelve-noon whistle groans out
its puff of steam partway up the smokestack.
Out of the brickwork the lace-workers
carry their empty black lunch-stomachs.
The noontime composition features
that one blurry bass note
in concert with the tenor of the stomachs.
The used-up lace-worker, who is about a hundred,
bicycles past, suctions together
mouth-matter, tongue-hurls it at the mill,
rattles away. The trajectory of gold rowels
its arc of contempt across a boy's memory.

2

Overhead the sea blows upside down across Rhode Island.
slub clump slub clump
Charlie drops out. Carl steps in.
slub clump
No hitch in the sequence.
Paddy stands down. Otto jumps up.
Otto in his lifetime clumped into place seven million bricks,
fell from the scaffolding,
clump.
slub clump slub clump
Jake takes over, slubs mortar onto brick, clumps brick onto mortar.
Does this. Does it again.
Topples over. No pause.

René appears. Homer collapses. Angelo springs up. No break in
    the rhythm.
slub clump slub clump
They wear in they wear out.
They lay the bricks that build the mills
that shock the Blackstone River into yellow froth.

3

Here come the joggers.
I am sixty-one. The joggers are approximately very young.
They run for fun through a world where everyone used to lay bricks
    for work.
Their faces tell there is a hell and they will reach it.

4

At the blast of the last whistle
the lace-workers straggle out again
from under the tragedy of bricks.
Some stand at the trolley stop, some trudge off,
some sit between two disks of piano wire
and, walking in air, wobble into the dusk.

5

A boy born among bricks
walks beside the brick walls.
Under his steps the packed snow
sounds the small crushed shrieks
of the former bricklayers who lie
stacked somewhere hereabout.
One of them patrols the roof of the mill,

carrying a lantern, like a father,
which has a tongue in it
that does not speak, like a father.
He is there to make sure no brick
fails in its duty. Suddenly the full
moon lays out across the imperfect
world everything's grave.
slub clump slub clump.
The boy knows his father and mother
will disappear before the least brick cracks
or tells its story: an order of going
formerly known as infernal corrosion.
Up in the future they are laying the footing
for the construction of the neutron bomb,
which evaporates the living forms
and spares the bricks and the mortar.

Kilauea

Here is a stone with holes in it,
like a skull. It has furrows,
like my father's brow. Once
he could get up when he wanted and go
into an untouched future; when I knew him
he was sprinting to get to death
before his cares could catch up
and kill him. The small rainbow
that forms around me now curves in,
like the birth-forceps that hoisted me out
— witness the depressions in the temple bones —

until its two ends almost touch
my feet. Could it be that *I*
am the pot of gold? Both pots,
one inside the other,
like the fire leaping inside the steel drum the night workers hold out
    their hands to, in the icy air before morning,
or the pitch-black of speech about to be born through scarlet lips,
or the child getting off her bicycle inside the old woman the priest has
    told to get ready to die,
or the father of Edinburgh rising early inside the son of Pawtucket —
    to whom on Sundays after church he read the funnies, Scripture
    in the father-tongue?
Now the rainbow throws its double onto the air above it —
as on those Sundays, when the first blessing was we were blessed,
and the second, we knew we were blessed.
In the fire pit, where patches
of black skin slide over fiery flesh,
a scrap of paper
the wind, agent
of Providence, tosses in
vanishes without a flame up or crackle —
and my balls, densest concentration of future anywhere in the body,
    suddenly hurt, with the claustrophobia of a million swimmers
    terrified they will never get out.

In the light before dawn
the blue glimmering fades
above four pillows dented all night by four dreaming heads.
The father, already in the cellar,
yanks the great iron lever, the iron teeth
gnash, ashes dotted with fire
crash into the ash pit; and shovels in

a new utopia of coal, in a black field,
which lies quiet, then jets up all over
in flickerings like little senseless bluets.
The pipes and radiators of the house
knock and bang in free un-unison.
In the bathroom he strops the razor,
hoots out last night's portion of disgust,
and shaves, a fleshy, rhythmic rasping, like a katydid's.

Memories of My Father

1

When we drove a spike too weak into wood too hard
we got, not
the satisfied grunt of everything organized to go downward,
but a sudden yodel,
like a funny bone singing.
I don't want to go back to that workbench
with its smell of spruce sawdust, where the voice
inside things cracks, and changes, ever again.

2

The sound doesn't come from the wheel-rims of the milk wagon
    rattling the milk and the cream down the hard earth of Oswald
    Street,
nor from the ice cream wagon of Peter Pellagi, whose horse, we all
    knew, dropped a horse bun under the wagon whenever Peter
    scooped ice cream inside it,
nor from the cart of the scissors-grinder, who frictioned black steel
    into Faustian sparkles,

nor from the wagon of the iceman, who stabbed out a block of that si-
   lenced water and lugged it in tongs into the house,
nor from the horse and team of the ragman, who from the next street
   began bellowing his indecipherable cry, possibly "Old rags!" or
   was it just the noise inside things that have turned into old rags,
   "AWWWWRAGHHH!"
The sound comes from none
of these now no ones, but from the no one himself,
the father, who neither brings up the rear nor goes on ahead,
and never rides alongside;
and it approaches closer and closer
and just before arriving goes farther and farther away.

3

In another generation
the father and son come skidding down
the embankment together. They wade
through the shallows, where the bright water
tumbles upon itself making self-licking noises,
then swim to the rock which, like a leak, lets bits of the river fly out.
Everywhere else the water lies flat
and yet seems to slide past faster than other water,
as if there is that force in it
that intimidates matter and can twist
the laws of physics, like the libido inside the lawn bowler's bowling
   ball, which dawdles it along well after it has used up its impetus.
The father and son laugh — unrhythmic, lovely noise — and, as if
   entropy just then curled its tongue inside it, the river cowlicks.
From a town somewhere a consecrated bell knocks
its mild accurate notes all the way to the river.
The boy picks up a pebble, puts it

in the pointed place at the bottom of his pocket,

first checking with a finger for a hole,

then they climb back up

to the path, which, in the schemelessness of things, soon works its
    way back down

to the banks of that secretly frantic water

still shedding its impressions of their bodies,

in which a few, small, horned fishes quietly drift.

4

Can a father give his son

what he himself never possessed,

or lacks the courage to wish up from his own deprivation?

Unlike the boy, who will turn into the father,

and unlike the father, who will turn into no one,

the pebble on the windowsill does not wrinkle, does not die,

though one day it will get lost,

or be thrown out,

maybe by the father the boy who stuck it in his pocket in the first
    place becomes,

when he forgets what it was he wanted the pebble to remember.

5

The motes inside the rays

of sun crossing the room of the childhood house

do not settle but keep turning

through themselves, like the $Z°$ bosons inside matter,

which know the moment they stop they get plucked up,

with a short sucking noise, like a camera shutter capturing a soul,

and belong to the past even before they exist;

in something of the way that childhood happened already;
or like the wedding kiss.

6

When I come back to my father's house,
it will be in any month, though I have loved
fall, and August, and the august moon,
and the moonstruck flagstones going to the door.
When I come back someone will be singing
in an upstairs room, and I will stop
just inside the door to hear who it is,
or is it someone I don't know, singing,
in my father's house, when I come back?

7

Those we love from the first
can't be put aside or forgotten,
after they die they still must be cried
out of existence, tears must make
their erratic runs down the face,
over the fullnesses, into
the craters, confirming,
the absent will not be present,
ever again. Then the lost one
can fling itself outward, its million
moments of presence can scatter
through consciousness freely, like snow
collected overnight on a spruce bough
that in midmorning bursts
into glittering dust in the sunshine.

The Auction

My wife lies in another dream.
The quilt covers her like a hill
of neat farms, or map of the township
that is in heaven, each field and pasture
its own color and sufficiency,
every farm signed in thread
by a bee-angel of those afternoons,
the tracks of her inner wandering.
In this bed spooled out of rock maple plucked
from the slopes above the farm, saints
have lain side by side, grinding their
teeth square through the winter nights,
or tangled together, the swollen
flesh finding among the gigantic
sleep-rags the wet vestibule, jetting
milky spurts into the vessel
as secret as that amethyst glass
glimpsed once overlaid with dust
in the corner of an attic.

2

Their babies have cried
their winter mornings
in this crib that rocks
calm into the jumble and holds
a woman-child the size of a peck
of onions, who still sleeps,
the lump of freestone

still warm at her feet,
under her own small hill.

3

Out now
in the cold air, under
the fading moon — the lithe-handled axe,
which has arrived like a guillotine
on the cords that tie up the brain-bags
of hen, wreaks down on maple-halves
harder to drive apart than
faithful lovers.

4

The fire inside the potbellied
stove wallows and sighs, blood of the
swollen iron of this squat god puffed up
and dreaming of smoke and waste-laying —
where the laid-out body of hen sweated grease
and freestone soaked up heat for the long night
and exhalations of small creatures bloated the globby batches in the
    shining pans,
and fire waved, in secret, jets of remembrance
out of the cloven
wood.

5

Rinse of ocher and lampblack
and skimmed milk drench the chest picked up
at the Federated Church auction the color of blood
spilled long ago — *All the old love letters*

go with it, all go! — this box-load
of antique affections whose bonds lie among sleepers
in the scythed, white-fenced precinct
on the Heights, their alphabets
now two scatterings of bones —
of a farmer who slew
the great trees and touched them to flames,
and dragged stones off their glacial graves,
and each dawn and each dusk squeezed
the alembicked juice of vetch and alfalfa into the barking pail bottom,
and of a farm wife
who sat in the dim parlor, easing
the spurting sorrow-milks of narrow rooms,
who touched the keys and trampled
the Holy Ghost into the machinery, and poured
Faith of Our Fathers
into the heavy Sunday, shifting
from Claribel to Dulciana to Vox Jubilante
to Vox Humana, where all the stops end,
saturating the air with such yearning
no one can sing it until the day when, crushed under
scored pistons on freeways not yet imagined,
exploded in oil, it comes back,
poisoned, purged of transcendence forever.
All the love letters go with it, all go.

6

On the shelf stands
a hand-blown whisky bottle
from the old days, blown askew

by the gray lungs of the Czechoslovak,
which a farmer — after a week
of dragging stones into the error
of walls, of squeezing and resqueezing
the exuberance of udders into
the squawking foam, of smiting
maple and ash into flame-chunks —
seized and doled to himself
in slow swigs through most of a Sunday,
lying at last stunned in the vapors
of corn-sap steamed from the rock-sucking fields,
while the jubilant pipes jetted Faith
of Our Fathers into the darkened house —
and so drank out his wandering.

7

These farm shoes by the door,
covered in dried mud, a hobnail
or two touched by first light,
hold the shapes a man trudged
into them a last time before dawn,
going out the other end of the barn,
straying across the pasture, climbing
all the way to the sugarbush
most of it sold off to the spindle mill,
passing beneath an owl, startling a few doves,
to see the sun come up.

The Massage

Hoisted onto the table, he lies limp.
He likes this — existence annihilated
into these two hands. How could anyone
willingly leave a world where they touch you
all over your body? He can almost feel
the hard skin, the crooked last
finger-joints — no one has touched him
so unstintingly since she unsafety-pinned
and talcum-slicked the tiny little body.
Only the hands of the hitter do not tire.
They alone know how to whack from deep down
the big double-salted tears that, licked
into the mouth, taste of the soul,
maybe the whiff of amniotic fluid once
at the birth-table. He lies bunched up,
in a corner, in remorse, eyes squeezed shut
and a tear popping out, like the tongue
of a snake through its closed smile.
The hands find coagulated rump-tissue — delve,
spear, grabble, until the buttocks want to jig.
He can hear a humming — the awakening
inside a teakettle, that will shriek
when hot enough to make its peaceful drink,
or the blades flinching away from each other overhead,
or the noises ironed flat in the horizontal plane
back in the kitchen where the sharp tongue
made its points while she puttered about,
that he was dumb, that he was worthless,

that he would never reach the future alone.
A siren struggles in the distance — maybe
an ambulance out prowling for a new geezer
to throw on the table and stroke, until he ramps,
and then agrees to croak. The hands separate
his hands into their fingers, using the tugs
of the sandwich-maker after Thanksgiving, who pries
flesh off little brown unidentifiable bones
of the creature who days before clomped about
abruptly gobbling as though thinking up jokes.
Far down inside his chest it feels sore.
The hands can't pass the twelve cartilaginous bars.
The future he dreaded seems to have dissolved
on approach, and reassembled behind as the past —
but slightly blurred, being mostly unlived.
The hands disappear. The horns of cars,
and a more urgent siren, possibly the police,
or a fire, touch through. The cadaver
two beds away spits out the scatological verbs,
as though he fears they will frisk his heart
in the next world. Through the wall,
from the next ward, come hard, uninhibited groans.

Judas-Kiss

Those who lie waiting know time
goes away eventually but in the meantime
sits there — oh maybe shuffles in its mechanisms
once in a while, skips a day, sometimes

behind you a whole year can get lost,
but basically sits there. Hair doesn't
turn white, skin refuses to mat
its spidery crushings over
the face-bones, the tiny ditched
carcasses of remembered acts
remain stuck nose and feet
to the amberish helix
of the heaven of childhood,
which droops down into the golden ringlet
of hell. Most can wait
for the capsule's slow burst
to lull them off, but some, dying
to get on with it, swill the whole
bottle-load down in one
foul gulp. Then somebody,
an ex-spouse, the woman downstairs,
or maybe the UPS man, will happen by,
discover the collapsed creature,
and never mind if it sleeps through
its last clutches, bend down,
and with the softest
part of the face, which hides
the hardest, Judas-kiss it,
with a click, like a conductor's
ticket-punch, this one here, God
of our Fathers, this one is the one.

The Man on the Hotel Room Bed

He shifts on the bed carefully, so as
not to press through the first layer
into the second, which is permanently sore.
For him sleep means lying as still as possible
for as long as possible thinking the worst.
Nor does it help to outlast the night —
in seconds after the light comes
the inner darkness falls over everything.
He wonders if the left hand of the woman
in the print hanging in the dark above the bed,
who sits half turned away, her right hand
clutching her face, lies empty,
or does it move in the hair of a man
who dies, or perhaps died long ago
and sometimes comes and puts his head in her lap,
and then goes back and lies under a sign
in a field filled nearly up to the roots
holding down the hardly ever trampled grass
with mortals, the once-lovers. He goes over
the mathematics of lying awake all night alone
in a strange room: still the equations require
multiplication, by fear, of what is,
to the power of desire. He feels around —
no pillow next to his, no depression
in the pillow, no head in the depression.
Love is the religion that bereaves the bereft.
No doubt his mother's arms still waver up
somewhere reaching for him; and perhaps
his father's are now ready to gather him

there where peace and death dangerously mingle.
But the arms of prayer, which pressed his chest
in childhood — long ago, he himself, in the name
of truth, let them go slack. He lies facedown,
like something washed up. Out the window
first light pinks the glass building across
the street. In the religion of love to pray
is to pass, by a shining word, into the inner chamber
of the other. It is to ask the father and mother
to return and be forgiven. But in this religion
not everyone can pray — least of all
a man lying alone to avoid being abandoned,
who wants to die to escape the meeting with death.
The final second strikes. On the glass wall
the daylight grows so bright the man sees
the next darkness already forming inside it.

PART II

The Cat

The first thing that happened
was that somebody borrowed the Jeep,
drove fifty feet, went off the road.
The cat may have stuck a tire iron
or baseball bat into the steering wheel.
I don't know if it did or didn't.
I do know — I don't dare say it aloud —
when the cat is around something goes wrong.
Why doesn't our host forewarn us? Well,
he tries. He gives each guest on arrival
a set of instructions about the cat.
I never was able to read mine,
for the cat was watching when I got it,
and I stuck it in my pocket to read later,
but the cat saw, leapt at me, nearly
knocked me down, clawed at the pocket,
would have ripped my clothes off
if I had not handed it over.
The guest book contains the name
of the young woman who was my friend,
who brought me here in the first place,
who is the reason I have come back,
to try to find out what became of her.
But no one will tell me anything.
Except tonight, my final evening,
at dinner, the host says, "There is
someone . . . someone . . . a woman . . .
in your life . . ." I know he means her,
but why the present tense? "Whom you have in . . ."

The next word sounds like "blurrarree"
but it could be "slavery." "Well, yes,"
I say. "Yes, but where is the cat?"
"It is an awful thing you are doing,"
he goes on. "Quite awful." "But who?"
I protest. "What are you talking about?"
"The cat," he says. "When you lock her up
she becomes dangerous." "The cat?
What cat?" I remember the kitten saved
out of the burlap sack, I was
mothering or fathering her, my father
or mother said, "Stop smothering her."
Now an electric force grabs my feet.
I see it has seized my host's, too —
he is standing up, his hands are flopping
in front of him. "What is it?" I whisper.
"I'm washing the dishes," he says.
"O my God," I think.
"I'm washing the dishes," he repeats.
I realize he is trying to get the cat to believe
he is not in a seizure but washing the dishes.
If either of us lets on about the seizure
it is certain the cat will kill us both.

Street of Gold

When I step forward to go to her
the concrete turns mushy and I sink in;
then it sets. Maybe she too stands
on a sidewalk somewhere, feet stuck.

More likely she sits on her bed,
bent forward, brushing yellow hair
over her head. If a few strands could
escape and blow here, that would be how
the wind passing under the streetlight
gets its glitter. A woman folds up
for the night on the bank steps,
a man works himself feet first into
a cardboard box — without a bedfellow,
or a face doughy from cold nights
a face could nuzzle. A bottle a passer
kicks into the street goes spinning across
the cobblestones' falsetto notes.
In a great hall a countertenor
rises up on tiptoe, opens his throat,
unspoons them into heaven. The bottle
chucks the cobblestones' fat cheeks.
A little girl wakes to ecstatic murder
taking place in some guttural language,
runs, peeks, watches a man and woman,
steady as a backyard oil jack,
pumping her back down into nonexistence.
A strand of yellow hair hits my forehead,
presses across it a familiar double-humped wobble.
The bottle stops. The man in the box
gropes in his fly, finds only a worm.
The woman on the steps finds a dry well
under the wilful hair. The wind turns cold.
The cobblestones soon will be rattling
in their sockets. What's going to happen?
Some will stay put. Some will change sleeping streets,

some will disappear for a stricter reason.
Enough will get bumped from home to replace them.
She will fly to California and marry.
The night runs out of gold. And I
am almost as old as my father.

Shooting Stars

It's empty, blank blue
up there, the sun's violent light
flies right through. Last night,
my God, the shooting stars!
The sky brilliant with them,
with meteors lined up, speeding
toward earth! — of which only
a few arrive unburned-up
into this swarm of lover
tangled upon lover. Yesterday,
because of the P-rade
(my G-d, can even p,a,r,a,d,e
form the Tetragrammaton?),
Nassau Street, too, was thronged,
as the graduated classes
passed in historical order —
first a solitary scout,
then a few stragglers, then
ever-larger bands
of rickety, well-wattled
old timers — including
my old friends and old strangers

of '48, all decked out
in black and orange
like rocket men. Last night,
deaths up there more brilliant
than lives — the way
they see us on the other side,
when we come through, red-faced,
cries foremost, as at birth,
still breathing heavily
from the hard labor
of dying. But today
it is clear again up there,
the escape-holes blued over,
the litter of scorched itineraries
broomed up. It is time for her
to go, who came down
from elsewhere, toward me
— startling herself,
not having guessed she could
crave love or take joy in it
so desperately — who is
by now an adept and could pluck
drunken flesh off a sidewalk
and with a kiss, or a
flurrying of lips at an ear,
come up with Adonis —
time to forget
about the criss . . . crissing
of earthly and heavenly bodies
torching each other

into bliss. On Nassau Street,
vacuumed, plucked of lint, again
the almost-black of the thick,
practically still wet flannel
of preachers' trousers, a man dressed
in the colors of soot and fire,
who last night could have flamed in inhuman arms,
imagined himself a god, staggers,
looking for the way out of here.

Agape

I want to touch her.
Once. Again. I will wait
if I must. Outwait.
Wait so long she will age,
pull even, pass. How
will she like it then if
when I bend to kiss wrinkles
ray out around her
mouth? I want to hold her.
In the flesh. All night.
Flesh like the bright
puffs the flower-god
puts on in spring, flimsy
for needing to last
but this one flashing
circuit through her
apparitions. Did she fear,

when I stood with the
precipice at my back
and beckoned, that I was a specter
she would plunge through?
At the agape love's addicts
lie back, drink, listen
to a priestess discourse
on love rightly understood.
As soon as cured anyone
can get up and go over
and bestow the Kiss
on anyone. Now the others
have disappeared — maybe
cured, probably joining lips
behind doors. It is
the Fourth Cup — the hour
for the breaking of the
transubstantiated body.
What if we break, the priestess
and I, the body
together? And I fall
in fear and longing? And
she commands me to
dissolve in the light
of love rightly understood,
or if I can't, to put
a gun to my head? I don't want
to know that on the other
side of the pillow nobody
stirs. I don't want ever

again to sit up half the night
and laugh and forget not
all of us will rejoice
like this always.

Who, on Earth

A ship sits on the sea raking
the water for fishes. A wave
flops heavily on top
of itself, defeat, and before
long does it again, defeat.
A skate, a baby, newly beached,
lies on the sand working her
sucking holes. Last night
I woke to a singing so high
it used only a soprano's
last outer notes, sometimes
sliding up into ultra-alts —
music a whale straying
into the Aegean long ago
might have keened through the wood walls
of ships in the black hours,
luring, wrecking
the sailors. I followed
down dark corridors to a lighted
courtyard where a woman sat
up to her waist in a pool,
singing. She turned

and kept singing, as though
she saw someone through me
and sang to him. Her breasts
were small and shapely,
like an athlete's, their
nipples never darkened
by the remorseless mouths
of babies. On the blurred
flesh under water black
dulse stirred — and down there too
was a sparkling, as of scales,
as if the submerged half of her
might be shutting itself up now
inside a fish tail — or, it could be,
pipping, busting, uncrumpling
a forked creature. On the beach,
pebbles, or maybe scales
shed on this spot at high tide
in some throe of metamorphosis,
gleam. In the skate
the mass of whatever
substance flesh on dying becomes
presses down into the sand,
trying to fall into the heaven
inside earth almost visible
through the half-washed windows
of stones. The sea
bristles up in waves. The largest
strikes the shore, gets upended,
leaps, lunges, crawls
all the way up to the skate,

then half sinking straight down,
half flowing back out, drags off
the carcass, leaving bubbles,
which pop, leaving the force
that crushes waves into nothing
to its victory. As when
mom harangues and pop icy-shoulders
the boy who can't think, can't yell,
explain himself, laugh, love, or sing;
can only fall in loneliness
with . . . but . . . who,
on earth?

The Ceiling

I don't like looking at
this ceiling of sprayed concrete
that would scrape the will out of anyone
who had decided to rise and pass through — just as
the trompe l'oeil of jagged rocks
on the Elmer Holmes Bobst Library floor
conjures up shattered flesh
in someone thinking of climbing over
those protruding balusters —
cruciform steel rods baring their row
of sharp crosses along the top, to interdict
the Christians, and make others imagine
being speared and hooked up halfway over.
But I don't want to wake up under
the smooth-plastered ceiling of my childhood either —

its cracks showed me the way but did not tell me the price.
A mild-spoken, uneasy man in a white jacket speaks
of Elavil, Lithane, Norpramin, Prozac, Desyrel, Xanax.
The woman with black eyes puts
the wafer she spirited out of Mass
under my pillow — scored with a Cross,
it will come apart into four, under
my heavy head, when we tumble,
or toss. I want a kiss
from red lips, like lip-petals in a garden,
speaking I don't know what to the morning.
I don't want to die.
I want to be born.

Oatmeal

I eat oatmeal for breakfast.
I make it on the hot plate and put skimmed milk on it.
I eat it alone.
I am aware it is not good to eat oatmeal alone.
Its consistency is such that it is better for your mental health if
    somebody eats it with you.
That is why I often think up an imaginary companion to have
    breakfast with.
Possibly it is even worse to eat oatmeal with an imaginary companion.
Nevertheless, yesterday morning, I ate my oatmeal with John Keats.
Keats said I was right to invite him: due to its glutinous texture, gluey
    lumpishness, hint of slime, and unusual willingness to disintegrate,
    oatmeal must never be eaten alone.

He said it is perfectly OK, however, to eat it with an imaginary
   companion, and he himself had enjoyed memorable porridges
   with Edmund Spenser and John Milton.
He also told me about writing the "Ode to a Nightingale."
He had a heck of a time finishing it — those were his words — "Oi
   'ad a 'eck of a toime," he said, more or less, speaking through his
   porridge.
He wrote it quickly, he said, on scraps of paper, which he then stuck in
   his pocket,
but when he got home he couldn't figure out the order of the stanzas,
   and he and a friend spread the papers on a table, and they made
   some sense of them, but he isn't sure to this day if they got it right.
An entire stanza may have slipped into the lining of his jacket
   through a hole in the pocket.
He still wonders about the occasional sense of drift between stanzas,
and the way here and there a line will go into the configuration of a
   Moslem at prayer, then raise itself up and peer about, then lay
   itself down slightly off the mark, causing the poem to move for-
   ward with God's reckless wobble.
He said someone told him that later in life Wordsworth heard about
   the scraps of paper on the table, and tried shuffling some stanzas
   of his own, but only made matters worse.
When breakfast was over, John recited "To Autumn."
He recited it slowly, with much feeling, and he articulated the words
   lovingly, and his odd accent sounded sweet.
He didn't offer the story of writing "To Autumn," I doubt if there is
   much of one.
But he did say the sight of a just-harvested oat field got him started
   on it,
and two of the lines, "For Summer has o'er-brimmed their clammy

cells" and "Thou watchest the last oozings hours by hours," came
   to him while eating oatmeal alone.
I can see him — drawing a spoon through the stuff, gazing into the
   glimmering furrows, muttering — and it occurs to me:
maybe there is no sublime, only the shining of the amnion's tatters.
For supper tonight I am going to have a baked potato left over from
   lunch.
I'm aware that a leftover baked potato can be damp, slippery, and
   simultaneously gummy and crumbly,
and therefore I'm going to invite Patrick Kavanagh to join me.

PART III

The Perch

There is a fork in a branch
of an ancient, enormous maple,
one of a grove of such trees,
where I climb sometimes and sit and look out
over miles of valleys and low hills.
Today on skis I took a friend
to show her the trees. We set out
down the road, turned in at
the lane which a few weeks ago,
when the trees were almost empty
and the November snows had not yet come,
lay thickly covered in bright red
and yellow leaves, crossed the swamp,
passed the cellar hole holding
the remains of the 1850s farmhouse
that had slid down into it by stages
in the thirties and forties, followed
the overgrown logging road
and came to the trees. I climbed up
to the perch, and this time looked
not into the distance but at
the tree itself, its trunk
contorted by the terrible struggle
of that time when it had its hard time.
After the trauma it grows less solid.
It may be some such time now comes upon me.
It would have to do with the unaccomplished,
and with the failing marriage

of solitude and happiness. Then a rifle
sounded, several times, quite loud,
from across the valley, percussions
of the rite of human mastery
over the earth — the most graceful,
most alert of the animals
being chosen to die. I looked
to see if my friend had heard,
but she was stepping about on her skis,
studying the trees, smiling to herself,
her lips still filled, for all
we had drained them, with hundreds
and thousands of kisses. Just then
she looked up — the way, from low
to high, the god blesses — and the blue
of her eyes shone out of the black
and white of bark and snow, as lovers
who are walking on a freezing day
touch icy cheek to icy cheek,
kiss, then shudder to discover
the heat waiting inside their mouths.

The Vow

When the lover
goes, the vow though
broken remains, that
trace of eternity love
brings down among us

stays, to give
dignity to the suffering
and to intensify it.

The Room

The door closes on pain and confusion.
The candle flame wavers from side to side
as though trying to break itself in half
to color the shadows too with living light.
The andante movement plays over and over
its many triplets, like farm dogs yapping
at a melody made of the gratification-cries
of cocks. I will not stay long.
Nothing in experience led me to imagine
having. Having is destroying, according
to my version of the vow of impoverishment.
But here, in this brief, waxen light,
I have, and nothing is destroyed. The flute
that guttered those owl's notes into the waste hours
of childhood joins with the piano
and they play, *Being is having.* Having
may be simply the grace of the shell
moving without hesitation, with lively pride,
down the stubborn river of woe. At the far end,
a door no one dares open begins opening.
To go through it will awaken such regret
as only closing it behind can obliterate.
The candle flame's staggering makes the room
wobble and shift — matter itself, laughing.

I can't come back. I won't change.
I have the usual capacity for wanting
what may not even exist. Don't worry.
That is dew wetting my face.
You see? Nothing that enters the room
can have only its own meaning ever again.

Divinity

When the man touches through
to the exact center of the woman,
he lies motionless, in equilibrium,
in absolute desire, at the threshold
of the world to which the Creator Spirit
knows the pass-whisper, and whispers it,
and his loving friend becomes his divinity.

Last Gods

She sits naked on a boulder
a few yards out in the water.
He stands on the shore,
also naked, picking blueberries.
She calls. He turns. She opens
her legs showing him her great beauty
and smiles, a bow of lips
seeming to tie together
the ends of the earth.
Splashing her image

to pieces, he wades out
and stands before her, sunk
to the anklebones in leaf-mush
and bottom-slime — the intimacy
of the visible world. He puts
a berry in its shirt
of mist into her mouth.
She swallows it. He puts in another.
She swallows it. Over the lake
two swallows whim, juke, jink,
and when one snatches
an insect they both whirl up
and exult. He is swollen
not with ichor but with blood.
She takes him and talks him
more swollen. He kneels, opens
the dark, vertical smile
linking heaven with the underearth
and murmurs her smoothest flesh
more smooth. On top of the boulder
they join. Somewhere
a frog moans, a crow screams.
The hair of their bodies
startles up. At last they call out
in the tongue of the last gods,
who refused to go,
chose death, and shuddered
in joy and shattered in pieces,
bequeathing their cries
into the human throat. Now in the lake
two faces float, looking up

at a great maternal pine whose branches
open out in all directions
explaining everything.

Flower of Five Blossoms

Flower of five blossoms
I have brought you with me here
because you might not still be blossoming when I go back,
and because you might not blossom again.
I watched each of your buds swell up,
like water collected on a child's lid, about to plop,
or the catch in a throat that turns into a sob,
or in a tenor's throat, on some nights into a hundred sobs.
But as the buds
became these blossoms,
I am trying to learn: time suffered
is not necessarily time destroyed.
Outside, snow falls down in big pieces, like petals,
while in here, fire blossoms
out of wood and goes up in flames,
which are not *things dying* but just the *dying*.
Above them on the mantelpiece,
how calm your blossoms appear, austere and orderly, like the faces
     of singers,
but singing in silence, like the child
half-hidden by the pew, who dares only to think the hymns.
Phalaenopsis, sensual Orchidaceae,
sometimes, out of the corner of the eye, your blossoms perched on
     their twigs seem true to your name, "moth-like,"

and there, in the salep risen out of the pot of chipped bark, is the
    origin of your family name, ὄρχις, "testicle."
A few minutes ago, I put on a sonata by Brahms
("Brahms," nearly the sound dwelling on you forms in my mouth)
and I was standing at the mantelpiece
just as the slowest passage began, that moment
when the bow rests nearly immobile on the strings
— as mouths might, on mouths, in stillest kissing,
when a lip could be lying against a tooth in the other mouth, one
    can't say —
the bow's tremblings at what is about to happen
all that shakes any sound out of the strings at all,
and I turned and saw
what everyone else perhaps sees at once:
that in each blossom
the calyx's middle petal curves up
and flows over the mons veneris and spreads across the belly,
and the petal on either side rises over the thigh, one edge following
    the ridge of the pelvic bone, which is prominent, for she lies on
    her back,
and the two petals that are set back hold the roundness of her
    buttocks,
and at the center, in the little crown,
the clitoris leans, above
the vestibule opening into the center of being;
and I wanted to lean close,
without sound, with my lips
touching lightly one of your blossoms,
and find there, like a kiss that has a soft lick in it, like "blossoms,"
the name of this place and speak it.
That's what two keep trying to do,

over and over, at night,

singing,

sometimes together, sometimes alone —

but in a little while they forget, and think they haven't found it,

and what is mute and wet waits again to be sung.

As the sonata ends,

your blossoms fall more profoundly still

— their lavender streaks suddenly empty, like staff-lines before any
      notes have been entered —

have a portion of death in them,

and watch,

intent, unblinking,

like the white, hooded faces of cobras

risen up to mesmerize, or to fling themselves forward into the
      deadly kiss;

though each wears the headdress of Mary.

Or am I myself the spellbinder and the killer?

Alone here, I often find myself thinking of women —

and now your blossoms could stand for five of them —

any five, if I were to try to name them —

one could be she to whom I was married for many years,

or she who merely exchanged a few words with me, across a table,
      under the noise of the conversation of the others,

or that pale, laughing beauty I hugged at the dancing lessons, when we
      were fifteen,

and another could be the woman whose strict intelligence I revere,
      whom I kiss on the forehead, a quarter inch away from the brain,
      the way Plato kissed,

and then the fifth blossom would be my mother, risen up at my
      bedside, wanting to please, but having, the next day or another,
      to crush —

strange,
for I began by speaking of sexual resemblance,
but not strange, for it was as a sexual creature she seized me into
 existence,
it was through her vagina, trespassed by man one way, transpierced
 by three babies the other,
I was dragged out alive, into the dead
of winter — a day
perhaps like this day, sixty years later, when out there earth
draws down on top of herself yet another of her freezing sleeping
 clothes,
but underneath is awakening . . .
besoming . . . blowsining . . . blissamous . . .
and in here, at the mantelpiece,
bending close to you, praying to you almost, standing almost in
 flames,
I wonder
what can come of these minutes,
each a hard inner tumbling, as when a key nearly won't turn,
or the note of a piano, clattered or stroked, ringing.
Everyone knows
everything sings and dies.
But it could be, too, everything dies and sings,
and a life is the interlude
when, still humming, we can look up, gawk about, imagine whatever,
 say it,
topple back into singing.
Oh first our voice be done, and then, before and afterwards and all
 around it, that singing.

Farewell

after Haydn's Symphony in F-sharp Minor

for Paul Zweig (1935–1984)

The last adagio begins.
A violinist gets up and leaves the stage.
Two cellists follow, bows held straight up, cellos dangling.
The flutist picks her way lifting the flute high as if to honor it for its
    pure hollow notes during the incessant rubbing.
Soon the bassoonist leaves, then the bass fiddler.
The fortepiano player abandons the black, closeted contraption and
    walks off shaking her fingers.

On going, each player stoops at the music stand and puffs
the flame off the top of the stalk of wax
in which fireweed, flame azalea, dense blazing star stored it a
    summer ago,
adding that quantity of darkness to the hall
and the same of light
to the elsewhere where the players reassemble,
like birds in a beech and hemlock forest just before first light,
and wait for the oboist to arrive with her reliable A,
so they can tune and play
the phrases inside flames wobbling on top of stems in the field,
and in greenish sparks of grass-sex of fireflies
and in gnats murmuring past in a spectral bunch,
and in crickets who would saw themselves apart to sing,
and in the golden finch atop the mountain ash, whose roots feed in
    the mouths of past singers.

By ones, the way we wash up on this unmusical shore,
and by twos, the way we pass into the ark each time the world begins,
the orchestra diminishes, until only two are left: violinists
who half face each other, friends who have figured out what they have
    figured out by sounding it upon the other,
and scathe the final phrases.

In the huge darkness above the stage I imagine
the face, very magnified, of my late dear friend Paul Zweig,
who went away, into Eternity's Woods, under a double singing of
    birds,
saying something like, "Let the limits of knowing stretch and
    diaphanize:
knowledge that leads to purer ignorance
gives the falling trajectory its grace."

Goodbye, dear friend.
Everything on earth, born only
moments ago, abruptly tips over
and is dragged, as if by mistake,
back into the chaotic inevitable.
Even the meantime, which is the holy time
of being on earth in simultaneous lifetimes, ends.

This is one of its endings.
The violinists drag their ignorant bows across
their know-nothing strings
a last time, the last
of the adagio flies out through the f-holes.
The audience straggles from the hall and at once disappears.

For myself I go on foot on Seventh Avenue
down to the small bent streets of the Village.
From ahead of me comes a *hic* of somebody drunk,
then a *nunc,* perhaps of a head bumping against a lamppost or scaf-
    folding.

PART IV

When One Has Lived a Long Time Alone

1

When one has lived a long time alone,
one refrains from swatting the fly
and lets him go, and one is slow to strike
the mosquito, though more than willing to slap
the flesh under her, and one hoists the toad
from the pit too deep to hop out of
and carries him to the grass, without minding
the poisoned urine he slicks his body with,
and one envelops, in a towel, the swift
who fell down the chimney and knocks herself
against window glass, and releases her outside
and watches her fly free, a life line flung at reality,
when one has lived a long time alone.

2

When one has lived a long time alone,
one grabs the snake behind the head
and holds him until he stops trying to stick
the orange tongue — which forks at the end
into black filaments and flashes out
like a fire-eater's breaths and bears little
resemblance to the pimpled pink lump
that mostly dozes inside the human mouth —
into one's flesh, and clamps it between his jaws,
letting the gaudy tips show, as children do
when concentrating, and as very likely
one does oneself, without knowing it,
when one has lived a long time alone.

3

When one has lived a long time alone,
among regrets so immense the past occupies
nearly all the room there is in consciousness,
one notices in the snake's eyes, which see behind
without giving any less attention to the future,
the opaque, milky-blue cloudiness that comes
when the snake is about to throw its skin
and become new — meanwhile continuing,
of course, to grow old — the same *bleu passé*
that bleaches the corneas of the blue-eyed
when they lie back at the end and look for heaven,
a fading one suspects means they don't find it,
when one has lived a long time alone.

4

When one has lived a long time alone,
one falls to poring upon a creature,
contrasting its eternity's-face to one's own
full of hours, taking note of the differences,
exaggerating them, making them everything,
until the other is utterly other, and then,
with hard effort, probably with tongue sticking out,
going over each difference again and this time
canceling it, until nothing is left but likeness
and suddenly oneness, and . . . minutes later
one starts awake, taken aback at how unresistingly
one drops off into the bliss of kinship,
when one has lived a long time alone.

5

When one has lived a long time alone
and listens at morning to mourning doves
sound their kyrie eleison, or to the small thing
spiritualizing upon a twig cry, "pewit-phoebe!"
or to grasshoppers scratch their thighs' needfire
awake, or to peabody birds at midday send their
schoolboys' whistlings across the field, and at dusk,
their undamped chinks, as from marble cutters' chisels,
or at nightfall to polliwogs just rearranged into frogs
raise their ave verum corpus — listens to those
who hop or fly call down upon us the mercy
of other tongues — one hears them as inner voices,
when one has lived a long time alone.

6

When one has lived a long time alone,
one knows that consciousness consummates,
and as the most self-conscious one among these
others uttering their seemingly compulsory cries —
the least flycatcher witching up "che-bec!"
or red-headed woodpecker clanging out his tunes
from a metal roof gutter, or ruffed grouse drumming
"thrump thrump thrump thrump-thrump-
thrump-thrump-rup-rup-rup-rup-rup-r-r-r-r-r-r"
deep in the woods, all of them in time's unfolding
trying to cry themselves into self-knowing —
one knows one is here to hear them into shining,
when one has lived a long time alone.

7

When one has lived a long time alone,
one likes alike the pig, who brooks no deferment
of gratification, and the porcupine, or thorned pig,
who enters the cellar but not the house itself
because of eating down the cellar stairs on the way up,
and one likes the worm, who by bunching herself together
and expanding works her way through the ground,
no less than the butterfly, who totters full of worry
among the day lilies as they darken,
and more and more one finds one likes
any other species better than one's own,
which has gone amok, making one self-estranged,
when one has lived a long time alone.

8

When one has lived a long time alone,
sour, misanthropic, one fits to one's defiance
the satanic boast, *It is better to reign
in hell than to submit on earth,* and forgets
one's kind — the way by now the snake does,
who stops trying to get to the floor and lingers
all across one's body, slumping into its contours,
adopting its temperature — and abandons hope
of the sweetness of friendship or love,
before long can barely remember what they are,
and covets the stillness of inorganic matter,
in a self-dissolution one may not know how to halt,
when one has lived a long time alone.

9

When one has lived a long time alone,
and the hermit thrush calls and there is an answer,
and the bullfrog head half out of water utters
the cantillations he sang in his first spring,
and the snake lowers himself over the threshold
and creeps away among the stones, one sees
they all live to mate with their kind, and one knows,
after a long time of solitude, after the many steps taken
away from one's kind, toward these other kingdoms,
the hard prayer inside one's own singing
is to come back, if one can, to one's own,
a world almost lost, in the exile that deepens,
when one has lived a long time alone.

10

When one has lived a long time alone,
one wants to live again among men and women,
to return to that place where one's ties with the human
broke, where the disquiet of death and now also
of history glimmers its firelight on faces,
where the gaze of the new baby meets the gaze
of the great granny, and where lovers speak,
on lips blowsy from kissing, that language
the same in each mouth, and like birds at daybreak
blether the song that is both earth's and heaven's,
until the sun rises, and they stand
in the daylight of being made one: kingdom come,
when one has lived a long time alone.

Imperfect Thirst

1994

To Bobbie

If your eyes are not deceived by the mirage
Do not be proud of the sharpness of your understanding;
It may be your freedom from this optical illusion
Is due to the imperfectness of your thirst.

— Sohrawardi

PROEM

The Pen

Its work is memory.

It engraves sounds into paper and fills them with pounded nutgall.

It can transcribe most of the sounds that the child, waking early, not
    yet knowing which language she will one day speak, sings.

Asleep in someone's pocket in an airplane, the pen dreams of paper,
    and a feeling of pressure comes into it, and, like a boy dreaming
    of Grace Hamilton, who sits in front of him in the fifth grade, it
    could spout.

An old pen with unresilient ink sac may make many scratches before
    it inks.

The pen's alternation of lifts and strokes keeps thoughts coming in a
    rhythmic flow.

When several thoughts arrive together, the pen may resort to scrib-
    bling "blah blah," meaning, come back to this later.

Much of what pens write stands for "blah blah."

In the Roman system, the pen moves to the right, and at the margin
    swerves backward and downward — perhaps dangerous directions,
    but necessary for reentering the past.

The pen is then like the person who gets out of the truck, goes around
    to the rear, signals to the driver, and calls, "C'mon back."

Under increased concentration the pen spreads its nib, thickening the
    words that attempt to speak the unspeakable.

These are the fallen-angel words.

Ink is their ichor.

They have a mineral glint, given by clarity of knowing, even in hell.

The pen also uses ink to obfuscate, like the cuttlefish, by inculcating the
    notions that reality happens one complete sentence after another,
    and that if we have words for an event, we understand it — as in:

How's your pa?

He died.

Oh.

When my father died, leaving my mother and me alone in the house, I don't know even now what happened.

What did Rilke understand on the death of his father, who by then had become a speck in the distance?

Did his mother suddenly become larger?

It seems that soon after she married him, Rilke's wife also began turning into a speck.

He told her in eloquent letters it was good for his artistic development for them to live apart; meanwhile women arrived from all over Europe, to spend their allotment of nights in his bed.

I called it "my work" when I would spend weeks on the road, often in the beds of others.

This Ideal pen, with vulcanite body, can't resist dredging up the waywardness of my youth.

Fortunately pens run out of ink.

Villon had to cut short the bitter bequests of *Le Lais* when his inkwell froze and his candle blew out.

Like a camel at an oasis with stomachs completely empty, the pen thrusts itself into the ink and suctions in near-silence.

Filled, it starts again laying trudge marks across the paper.

Yesterday, when trying to write about my sister Wendy, my little mother in childhood, I couldn't find the words in the ink.

Then I had a visit from a poet a few years widowed, who talked about her husband and how she felt thwarted in her writing and had lost her way — though in the rhythmical tumbling forth of her words she seemed to be finding it.

I wished I had collected some of the mascara-blackened fluid on her
   cheeks to mix into my ink.

But when I started writing about Wendy again, the ink had replen-
   ished its vocabulary, and from the street came the bleats of a truck
   in reverse gear and a cry, "C'mon back, c'mon back."

I

My Mother's R & R

She lay late in bed. Maybe she was sick,
though she was never sick. Pink flowers
were in full blossom in the wallpaper
and motes like bits of something ground up
churned in sun rays from the windows.
We climbed into bed with her.
Perhaps she needed comforting,
and she was alone, and she let us take
a breast each out of the loose slip.
"Let's make believe we're babies,"
Derry said. We put the large pink
flowers at the end of those lax breasts
into our mouths and sucked with enthusiasm.
She laughed and seemed to enjoy our play.
Perhaps intoxicated by our pleasure,
or frustrated by the failure of the milk
to flow, we sucked harder, probably
our bodies writhed, our eyes flared,
certainly she could feel our teeth.
Abruptly she took back her breasts
and sent us from the bed, two small
hungry boys enflamed and driven off
by the she-wolf. But we had got our nip,
and in the empire we would found,
we would taste all the women and expel them
one after another as they came to resemble her.

Showing My Father Through Freedom

His steps rang in the end room
of the henhouse of ten rooms in a row
someone had lent my father as a place
to put the family for the summer
while he stayed behind doing his odd jobs.
This would be his one visit, and I ran
through the dark of the empty rooms
until he bent down out of the gloom like a god
and picked me up and carried me back into the lamplight.
The next day my mother and I showed him through Freedom.
The strawberry ice cream in the Harmony Tea Shop,
which my mother called the Patisserie, was pink
with red bruises. Lettie the postmistress
said, with her sweet regretfulness, perhaps acquired
from palping whatever billets-doux passed
in or out of Freedom, as she said nearly every day
to one or another of us children, "Nothing today, dear."
John, who pumped gas probably no more
than a dozen times a day, sat back in his chair
under the sign of Pegasus. I ran to him,
to get on the knee where he put me
whenever my mother and I came by, happy
that my father would see this full-grown
man was my friend, and would respect me.
But after he greeted us, John turned and, when he sat again,
leaned forward and put his elbows on his knees.
The three of them conversed. My father did his best.
"Yes, it *has* been," of the wet summer.
"They *are* sudden," of the lightning storms.

I lingered at the knee. My sitting on it,
and my mother and John talking while I sat,
was that a secret? Suddenly I was like
somebody propped up in a hospital bed,
who can see, hear, almost understand,
and is unable to speak.

Hitchhiker

After a moment, the driver, a salesman
for Travelers Insurance heading for
Topeka, said, "What was that?"
I, in my Navy uniform, still useful
for hitchhiking though the war was over,
said, "I think you hit somebody."
I knew he had. The round face, opening
in surprise as the man bounced off the fender,
had given me a look as he swept past.
"Why didn't you say something?" The salesman
stepped hard on the brakes. "I thought you saw,"
I said. I didn't know why. It came to me
I could have sat next to this man all the way
to Topeka without saying a word about it.
He opened the car door and looked back.
I did the same. At the roadside,
in the glow of a streetlight, was a body.
A man was bending over it. For an instant
it was myself, in a time to come,
bending over the body of my father.
The man stood and shouted at us, "Forget it!

He gets hit all the time!" Oh.
A bum. We were happy to forget it.
The rest of the way, into dawn in Kansas,
when the salesman dropped me off, we did not speak,
except, as I got out, I said, "Thanks,"
and he said, "Don't mention it."

The Man in the Chair

I glanced in as I walked past
the door of the room where he sat
in the easy chair with the soiled area
along the top from the olive oil.
I think I noticed something—
a rigidity in the torso, making it
unable to settle into the cushions,
or a slackness in the neck,
causing the head to tilt forward,
or a shaking in the lifted left fist,
as though he were pushing a hammer
handle back with all his force, to pull
a spike driven nineteen years before
the end of the nineteenth century
into lignum vitae so dense the steel
may have cried out in excruciated singsong,
or an acute angle in the knees,
as if he were holding his feet inches off
the floor to keep them from a whitish
wash of mist from some freshly
dug pit simmering across it,

or the jerk of a leg, as if a hand
just then had reached up through the floor
and tried to grab it. I think I noticed,
yet I did not stop, or go in, or speak.
For his part he could not have spoken,
that day, or any day, he had a human
version of the pip, the disease that thickens
birds' vocal cords and throttles their song.
I had it too, no doubt caught from him,
and I could not speak truly except
to the beings I had invented far within.
I walked past, into my room, shut
the door, and sat down at the desk,
site of so many hours lost
passing one number through another
and drawing a little row of survivors on top,
while my mother sat across from me
catching my mistakes upside down.
I wrote, and as I did I allowed
to be audible in the room only
the scritches of the pen nib, a sound
like a rat nosing around in the dark
interior of a wall, making a nest of shreds.
All other sounds, including the words
he never said to me, my cries to him
I did not make, I forced down
through the paper, the desk, the floor,
the surface of the earth, the roof
of that dismal region where they stood,
two or three of them, who had reached up
and had him by the foot, and were pulling hard.

438

Picnic

When my father was three years dead and dying
away more quickly than other dead fathers do,
I took my mother in my 1935 green Ford
for a picnic on the Back Shore of Cape Cod,
where Henry Beston had gone alone
and chronicled a year spent attempting to feel
kinship with the elements and the beach creatures,
who demanded nothing and did not expect to be loved.
I swam, not far out; I have always felt fear
when swimming on top of very deep water.
When I came back I sat next to my mother on the towel,
and we ate the lunch she had wrapped in the same
Cut-rite wax paper she had wrapped my sandwiches in
in J. C. Potter School, paraffined to the degree
of cloudy translucency that indicated the extent
we saw, and the extent we did not see,
ourselves as two who had done nothing
to avert the explosion in my father's chest.
As I rubbed myself with sun oil, concentrating
in the way I concentrated on anything that
did not entail knowing what it meant
for me to be a son of him or her, she said, "Oh,
you have hair on your legs, I never thought you did."

II

The Cellist

At intermission I find her backstage
still practicing the piece coming up next.
She calls it the "solo in high dreary."
Her bow niggles at the strings like a hand
stroking skin it never wanted to touch.
Probably under her scorn she is sick
that she can't do better by it. As I am,
by the dreary in me, such as the disparity
between all the tenderness I've received
and the amount I've given, and the way
I used to shrug off the imbalance
simply as how things are, as if the male
were constituted like those coffeemakers
that produce less black bitter than the quantity
of sweet clear you pour in — forgetting about
how much I spilled through unsteady walking,
and that lot I flung on the ground
in suspicion, and for fear I wasn't worthy,
and all I threw out for reasons I don't understand yet.
"Break a leg!" somebody tells her.
When she comes out, she seems nervous,
her hand shakes as she re-dog-ears the big pages
that appear about to flop over on their own.
Now she raises the bow — its flat bundle of hair
harvested from the rear ends of horses — like a whetted
scimitar she is about to draw across a throat,
and attacks. In a back alley a cat opens
its pink-ceilinged mouth, gets netted
in full yowl, clubbed, bagged, bicycled off, haggled open,

441

gutted, the gut squeezed down to its highest pitch,
washed, and sliced into cello strings that bring
a screaming into this duet of hair and gut.
Now she is flying — tossing back the goblets
of Saint-Amour standing empty,
half-empty, or full on the tablecloth-
like sheet music. Her knees tighten
and loosen around the big-hipped creature
wailing and groaning between them
as if locked with her in syzygial amplexus.
The music seems to rise from the crater left
when heaven was torn up and taken off the earth;
more likely it comes up through her priest's dress,
up from beneath that clump of hair that now
may be so wet with its waters, miraculous
as those the fishes multiplied in at Galilee,
that each strand wicks a portion all the way out
to its tip and fattens it into a droplet
on the bush of half notes glittering in that dark.
Now she lifts off the bow and sits back.
Her face shines with the unselfconsciousness of a cat
screaming at night and the teary radiance of one
who gives everything no matter what has been given.

Running on Silk

A man in the black twill and gold braid of a pilot
and a woman with the virginal alertness
flight attendants had in the heyday
of stewardesses go running past

as if they have just hopped off one plane
and now run to hop on another.
In the verve and fleetness of their sprint
you can see them hastening toward each other
inside themselves. The man pulls a luggage
cart with one suitcase bungeed on top of another,
and the woman . . . my God, she holds her
high heels in her hand and runs on silk!
I see us, as if preserved in the amber
of forty-year-old Tennessee sour-mash whiskey
splashed over cherishing ice, put down
our glasses, sidestep through groups
and pairs all gruffing and tinkling
to each other, slip out the door,
hoof and click down two flights of stairs.
Maybe he wonders what gives with his wife
and that unattached young man he left her
laughing with — and finds them not
where they last were, not in the kitchen,
not anywhere, and checking the hall
hears laughter jangling in the stairwell
cut off by the bang of the outside door. In the street
she pulls off her shoes and runs on stocking feet
— laughing and crying *taxiii! taxiii!*
as if we were ecstatic worshipers springing
down a beach in Bora-Bora — toward a cab
suffusing its back end in red brake light.
As I push her in, a voice behind us calls
bop! bop! like a stun gun, or a pet name.
Out the taxi's rear window I glimpse him,
stopped dead, one foot on the sidewalk,

one in the gutter, a hand on his heart. *Go! go!*
we cry to the driver. After we come together,
to our surprise, for we are strangers,
my telephone also starts making a lot
of anxious, warbling, weeping-like noises.
I put it on the floor, with a pillow on it,
and we lie back and listen with satisfaction
to the stifled rings, like dumdum bullets
meant for us, spending their force in feathers.
A heavy man trotting by knocks my leg with his bag;
he doesn't notice or care and trots on.
Could he be pursuing those two high-flyers
who have run out of sight? Will I find him, up ahead,
stopped at a just-shut departure gate, like that man
that night forty years ago, as if turned to wood
and put out by his laughing murderers to sell cigars?

The Deconstruction of Emily Dickinson

The lecture had ended when I came in,
and the professor was answering questions.
I do not know what he had been doing with her
poetry, but now he was speaking of her
as a victim of reluctant male publishers.
When the questions dwindled, I put up my hand.
I said that the ignorant meddling of the Springfield *Republican*
and the hidebound response of literary men,
and the gulf between the poetic wishfulness
then admired and her own harsh knowledge,
had let her see that her poems

would not be understood in her time;
and therefore, passionate to publish,
she vowed not to publish again. I said
I would recite a version of her vow,

> Publication — is the Auction
> Of the Mind of Man —

but before I could, the professor broke in.
"Yes," he said, "'the Auction' — 'auction,' from *augere, auctum,* to
    augment, to author . . ."
"Let's hear the poem!" "The poem!" several women,
who at such a moment are more outspoken than men, shouted,
but I kept still and he kept going.
"In *auctum* the economy of the signifier is split, revealing an uncon-
    scious collusion in the bourgeois commodification of conscious-
    ness. While our author says 'no,' the unreified text says 'yes,' yes?"
He kissed his lips together and turned to me
saying, "Now, may we hear the poem?"
I waited a moment for full effect.
Without rising to my feet, I said,
"Professor, to understand Dickinson
it may not always be necessary to uproot her words.
Why not, first, try *listening* to her?
Loyalty forbids me to recite her poem now."
No, I didn't say that — I realized
she would want me to finish him off with one wallop.
So I said, "Professor, I thought you
would welcome the words of your author.
I see you prefer to hear yourself speak."
No, I held back — for I could hear her

urging me to put outrage into my voice
and substance into my argument.
I stood up so that everyone might see
the derision in my smile. "Professor," I said,
"you live in Amherst at the end of the twentieth century.
For you 'auction' means a quaint event
where somebody coaxes out the bids
on butter churns on a summer Saturday.
Forget etymology, this is history.
In Amherst in 1860 'auction' meant
the slave auction, you dope!"
Well, I didn't say that either,
although I have said them all,
many times, in the middle of the night.
In reality, I stood up and recited the poem
like a schoolboy called upon in class.
My voice gradually weakened, and the women
who had cried out for the poem
now looked as though they were thinking
of errands to be done on the way home.
When I finished, the professor smiled.
"Thank you. So, what at first some of us may have taken as a simple
    outcry, we all now see is an ambivalent, self-subversive text."
As people got up to go, I moved
into that sanctum within me where Emily
sometimes speaks a verse, and listened
for a sign of how she felt, such as,
"Thanks — Sweet — countryman —
for wanting — to Sing out — of Me —
after all that Humbug." But she was silent.

The Night

Just as paint seems to leap from the paintbrush
to clapboards that have gone many years unpainted
and disappear into them almost with a slurp,
so their words, as they lie and talk, their faces
almost touching, jump from one mouth to the other
without apparent sound except little lip-wetting smacks.
When their mouths touch at last they linger, making
small eating motions and suction squeaks.
She licks three slithery syllables on his chest,
looks up, smiles, shines him the same three.
In his gasps suspense and gratefulness mix,
as in the crinkling unwrapping of Christmas packages.
Where he touches her she glisses smooth and shining
as the lower lip of a baby tantalizing its gruel bowl
with lengthening and shortening dangles of drool.
Her moans come with a slight delay, as if the sequence
happens across a valley, the touch and then the cry.
Their bones almost hit — the purpose of flesh
may be to keep the skeletons from bruising each other.
One of them calls out in cackling, chaotic rattles,
like a straw suddenly sucking the bottom. Then, with a sound
like last bathwater seized by the Coriolis force,
the other calls out. They lie holding each other.
For a moment the glue joining body and soul does not ache.
They are here and not here, like the zebra,
whose flesh has been sliced up and reassembled
in alternating layers with matter from elsewhere.
The sense that each one had of being divided in two

has given way to the knowledge that each is half
of the whole limb-tangle appearing like a large
altricial hatchling occupying much of the bed.
The man squinches himself up against the back
of the woman, an arm crooks over her waist,
his hand touches sometimes her hand, sometimes her breast,
his penis settles along the groove between her buttocks,
falls into deep sleep, almost starts to snore.
If someone were to discover them this way,
him like the big, folded wings of her,
they might stay as they are, the way the woodcock,
believing herself safe in her camouflage, sometimes
sits still until a person stoops and reaches out to pet her —
then jumps six feet straight up and wherries off.
When the sun enters the room, he wakes and watches her.
Her hair lies loose, strewn across the pillow
as if it has been washed up, her lips are blubbed,
from the kissing, her profile is fierce,
like that of a figurehead seeing over
the rim of the world. She wakes.
They do not get up yet. It is not easy
to straighten out bodies that have been lying
all night in the same curve, like two paintbrushes
wintering in a coffee can of evaporated turpentine.
They hear the clangs of a church clock. Why only nine?
When they have been lying on this bed since before the earth began.

Trees

I sneaked out of the house after helping with the dishes. I
made my way to the deepest center of the woods and climbed
a young maple tree and gazed up into the deepening sky
above. I must have dozed off for a few minutes, because quite
suddenly the stars emerged in a blacker sky. Although I did
not know their names — in fact, I did not even know they
had names — I began to address them quietly, for I never
spoke with "full-throated ease" until hidden by the cover of
total darkness. A soft wind shook the leaves around me. From
my own hands I caught the smell of earth and iron.

— Philip Levine

I would leave by the back door
and make my way to the woods, on paths
I thought were trails of the Wampanoags,
paths at that hour still woven over
with scaly, cobwebby stuff
that had dew under it and dew on top.
I pressed myself to a white oak
and climbed. On the way up gravity
seemed to start pulling me from above.
At the top of this somnolent fountaining
of trunk, boughs, branches, twigs, leaf-splashes,
all of it tinned with the industrial dust
of Pawtucket in Depression,
I gave my ape-cry.
I knew the oaks' sermon to us
has to do with their verticality,
and their muted budding and brilliant decay,

and their elasticity, and their suthering and creaking,
and now and then their dispersal at the top into birds.
But I knew it had to do even more
with this massive, stunting halt
and the 360° impetus to spill outward
and downward and hover above their twin
glooming open under the ground
— at Loon Lake I had seen this in visions.
Out of the hush and rustlings came
chirrups, whistlings, tremolos, hoots,
noises that seemed left poking up
after some immense subtraction.
Tok-tok-tok-tok, as from somebody
nailing upholstery, started up nearby:
the bird with a bloodmark on the back
of his head clung, cutting with
steady strokes his cave of wormwood.
On another tree, a smaller bird,
in gray rags, put her rump
to the sky and walked headfirst
down the trunk toward the earth
and the earth under the earth.
Drops of rain plopped into my hair.
I looked up and bigger drops tapped
my lips and cheeks. Unlike the cat,
who loves climbing but not coming down,
I came swinging and sliding down,
hanging by my knees on the last branch,
and, as if the tree were one bell
of an hourglass which had been taken up

and turned over while I was up in it
and just as I slid through set down hard,
I landed with a jounce. The drops
chuting earthward all around me
were bringing back a kind of time
that falls and does not fly.
The red-topped bird kept working in the rain.
I had seen my father stand most of a
day pushing and lifting
his handsaw. All hand tools, I thought,
were the trees' equals, working wood
no more easily than a woodpecker's auger.
I had not yet caught in the crosscut's
grunts and gasps the screams, in time
to come, of chainsaws, or in the steady,
drudging *hunhs!* of the ripsaw the howls
of supersaws clear-cutting the mountainsides,
or in the *har-har* and handshake
of the developer the loud bellowing
and hard squeeze of tree harvesters; I had not
conceived its own pulverized
pulp being ripped out in an arc at the foot
of every tree, I had not witnessed
the imperceptible budge, the dryadic pop,
the slow tilt and accelerating topple,
the dry splintering crash of tree
after tree like the end of history.
And yet — as I walked — a scrub pine brushed
dust off my pants, a birch branch knocked
debris of bark from my shirt, a leaf-clump

of a white cedar seemed to reach down and,
as if to preempt the work of the hairbrush
ready to harrow its spiky bristles across
my brain-skin in the morning at the front door
on my way to Sunday school, smoothed my sodden hair.

III

SHEFFIELD
GHAZALS

The Biting Insects

The biting insects don't like the blood of people who dread dying.
They prefer the blood of people who can imagine themselves entering
    other life-forms.
These are the ones the mosquito sings to in the dark and the deer fly
    orbits and studies with yellow eyes.
In the other animals the desire to die comes when existing wears out
    existence.
In us this desire can come too early, and we kill ourselves, or it may
    never come, and we have to be dragged away.
Not many are able to die well, not even Jesus going back to his father.
And yet dying gets done — and Eddie Jewell coming up the road with
    his tractor on a gooseneck trailer and seeing an owl lifting its
    wings as it alights on the ridgepole of this red house, Galway, will
    know that now it is you being accepted back into the family of
    mortals.

Paradise Elsewhere

Some old people become more upset about human foibles than they
    did when they were younger — part of getting ready to leave.
For others, human idiocy becomes increasingly precious; they begin to
    see in it the state of mind we will have in heaven.
"What about heaven?" I said to Harold, who is ninety-four and lives
    in the VA Hospital in Tucson.
He said, "Memory is heaven."
The physicist emeritus tottering across the campus of Cal Tech
    through the hazy sunshine occasionally chuckles to himself.

454

Yet it has happened to many others, and to you, too, Galway — when
illness, or unhappiness, or imagining the future wears an empty
place inside us, the idea of paradise elsewhere quickly fills it.

Collusion of Elements

On the riverbank *Narcissus poeticus* holds an ear trumpet toward the
canoe apparitioning past.
Cosmos sulphureous flings back all its eyelashes and stares.
The canoe enacts the Archimedean collusion of elements: no matter
how much weight you try to sink it with, the water as vigorously
holds it up.
Up to a point.
Likewise, the more pressure the fuel exerts on the O-rings, the more
securely they fit into their grooves and keep the fuel from escaping.
At certain temperatures.
Pain is inherently lonely.
Of all the varieties of pain, loneliness may be the most lonely.
The Queen Charlotte Islanders used the method of fire to hollow a
canoe out of a single log.
If there are burn-throughs, a vessel could founder; if cold O-rings,
blow up.
As for you, Galway, the more dire the burn-throughs, the looser the
O-rings, the greater the chance you could float or fly.

Driving West

A tractor-trailer carrying two dozen crushed automobiles overtakes a
tractor-trailer carrying a dozen new.

Oil is a form of waiting.

The internal combustion engine converts the stasis of millennia into
motion.

Cars howl on rain-wetted roads.

Airplanes rise through the downpour and throw us through the
blue sky.

The idea of the airplane subverts earthly life.

Computers can deliver nuclear explosions to precisely anywhere on
earth.

A lightning bolt is made entirely of error.

Erratic Mercurys and errant Cavaliers roam the highways.

A girl puts her head on a boy's shoulder; they are driving west.

The windshield wipers wipe, homesickness one way, wanderlust the
other, back and forth.

This happened to your father and to you, Galway — sick to stay, long-
ing to come up against the ends of the earth, and climb over.

Passing the Cemetery

Desire and act were a combination known as sin.

The noise of a fingernail on a blackboard frightened our bones.

The stairwell on the way up to the dentist's smelled of the fire inside
teeth.

Passing the cemetery, I wondered if the bones of the dead become
brittle and crumbly, or if they last.

A dog would gnaw its own skeleton down to nothing, if possible.

On Holytide Wednesday a number of children came to school with
foreheads smudged, in penance beforehand, with what will be left
of them.

The old sermons on the evils of the flesh often caused portions of flesh
to lose feeling, sometimes to drop off.

If we press our frontal bones to the madrone, the chill of the under-
earth passes up into us, making us shiver from within.

A deathbed repentance intended to pluck out one bright terrible
thread could unravel a lifetime — and the lifetimes of those left
behind.

Fishes are the holy land of the sea.

In them spirit is flesh, flesh spirit, the brain simply a denser place in
the flesh.

The human brain may be the brightest place on earth.

At death the body becomes foreign substance; a person who loved
you may wash and dress this one you believed for so long was you,
Galway, a few embrace the memory in it, but somewhere else will
know it and welcome it.

IV

Parkinson's Disease

While spoon-feeding him with one hand
she holds his hand with her other hand,
or rather lets it rest on top of his,
which is permanently clenched shut.
When he turns his head away, she reaches
around and puts in the spoonful blind.
He will not accept the next morsel
until he has completely chewed this one.
His bright squint tells her he finds
the shrimp she has just put in delicious.
She strokes his head very slowly, as if
to cheer up each hair sticking up
from its root in his stricken brain.
Standing behind him, she presses
her cheek to his, kisses his jowl,
and his eyes seem to stop seeing
and do nothing but emit light.
Could heaven be a time, after we are dead,
of remembering the knowledge
flesh had from flesh? The flesh
of his face is hard, perhaps
from years spent facing down others
until they fell back, and harder
from years of being himself faced down
and falling back, and harder still
from all the while frowning
and beaming and worrying and shouting
and probably letting go in rages.

His face softens into a kind
of quizzical wince, as if one
of the other animals were working at
getting the knack of the human smile.
When picking up a cookie he uses
both thumbtips to grip it
and push it against an index finger
to secure it so that he can lift it.
She takes him to the bathroom,
and when they come out, she is facing him,
walking backwards in front of him
holding his hands, pulling him
when he stops, reminding him to step
when he forgets and starts to pitch forward.
She is leading her old father into the future
as far as they can go, and she is walking
him back into her childhood, where she stood
in bare feet on the toes of his shoes
and they foxtrotted on this same rug.
I watch them closely: she could be teaching him
the last steps that one day she may teach me.
At this moment, he glints and shines,
as if it will be only a small dislocation
for him to pass from this paradise into the next.

Telephoning in Mexican Sunlight

Talking with my beloved in New York
I stood at the outdoor public telephone
in Mexican sunlight, in my purple shirt.

Someone had called it a man/woman
shirt. The phrase irked me. But then
I remembered that Rainer Maria
Rilke, who until he was seven wore
dresses and had long yellow hair,
wrote that the girl he almost was
"made her bed in my ear" and "slept me the world."
I thought, OK this shirt will clothe the other in me.
As we fell into long-distance love talk
a squeaky chittering started up all around,
and every few seconds came a sudden loud
buzzing. I half expected to find
the insulation on the telephone line
laid open under the pressure of our talk
leaking low-frequency noises.
But a few yards away a dozen hummingbirds,
gorgets going drab or blazing
according as the sun struck them,
stood on their tail rudders in a circle
around my head, transfixed
by the flower-likeness of the shirt.
And perhaps also by a flush rising into my face,
for a word — one with a thick sound,
as if a porous vowel had sat soaking up
saliva while waiting to get spoken,
possibly the name of some flower
that hummingbirds love, perhaps
"honeysuckle" or "hollyhock"
or "phlox" — just then shocked me
with its suddenness, and this time
apparently did burst the insulation,

letting the word sound in the open
where all could hear, for these tiny, irascible,
nectar-addicted puritans jumped back
all at once, fast, as if the air gasped.

"The Music of Poetry"

And now — after putting forward a "unified theory":
that the music resulting from any of the methods
of organizing English into rhythmic surges
can sound like the music resulting from any other,
being the music not of a method but of the language;
and after proposing that free verse is a variant
of formal verse, using unpredictably the acoustic
repetitions which formal verse employs regularly;
and after playing recordings of the gopher frog's
long line of glottal stops, sounding like rumblings
in an empty stomach, and the notes the hermit thrush
pipes one after another, then twangles together,
and the humpback whale's gasp-cries as it passes
out of the range of human perception of ecstasy,
and the wolf's howls, one, and then several,
and then all the pack joining in a polyphony
to whatever in the sunlit midnight sky
remains keeper of the axle the earth and
its clasped lovers turn upon and cry to;
and after playing recordings of an angakoq
chanting in Inuktitut of his trance-life as a nanuk,
a songman of Arnhem Land, Rahmani of Iran,

Neruda of Chile, Yeats, Thomas, Rukeyser,
to let the audience hear that our poems
are of the same order as those of the other animals
and are composed, like theirs, when we find ourselves
synchronized with the rhythms of the earth,
no matter where, in the city of Brno, which cried
its vowel too deep into the night to get it back,
or at Ma'alaea on Maui in Hawaii, still plumping
itself on the actual matter of pleasure there,
or here in St. Paul, Minnesota, where I lean
at a podium trying to draw my talk to a close,
or on Bleecker Street a time zone away in New York,
where only minutes ago my beloved may have
put down her book and drawn up her eiderdown
around herself and turned out the light —
now, causing me to garble a few words
and tangle my syntax, I imagine I can hear
her say my name into the slow waves
of the night and, faintly, being alone, sing.

Rapture

I can feel she has got out of bed.
That means it is seven A.M.
I have been lying with eyes shut,
thinking, or possibly dreaming,
of how she might look if, at breakfast,
I spoke about the hidden place in her
which, to me, is like a soprano's tremolo,

and right then, over toast and bramble jelly,
if such things are possible, she came.
I imagine she would show it while trying to conceal it.
I imagine her hair would fall about her face
and she would become apparently downcast,
as she does at a concert when she is moved.
The hypnopompic play passes, and I open my eyes
and there she is, next to the bed,
bending to a low drawer, picking over
various small smooth black, white,
and pink items of underwear. She bends
so low her back runs parallel to the earth,
but there is no sway in it, there is little burden, the day has hardly
     begun.
The two mounds of muscles for walking, leaping, lovemaking,
lift toward the east — what can I say?
Simile is useless; there is nothing like them on earth.
Her breasts fall full; the nipples
are deep pink in the glare shining up through the iron bars
of the gate under the earth where those who could not love
press, wanting to be born again.
I reach out and take her wrist
and she falls back into bed and at once starts unbuttoning my pajamas.
Later, when I open my eyes, there she is again,
rummaging in the same low drawer.
The clock shows eight. Hmmm.
With huge, silent effort of great,
mounded muscles the earth has been turning.
She takes a piece of silken cloth
from the drawer and stands up. Under the falls
of hair her face has become quiet and downcast,

as if she will be, all day among strangers,
looking down inside herself at our rapture.

The Road Across Skye

> What is the "this"? The weasel's shriek, only that.
> — Lucien Stryk

Through the open window I can see the road
that climbs the flank of Sgurr na Connaich,
dips out of sight, reappears, twists
over the topmost ridge, and vanishes —
reminding me of the roads winding away
over rising land, which I cut out and pasted
into a childhood scrapbook, all of them
leading out of the mill town hidden
below the bottom edge of each picture.
A cow with draggled petticoat, her flat face
shoveling the way for the rest of her
through the soft-cornered geometry
of the trajectories of flies, approaches,
raises her head, half sticks it in the window,
and gives a low cry. Behind her,
on the wire of the fence, a coal tit
tweets — loudly, given his size. Behind him,
in the pasture, three lambs shove at each other
under the udder of a ewe, who now gives two of them
discouraging kicks and the third a welcoming bleat.
If I hadn't been watching I might have heard
only an ordinary rattle in a sheep's throat.

In the greengrocer's on Wednesday a poster
announced LIFE HAS MEANING and if we tune in
to the wireless next Thursday, Friday, and Saturday
Billy Graham will tell us what it is.
From the next room my beloved calls,
in high notes, as from a treetop, "Some *tea*?"
and my head, fallen forward
at the thought of Billy Graham, pops up,
the way a weasel sticks his head out of his hole
at the vibration of footsteps. The dying Zen master
Daibei, hearing a weasel shriek, sat down
and composed his unrenounceable *jisei* —
"I am one with this, this only," it begins —
and told his disciples to remember to point out,
when they recited it, that the "this"
was the shriek, only that, and toppled over. "Yes,"
I call back. "With a little honey. And your company."
A baby named Hunter dribbles milk down his chin,
lies back, holds his left arm out straight
as if gripping the bow and his right bent over
the top of his head as if drawing the string,
and sleeps, in the night sky, all over the half-world,
on Thursday. On Friday and Saturday, *taisches,*
spirits of people who are about to die, wander the fields,
composing their farewells; those could be two,
there, perched on either side of the tit,
passing their last afternoon as feathery puffs
with quick hearts, to make musical *jisei.*
What sets the road climbing across Skye
apart from the roads in the scrapbook
is that, as it goes, it leaves me content to be

left here with all this. I think I might yet
get conscripted into the choir of the coal tit,
the cow, the ewe, the lambs, the weasel, Daibei,
the *taisches,* even the Reverend Billy, and especially
she who just cried to me from a treetop,
if I could sing all this to her without ceasing
so that it will not turn into all that.

V

Lackawanna

Possibly a child is not damaged immediately
but only after some time has passed.
When the parent who sits on the edge
of the bed leans over and moves an elbow
or a forearm or a hand across the place
where the child's torso divides into legs
at last gets up and goes to the door and turns
and says in an ordinary voice, "Good night,"
then in exactly eight minutes a train
in the freight yards on the other side of town
howls, its boxcar loaded up, its doors
rusted shut, its wheels clacking
over the tracks   *lacka   wanna   lacka.*
It may be that the past has the absolute force
of the law that visits parent upon child
unto the third or fourth generation, and the implacability
of vectors, which fix the way a thing
goes reeling according to where it was touched.
What is called spirit may be the exhaust-light
of toil of the kind a person goes through
years later to take any unretractable step
out of that room, even a step no longer
than a platinum-iridium bar in a vault in Paris,
and flesh the need afterwards to find
the nearest brasserie and mark with both elbows
on the zinc bar the start and the finish.
Never mind. The universe is expanding.
Soon they won't know where to look to find you.
There will be even more room when the sun dies.

It will be eight minutes before we know it is dead.
Plenty of time for the ordinary human acts
that will constitute our final mayhem.
In the case of a house there may be less room
when the principal occupants die, especially
if they refuse to leave and keep on growing.
Then in a few years the immaterial bulk
of one of them padding up from the dark
basement can make the stairs shriek
and the sleeper sit up, pivot out of bed, knock
an arm on the dresser, stand there shaking
while the little bones inside the elbow cackle.
The mind can start rippling again at any time
if what was thrown in was large, and thrown in early.
When the frequency of waves increases,
so does the energy. If pressure builds up,
someone could die from it. If they had been
able to talk with him, find out what he was going through,
the children think it would not have been him.
Inquiring into the situation of a thing
may alter the comportment, size, or shape of it.
The female nurse's elbow, for instance,
bumping a penis, could raise it up,
or the male doctor's hand, picking it up
and letting it drop a couple of times for
unexplained medical reasons, could slacken it.
Or vice versa. And the arm passing across it,
like Ockham's razor grabbed off God's chin
eight minutes before the train howls,
could simplify it nearly out of existence.
Is it possible, even, that Werner Heisenberg,

boy genius, hit on his idea in eight minutes?
The train sounds its horn and clickets over
the tracks *lacka   wanna*   shaking up
a lot of bones trying to lie unnoticed
in the cemeteries. It stops to let off
passengers in a town, as the overturned grail
of copper and tin, lathed and fettled off
to secure its pure minor tierce, booms out
from the sanctus-turret those bulging notes
which, having been heard in childhood,
seem to this day to come from heaven.
So in memory, an elbow, which is without flesh,
touching a penis, which is without bone,
can restart the shock waves of being the one chosen,
even in shame, in a childhood of being left out.
But no one gets off. And a hand
apports in the center of a room suddenly
become empty, which the child has to fill
with something, with anything, with the ether
the Newtonian physicists manufactured
to make good the vacuums in the universe
or the nothing the God of the beginning
suctioned up off the uninhabited earth
and held all this time and now must exhale
back down, making it hard, for some, to breathe.
The hand suspended in the room still has
a look of divinity; every so often
it makes sweet sounds — music can't help it; like maggots
it springs up anywhere. The umbilical string
rubs across the brain, making it
do what it can, sing.

Holy Shit

Parmenides: Would you feel, Socrates, that mud or hair or that matter that is even more worthless and vile has an idea which is distinct from the thing we can see and touch?

Socrates: Certainly not. Things of that kind are exactly as they appear. Though sometimes I become troubled and think that everything must have an idea. But the moment I think this, I run from the thought, in fear that I will fall into a bottomless pit of nonsense and perish.

— Plato

Jesus ate and drank but did not defecate.

— Valentinus

The trees and the herbs of the earth bring forth boughs, leaves, flowers, and fruits. A man brings forth nits, lice, and tapeworms. They distill and pour out oil, wine, and balms, and a man makes excrements of spittle, piss, and shit. They smell and breathe all sweetness, whereas man belches, breaks wind, and stinks.

— Innocent III

A man is, first, fetid sperm, then a sack of excrement, then food for worms.

— Saint Bernard

And þarfor says Saynt Bernard right:
> *Si diligenter cansideres quid per os,*
> *quid per nares, ceterosque meatus*
> *corporis egreditur, vilius sterquilinium*
> *nunquam vidisti.*

"If þow wille," he says, "ententyfly se,
And by-hald what comes fra þe
What thurgh mouthe, what thurgh nese, commonly,
And thurgh other overtes of his body,
A fouler myddyng saw þow never nane,"
Þan a man es, with flesche and bane.
                              — Richard Rolle of Hampole

O wombe! O bely! O stynkyng cod,
Fulfilled of dong and of corrupcioun!
At either end of thee foul is the soun.
                              — Chaucer's Pardoner

Through the pores there is an incessant oozing and trickling as from
a kettle of fat. The body is always discharging matter, like a ripe boil,
through its nine orifices. Matter is secreted from the eyes, wax from
the ears, snot from the nostrils, food, bile, phlegm, and blood from
the mouth, shit and piss from the two lower orifices, and from the
ninety-nine thousand pores, a foul sweat that attracts flies and other
insects.
                              — Buddhaghosa

Blessed are you, Adonai, Eloheinu, King of the World, who has
formed the human body in wisdom and created in it cavities and
orifices. It is well known before your seat of glory that if any of these
be opened or any of these be blocked, it is impossible to stand before
you, blessed Adonai, physician to all flesh, wondrous maker.
                              — *Shacharit*

Let us also consider the gifts of the belly and hind end, how necessary they be, without which we cannot live. A man or woman may live without eyes, ears, hands, feet, etc.; but (*salva reverentia*) without the hind end no human creature can survive; so great and necessary is the use and profit of this one part, that to it belongeth the preservation of human existence. Therefore St. Paul saith well (1 Cor. xii), "Those parts of the body that we think less honorable we clothe with greater honor, and our less respectable parts are treated with greater respect."

— Martin Luther

All attitudes, all the shapeliness, all the belongings of my or your body
    or of any one's body, male or female,
The lung-sponges, the stomach-sac, the bowels sweet and clean . . .
O I think now these are not the parts and poems of the body only but
    of the soul,
O I think these are the soul!

— Walt Whitman

I gathered all my courage, as though I were about to leap forthwith into hell-fire, and let the thought come. I saw before me the cathedral, the blue sky. God sits on His golden throne, high above the world — and from under the throne an enormous turd falls upon the sparkling new roof, shatters it, and breaks the walls of the cathedral asunder . . . Why did God befoul His cathedral? That, for me, was a terrible thought. But then came the dim understanding that God could be something terrible. I had experienced a dark and terrible secret. It overshadowed my whole life, and I became deeply pensive.

— C. G. Jung

Often we forget, and imagine we're immortal.
If the gods don't shit, why must we?
And we would feel distinctly less like animals
if only we could sever the chain of linked turds
tying us to some hole in the ground —
the cesspool Dante used as his model for hell
or the pit Martin Luther squatted over,
after six days of clogged bowels, while
receiving the doctrine of justification by faith,
an epiphany that came with a stink
of the kind Swift's alter ego met on lifting
the lid of his beloved's chamber pot
(he was slow to believe it): "Oh Celia, Celia,
Celia shits!" But think, last night
you took what you liked from a carrot;
today you give back the rest.
For hours each day the child Genet
roosted in the silken peace of the outhouse,
a confessional where we bare our intimate parts,
feeding his imagination on the odor and darkness.
For myself, it was many years before I could
get near the poetry section in a bookstore
or PS3521 in library stacks
without a sudden urge to shit,
I don't know why, unless envy, or emulation,
a need, like a coyote's or hyena's,
to set down my identity in scat.
The white-tailed deer stops and solfs her
quarter notes the size and color
of niçoise olives onto the snow. The canary
sands off the hull with her gizzard

and sleets it to the cage floor, trilling
the entire kernel of the seed into song.
My father grunted — I heard him —
on the horseshoe of the toilet seat;
I pictured one of the *noctis equii*
kicking him in the rear end, knocking a lump
out of him, into the still water, causing
its surface, thinner than brow skin, to worry all over.
Thirty-five thousand feet up a fountain pen sheisses
into a shirt pocket a purplish black gush that can now
never become one of the great elemental words —
fire   night   wind   shit.*
Coming home, she said, "Yes, there's
the bag, and the fuss, and the mess.
But what I hate most is that I'll never
sit down ever again and take a good shit."
After five years of captivity the ex-hostage said,
"Nobody says it, but one of the blessings
of being free is going to the bathroom when you want."
A horsebun turns golden in the September sun,

---

* *Shit:*   And yet seen as an indecent word,
              which the newspapers that were enamored
              of the smart weapons of the Gulf War,
              which kill so far away you could never
              hear the screams or see the blood,
              won't print, despite a lineage going back
              to the Indo-European, from *skheid,*
              to shed, to drop, and its wide lead
              over the other expletives in frequency
              of use, even the divine three,
              God, Christ, and fuck.

a cowflap in a pasture wrinkles pinkish.
On the kitchen shelf a fieldmouse lays its
turds at the foot of a box of whole-grout oats.
The black bear who swatted down the apples
from the lower branches began before first light
expelling foot-long cylinders of apple-chompings
— some apple nectar removed, some bear nectar added —
which could almost be served up in a restaurant
in Lyons or Paris as Compote de Pommes des Dieux.
Well, we eat shit anyway. Consider
andouilles and *boudins noirs*.
And don't *boeuf,* whom we castrate and strip
of all function except to divide grass
into shit and flesh that soon will be mostly shit,
look like lumps skheided into the field
by a something else? Of course, as cummings'
Olaf, "whose warmest heart recoiled at war,"
declared, "there is some s. I will not eat."
Like the s. of having to print it as *s.*
Or of imagining we are a people who don't die,
who come out of the sky like gods and drop
not shit but bombs on people who shit.
We don't know what life is, but we know
all who live on earth eat, sleep, mate, work,
shit, and die. Let us remember this is our home
and that we have become, we mad ones, its keepers.
Let us sit bent forward slightly, and be opened a moment,
as earth's holy matter passes through us.

Flies

Walt Whitman noticed a group of them
suspended near his writing table at lunchtime;
at sunset he looked up and there they still were,
"balancing in the air in the centre of the room, darting athwart, up
    and down, casting swift shadows in specks on the opposite wall
    where the shine is."
When a person sits concentrating hard,
flies often collect in one spot, in a little bunch,
not far from that person's brain, and fly through each other.
The next day you can see them in a shaft of sun
in the barn, going over an intricacy.
Sometimes they alight on my writing-fingers
as I form letters that look like drawings of them,
or sit on the typewriter watching the keys hit,
perhaps with some of the alert misapprehension
of my mother, when I was in high school,
at the sporadic clacking coming from my room.
Karl Shapiro addressed a fly:
"O hideous little bat, the size of snot."
Yesterday I killed a fly that had been trying
to crawl up a nostril and usurp a snot's niche.
On being swatted, it jettisoned itself
into my cup of coffee. When I swat and miss,
the fly sometimes flies to the fly swatter,
getting out of striking range by going deeper
inside it, like a child hugging the person who has just
struck her. Or it might alight on my head.

Miroslav Holub says that at the battle of Crécy a fly

        alighted
    on the blue tongue
    of the Duke of Clervaux.

When Emily Dickinson's dying person dies, a fly's
"Blue — uncertain stumbling Buzz" goes with her
as far as it can go. If you fire the stoves
in a closed-up house in the fall, the cluster flies,
looking groggy, will creep from their chinks
and sleeping-holes, out of seeming death.
Soon, if the sun is out, hundreds will appear,
as if getting born right there on the window glass.
When so many vibrate together, the murmur
Christopher Smart called the "honey of the air"
becomes a howl. Seiki observes in himself
what is true of me too:

    Once I kill
    A fly I find I
    Want to massacre them all.

Then Antonio Machado cries, *But . . . but . . . they*

        have rested
    upon the enchanted toy,
    upon the large closed book,
    upon the love letter,

upon the stiffened eyelids
of the dead.

John Clare, who came like the Baptist to prepare us
for the teachings of Darwin, tells us flies
"look like things of the mind or fairies, and seemed pleased or dull as
    the weather permits in many clean cottages, and genteel houses,
    they are allowed every liberty to creep, fly or do as they like, and
    seldom or ever do wrong, in fact they are the small or dwarfish
    portion of our own family."
James K. Baxter said New Zealand flies regard him as their *whenua,*
which in Maori means both placenta and land.
In the year of Clare's birth, William Blake asks:

    Am not I
    A fly like thee?
    Or art not thou
    A man like me?

He could not have known the tsetse spits into its bite
the trypanosome, which releases into us
a lifetime supply of sleep, even some extra,
or that the flashy, green, meat-eating botfly
needs flesh to bury its eggs in, living flesh will do,
or that his diminutive cousin, that fly
walking on the lips of his baby, scatters manure
behind him as copiously as the god Sterquilius.
Martin Luther said, "I am a bitter enemy to flies. When I open a book
    for the first time, flies land on it at once, with their hind ends, and
    choose a spot, as if they would say, 'Here we will squat, and be-
    smirch this book with our excrement.'"

The wanton among us, who kill flies for our sport,
like to hear of the evil flies do. Then we swat
with more pleasure, as if we did God's work.
"Is this thy play?" Edward Taylor cries. "For why?"
I think I have a fly inside me.
It drones through me,
at three A.M., looking for what stinks,
the more stinking the better, a filth heap
old or new, some regret, or guilt, or humiliation,
and finds it, and feeds, waking me,
and I live it again. Then, with an effort
of will feeble enough if compared with my mother's
when I arrived almost too late at her deathbed
and she broke back through her last coma and spoke,
I swat at it, and it jumps up and swerves away.
I do not think this fly will ever go.
It feels like part of me, and can't leave until
I rattle out a regret sufficient to the cause
and thus close the account. Then
it could steal out and, if the stove is lit
and the fall sun bright, fly to the window
above the table, or, if the day is gloomy,
crawl up my upper lip and hole up
in that nostril at last. So I swat,
flailing at the window almost without aiming,
until the windowsill, and the big, open
Webster's First, and the desk and part of the floor
are speckled with the flies' paltry remains,
strewn thick as the human dead in the Great War.
One of them rights itself, and walks,
and seems to feel OK, and flies.

My father righted himself out of the muck
where many thousands of dead
stuck out their blue tongues. The Preacher says,
"Dead flies cause the ointment of the apothecary to send forth a
    stinking savour."
Would that muck were an ointment some chthonic
apothecary oozes up in earth's devastated places.
But no one who rights himself out of it
and walks and feels OK
is OK.
He knows something, and wants to keep others
from smelling it on him and knowing that
he is the fly in the ointment, wherever he flies.
As the treetops' shadow creeps up the window
the flies creep just ahead of it. They often
collide, and seem troubled and confused,
as though they came here for something
and have forgotten what, and keep looking anyway,
like my father, on coming to America.
When a fly stands motionless on a window pane,
I wonder if it is looking through the bottom
facets of its eye at the outdoors.
Federico García Lorca said that if
a fly buzzes inside a window,

           I think of people
           in chains.
           And I let it go free.

A fly may not always want to go free,
even if radiant heat through the barrier of glass

lets it imagine that it does. In this
it would be like my mother, in her ardor
for poetry, before she realized that poetry
was what I was up to in my life
— though not in her craving for love in her own life.
When she looked out with her blue eye I'm sure
it seemed wild and fiery there and she knew she must go.
I find it hard to think that she did not,
at some point, with her big, walker's feet, tread hard
and break through. More than once I felt
a draft of icy air. But my sisters say no.

The Striped Snake and the Goldfinch

I

When I pick up the corner of the sheet of black
plastic spread over last year's potato patch,
a striped snake two feet long lifts her head.
When I take her by the back of the neck, she writhes,
seeking purchase so she can throw herself and bite,
her tongue zzzing like an arc welder rumpling out
a brass bandage, rough as the gossamers snakes
slough on mountain paths, which crested flycatchers
snatch up and weave into their nests to hex cowbirds.
Trying to slide away, she goes through one of my hands
and finds the other waiting to draw her back.
Up on my shoulder, she drags herself across my nape,
turns, drags herself back again across my Adam's apple,
making me think of one of those high-limb rope saws
you work from the ground by pulling alternately

on the two control cords, sawing off my head.
Now she crawls over me more slowly and drapes herself,
and I can feel what seems her pleasure, and
I am happy to be her somewhat living warm object.
Sliding halfway off my hand, she holds herself
with forepart pulled down like a wand of applewood
straining toward water under the black soil
where the worms rumba, streams to the ground
like a spirit going from me, wriggles over
to the black plastic, pauses, and slides under.

2

Stepping into the woods, I remember going
alone into Seekonk Woods when I was ten,
sometimes wondering: Who would I be?
Would I find work I could do? Could I love,
or be loved? Was being, for me, even possible?
Looking back, I have to squint, to see those days
which I spent as if walking at night in a village
high in the Alps, when the lights in the valley
seem farther away than the stars, passing houses
where a man and a woman lie asleep
in one room, and children sleep in another,
and in a courtyard a dog, hearing someone
unfamiliar walking at the wrong hour, wakes —
someone smoking a cigarette, like the cigarette my father
dragged on, as he sat in mud, its periodic glow
proof he existed, while shells shrieked overhead
and exploded in other trenches, the trench
where his brother David blew up many times
in imagination, wrote one letter to his mother

praying he might live to come home, blew up
into parts some of which may have got mixed up
with some of someone else's — and barks, *proof,*
and again, double-checking, *proof proof,* and then,
hearing no one, goes back to sleep, and the village
snow creaks as if the press of nightwalking hurt it.

3

How much do I have left of the loyalty to earth,
which human shame, and dislike of our own lives,
and others' deaths that take part of us with them,
wear out of us, as we go toward that moment
when we find out how we die: clinging and pleading,
or secretly relieved that it is all over,
or despising ourselves, knowing that death
is a punishment we deserve, or like an old dog,
off his feed, who suddenly is ravenous,
and eats the bowl clean, and the next day is a carcass.
There is an unfillableness in us — in some of us,
a longing for that blue-shaded black night
where the beloved dead, and all those others
who suffered and sang and were not defeated —
the one who hushed them by singing "Going Home"
when they lynched him on Bald Mountain,
the klezmer violinists who pressed bows
across strings until eyes, by near-starvation
enlarged, grew wet and sparkled — have gone.
Yet I know more than ever that here is the true place,
here where we sit together, out of the wind,
with a loaf of country bread, and tomatoes still warm
from the distant sun, and wine in glasses that are,

one for each of us, the upper bell of the glass
that will hold the last hour we have to live.

4

Coming out of the woods I cross the field,
check the black plastic — nobody — and go up
to the house. Inside there is a flurry of clicks —
a goldfinch, who must have flown in the open door
on seeing sky in the window in the opposite wall,
flies at window glass, beak and talons hitting
it like a telegraph key sending · · · — — — · · ·
Holding a towel to the glass, I bunch it around the bird,
take the bundle to the door, reach in
and draw the soft-surfaced, distinct body
into the brilliant sunshine. He looks at me, his eye guarded,
unforthcoming, with the blankness of an old person
on a gurney staring at corridor ceilings
on the way to surgery. Perhaps also with defiance.
I search it for signs of eros — before long
a bird can start courting us, if we have rescued it,
put splints on a leg or wing, eyedroppered it sugary water,
deposited mealworms and pieces of fruit
down its throat, surrounded it in a warm hand
that brings back an embryo-memory of the hot,
featherless brood patch which darkened upon the egg,
like the lead aprons the good dentists Landa
and Silloway have spread, huge and heavy, on me,
or the tongue of God pressed to a body just
before giving it that vast lick from head to tail.

5

When I open my hand, wherever I had touched him
looks corroded; wherever I had not shines
his original lemon yellow. He sits a moment,
as if half-limed. But, his *odorat* undeveloped,
unresponsive to the 2-methyl-3-hexanoic
which the lipophilic diphtheroids of my hand
release through the wrinkles cross-stitching
each other down the heart line, he flies,
dipping and lifting like a needle basting a hem,
disappears into the intertangled branches of the birches
Inés and I planted in the spring of our marriage
six hundred and thirteen years ago, if you go
by the affection-rings and the weariness-rings
inside the trunk when the magician saws it through,
and opens it, and finds each of you cut in half,
separated from yourself at the waist. There he is,
in a birch top, its crown. Meanwhile the snake
may have crawled up my spine to sit in my mouth
and utter an unsteady flame. I think I will fly
for a while now in the world that exists
the height of the human head above the ground.
A boy who stood in Seekonk Woods might like
living out this life; he might even count it a worthy destiny
to pass, in rhythmic flight, with zzzing tongue,
through this heaven, some moments, on the way to death.

Neverland

Bending over her bed, I saw the smile
I must have seen when gaping up from the crib.
Knowing death will come, sensing its onset,
may be a fair price for consciousness.
But looking at my sister, I wished
she could have died by surprise,
without ever knowing about death.
Too late. Wendy said, "I am in three parts.
Here on the left is red. That is pain.
On the right is yellow. That is exhaustion.
The rest is white. I don't know yet what white is."
For most people, one day everything is all right.
The next, the limbic node catches fire. The day after,
the malleus in one ear starts missing the incus.
Then the arthritic opposable thumb no longer opposes
whoever last screwed the top onto the jam jar.
Then the coraco-humeral ligament frizzles apart,
the liver speckles, the kidneys dent,
two toes lose their souls. Of course,
before things get worse, a person could run for it.
I could take off right now, climb the pure forms
that surmount time and death, follow a line
down Avenue D, make a 90° turn right on 8th Street,
90° left on C, right on 7th, left on B, then cross
to Sixth Avenue, catch the A train
to Nassau, where the A pulls up beside the Z,
get off, hop on the Z, hurtle under the river
and rise on Euclid under the stars and taste,
with my sweetheart, in perfectly circular kisses,

the actual saliva of paradise.
Then, as if Wendy suddenly understood
this flaw in me, that I could die
still wanting what is not to be had here, drink
and drink and yet have most of my thirst
intact for the water table, she opened her eyes.
"I want you to know I'm not afraid of dying,"
she said. "I just wish it didn't take so long."
Seeing her appear so young and yet begin to die
all on her own, I wanted to whisk her off.
Quickly she said, "Let's go home." From outside
in the driveway came the gargling noise
of a starter motor, and a low steady rumbling, as if
my car had turned itself on and was warming up the engine.
She closed her eyes. She was entirely white,
as if freshly powdered with twice-bleached flour.
Color flashed only when she opened her eyes.
Snow will come down next winter, in the woods;
the fallen trees will have that flesh on their bones.
When the eye of the woods opens, a bluejay shuttles.
Outside, suddenly, all was quiet,
I realized my car had shut off its engine.
Now a spot of rosiness showed in each cheek:
blushes, perhaps, at a joy she had kept from us,
from somewhere in her life, perhaps two mouths,
hers and a beloved's, near each other, like roses
sticking out of a bottle of invisible water.
She was losing the half-given, half-learned
art of speech, and it became for her a struggle
to find words, form them, position them,
quickly say them. After much effort she said,

"Now is when the point of the story changes."
After that, one eye at a time, the left listened,
and drifted, the right focused, gleamed
meanings at me, drifted. Stalwart,
the halves of the brain, especially the right.
Now, as they ratchet the box that holds
her body into the earth, a voice calls
back across the region she passes through,
a far landscape I seem to see from above,
in prolonged, even notes that swell and diminish.
Now it sounds from beneath the farthest horizon,
and now it grows faint, and now I cannot hear it.

Strong Is Your Hold

2006

To Bobbie

Tenderly — be not impatient,
(Strong is your hold O mortal flesh,
Strong is your hold O love.)

— Walt Whitman

I

The Stone Table

Here on the hill behind the house,
we sit with our feet up on the edge
of the eight-by-ten stone slab
that was once the floor of the cow pass
that the cows used, getting from one pasture
to the other without setting a hoof
on the dirt road lying between them.

From here we can see the blackberry thicket,
the maple sapling the moose slashed
with his cutting teeth, turning it
scarlet too early, the bluebird boxes
flown from now, the one tree left
of the ancient orchard popped out
all over with saffron and rosy,
subacid pie apples, smaller crabs grafted
with scions of old varieties, Freedom,
Sops-of-Wine, Wolf River, and trees
we put in ourselves, dotted with red lumps.

We speak in whispers: fifty feet away,
under a red spruce, a yearling bear
lolls on its belly eating clover.
Abruptly it sits up. Did I touch my wine glass
to the table, setting it humming?
The bear peers about with the bleary undressedness
of old people who have mislaid their eyeglasses.
It ups its muzzle and sniffs. It fixes us,

whirls, and plunges into the woods —
a few cracklings and shatterings, and all is still.

As often happens, we find ourselves
thinking similar thoughts, this time of a friend
who lives to the south of that row of peaks
burnt yellow in the sunset. About now,
he will be paying his daily visit to her grave,
reading by heart the words, cut into black granite,
that she had written for him, when they
both thought he would die first:
I BELIEVE IN THE MIRACLES OF ART BUT WHAT
PRODIGY WILL KEEP YOU SAFE BESIDE ME.
Or is he back by now, in his half-empty house,
talking in ink to a piece of paper?

I, who so often used to wish to float free
of earth, now with all my being want to stay,
to climb with you on other evenings to this stone,
maybe finding a bear, or a coyote, like
the one who, at dusk, a week ago, passed
in his scissorish gait ten feet from where we sat —
this earth we attach ourselves to so fiercely,
like scions of Sheffield Seek-No-Furthers
grafted for our lifetimes onto paradise root-stock.

Everyone Was in Love

One day, when they were little, Maud and Fergus
appeared in the doorway naked and mirthful,
with a dozen long garter snakes draped over
each of them like brand-new clothes.
Snake tails dangled down their backs,
and snake foreparts in various lengths
fell over their fronts. With heads raised and swaying,
alert as cobras, the snakes writhed their dry skins
upon each other, as snakes like doing
in lovemaking, with the added novelty this time
of caressing soft, smooth, moist human skin.
Maud and Fergus were deliciously pleased with themselves.
The snakes seemed to be tickled, too.
We were enchanted. Everyone was in love.
Then Maud drew down off Fergus's shoulder,
as off a tie rack, a peculiarly
lumpy snake and told me to look inside.
Inside the double-hinged jaw, a frog's green
webbed hind feet were being drawn,
like a diver's, very slowly as if into deepest waters.
Perhaps thinking I might be considering rescue,
Maud said, "Don't. Frog is already elsewhere."

It All Comes Back

We placed the cake, with its four unlit candles
poked into thick frosting, on the seat
of his chair at the head of the table
for just a moment while Inés and I unfolded
and spread Spanish cloth over Vermont maple.

Suddenly he left the group of family,
family friends, kindergarten mates, and darted
to the table, and just as someone cried *No, no!*
Don't sit! he sat down right on top of his cake
and the room broke into groans and guffaws.

Actually it was pretty funny, all of us
were yelping our heads off, and actually
it wasn't in the least funny. He ran to me
and I picked him up but I was still laughing,
and in indignant fury he hooked his thumbs

into the corners of my mouth, grasped
my cheeks, and yanked — he was so muscled
and so outraged I felt he might rip
my whole face off. Then I realized
that was exactly what he was trying to do.

And it came to me: I was one of his keepers.
His birth and the birth of his sister
had put me on earth a second time,
with the duty this time to protect them
and to help them to love themselves.

And yet here I was, locked in solidarity
with a bunch of adults against my own child,
heehawing away, all of us, without asking
if, underneath, we weren't striking back, too late,
at our own parents, for their humiliations of us.

I gulped down my laughter and held him and
apologized and commiserated and explained and then
things were set right again, but to this day it remains
loose, this face, seat of superior smiles,
on the bones, from that hard yanking.

Shall I publish this story from long ago
and risk embarrassing him? I like it
that he fought back, but what's the good,
now he's thirty-six, in telling the tale
of that mortification when he was four?

Let him decide. Here are the three choices.
He can scratch his slapdash check mark,
which makes me think of the rakish hook
of his old high school hockey stick,
in whichever box applies:

❑ *Tear it up.*
❑ *Don't publish it but give me a copy.*
❑ *OK, publish it, on the chance that somewhere someone*
    survives of all those said to die miserably every day for lack
    of the small clarifications sometimes found in poems.

Inés on Vacation

We came down the common road
thinking of nothing much. Summer day.
Maud holding one hand. Fergus holding the other.
Familiar arrangement. We came to the honeysuckle.
Bees were going and coming.
No weariness in their drone. Blossoms
bathed in the lush breeze. We were waiting
for Inés to come back to us tomorrow.
Or, if not tomorrow, then tomorrow.

Dinner Party

I

In a dream, as in a dream,
they sit around a round
table, seven of them, friends
of each other and of me too,
including two of my oldest
and closest. They look like
a bunch so loving they have
made it into paradise, as, in fact,
in life, they actually have — so far,
Aristotle would have us add.
Chunks of tiny sakras, bright
with the light drained from
the worldly sky, fulge from
the tips of the waxen stalagmites,
like heads of salamanders

that have wiggled themselves
into the air. At the table
they talk a kind of talk
I know I don't know, sometimes
they smile it, sometimes chuckle
to each other their arrays
of oral finery. At these moments
their ears bunch up in the somewhat
bizarre natural screwiness
of ears at any sudden thrill.

2

In space as yet untracked
by feet of flies, still unpurged
by Pontic waters or by the Ajax
of the love of things earthly,
they look up, and smile.
"This empty chair. It's for you.
Come." Oh my dears. Yes, except
of course I'm only dreaming you,
the impossibility of you, of being
one of you. I can't. They take
the straitjacket off. So what?
The lunatic continues to hug himself.
Across the table I clink
eyeballs with several of you.
Space sings. My ears gaggle. Why?
I'm making you up as I glidder
through the human dream.
Sometimes, rising from my desk

thick with discarded wretched
beginnings, the only way
I know I'm alive is
my toe- and fingernails grow.
Oh what I could have written! Maybe
will have written . . . Tonight
I will work late, then bed,
then up, then . . . then we'll see.
By then the busgirls and busboys
may have already come and lapsed
me into the lapping waters of ever
more swiftly elapsing time, and then
sat me down propped up on a chair,
alone with knife, fork, and spoon
and many bright empty glassfuls of desire.

Hide-and-Seek 1933

Once when we were playing
hide-and-seek and it was time
to go home, the rest gave up
on the game before it was done
and forgot I was still hiding.
I remained hidden as a matter
of honor until the moon rose.

Conversation

For Maud

—*How* old?

—It was completely inadvertent.
  It was more or less late afternoon
  and I came over a hilltop
  and smack in front of me was the sunset.

—Couldn't you have turned around and gone back?

—Wherever you turn, a window
  in a childhood house fills with fire.

—Remember the pennies we put on the track,
  how the train left behind only the bright splashes?

—Everything startles with its beauty
  when assigned value has been eradicated,
  especially if the value assigned is one cent.

—Does the past ever get too heavy to lug around?

—If your rucksack is too full it could
  wrestle you down backwards.

—Does it ever get lighter?

—Yes, when so-called obsolete words start
  falling off the back end of the language.

— Is it easier to figure things out when you're old?

— I once thought so. Once I said to myself,
   "If I could sit in one place on earth
   and try to understand, it would be here."

— Nice thought.

— Yes, but where on earth was I when I thought it?

— Where do you think you might have
   ended up if you had turned around?

— Where the swaying feet of a hanged man
   would take him, if he were set walking.

— Maybe only half of you is a hanged man.

— Conscious mind would be much
   more dangerous if it had more than one body.

— Do you feel a draft?

— It could be a lost moment, unconnected
   with earth, just passing through.

— Or did I forget to shut the front door?

— Maybe a window exploded.

— Have you noticed the lightbulb in the cellar
   blows out about every two months?

— When ordinary things feel odd
    and odd things normal, be careful.

— I like it best when everything's
    doing what it's supposed to.

— Kissers kiss, roofers roof, matter matters.

— Don't forget to call your friend in Des Moines.

— I called him. He said he's feeling good.
    He said he had just finished eating an orange.

— Where would you like to be right now?

— I'd like to be at McCoy Stadium
    watching a good game of baseball.

— I like it when there's a runner on third.
    At each pitch he hops for home,
    then immediately scurries back.

— If it's a wild pitch, he hovers
    a moment to be sure it's really wild
    and then is quick — like a tear,
    with a tiny bit of sunlight inside it.

— Why the bit of sunlight?

— It would be his allotment of hope.

II

Ode and Elegy

A thud. Shrieks. Frantic
wingbeats like a round
of soft applause.
The hawk jumps on top
of the jay knocked to the grass,
presses his wings to the ground,
digs his claws into the jay's
back, chops at the neck,
scattering
blue feathers. Then,
as easily as a green wave
in heavy seas lifts a small boat
and throws it upside down,
still afloat but keel up, so
the hawk flips the jay,
then tears at his throat.

A blue wing wrests itself free, flaps
like a flag crying *I will fight you!*
The hawk stuffs the wing
back down into place,
clamps it there with a foot.
Now jay and hawk stare
at each other beak to beak,
as close as Jesus and Judas at their kiss.
The hawk strikes, the jay struggles,
but his neck breaks, his eyes
shrink into beads of taxidermists' glass.
As a grape harvester trampling out

the last juices of grape, so the hawk
treads the jay's body up and down
and down and up. He places
a foot on the throat and a foot
on the belly, flaps his wings,
repositions his feet, flaps again,

and lifts off, clutching transversely
the body of the jay, which is like a coffin
made in the shape and color of the dead.

Much as in the *décollage à l'américain*
of the Lafayette Escadrille, when
the pilots fly a long time only yards
above the tarmac, to gain speed, then pull back
hard on the joystick, zooming into nearly
vertical ascent, just so
the sharp-shinned hawk, carrying
his blue load glinting in the sunlight
low to the ground, now suddenly
climbs steeply and soars over the tops
of the Norway spruce and the tamarack.

Feathering

Yesterday she took down from the attic
an old lumpy tea-colored pillow — stained
with drool, hair grease, night sweats, or what!
which many heads may have waked upon
in the dark, and lain there motionless, eyes open,

wondering at the strangeness within themselves —
took it and ripped out the stitching
at one end, making of it a sack.

She stands on a bench in the garden
and plunges a hand into the sack and lifts
out a puffy fistful of feathers.
A few accidentally spill and drift,
and tree swallows appear. She raises
the hand holding the feathers straight up
over her head, and stands like a god
of seedtime about to scatter bits of plenitude,
or like herself in a long-ago summer, by a pond,
chumming for sunfish with bread crumbs.

When the breeze quickens she opens
her fist and more of these fluffs
near zero on the scale of materiality
float free. One of the swallows
looping and whirling about her
snatches at a feather, misses, twists round
on itself, streaks back, snaps its beak
shut on it, and flings itself across the field.
Another swallow seizes a feather
and flies up, but, flapping and turning,
loses it to a third, who soars
with it even higher and disappears.

After many tosses, misses, parries, catches,
she ties off the pillow, ending for now
the game they make of it when she's there,

the imperative to feather one's nest,
which has come down in the tree swallow
from the Pliocene. She returns to the house,
a slight lurch in her gait — not surprising,
for she has been so long at play with these
acrobatic, daredevil aerialists, she might
momentarily have lost the trick of walking on earth.

Burning the Brush Pile

I shoved into the bottom of the brush
pile two large grocery bags holding
chainsaw chaff well soaked
in old gasoline gone sticky — a kind
of homemade napalm, except, of course,
without victims, other than boughs,
stumps, broken boards, vines, crambles.

I braced my knees against the next-
to-the-top roundel of the twelve-foot
apple-picker stepladder
and poured diesel gurgling
and hiccupping into the center of the pile,
then climbed down and sloshed
the perimeter with kerosene and sludge.

Stepping back, I touched a match
to the oil rag knotted to the thick end
of a thick stick and hurled it, javelin
style, into the core of the pile,

which gasped, then illuminated:
red sunset seen through winter trees.
A small flame came curling out from either
side of the pile and quietly wavered there,
as if this were simply the way matter burns.
Suddenly the great loaded shinicle roared
into flames that leapt up sixty, seventy feet,
swarming through the hole they had heated
open in the chill air to be their chimney.

At noon I came back with a pitchfork
and flicked into the snapping flames
charred boughs, burnt-off twig ends,
that lay around the edges of the fire
as if some elephantine porcupine had been
bludgeoned on its snout, on this spot,
and then, rotting away, had left a rough circle
of black quills pointing to where it had been.

In the evening, when the fire had faded,
I was raking black clarts out of the smoking dirt
when I felt a tine of my rake snag on a large lump.
I jerked, shook, beat it apart, and out fell
a small blackened snake, the rear half
burnt away, the forepart alive. When
I took up this poor Isaac, it flashed its tongue,
then struck my hand a few times; I let it.

Already its tail was sealing itself off,
fusing shut the way we cauterize unraveling
nylon line by using its own hot oozings

as glue. I lowered it into the cool grass,
where it waggled but didn't get very far.
Gone the swift lateral undulation, the whip-tail,
the grip that snakes bring into the world.

It stopped where the grass grew thick
and flashed its tongue again, as if trying
to spit or to spirit away its pain,
as we do, with our growled profanities,
or as if uttering a curse, or — wild fantasy —
a benediction. Most likely it was trying to find
its whereabouts, and perhaps get one last take
on this unknown being also reeking of fire.
Then the snake zipped in its tongue
and hirpled away into the secrecy of the grass.

Pulling a Nail

In the year of my birth
my father buried this spike,
half in hemlock half in oak,
battered the flat of its head
into the dead center
of the round dent of his last blow.

He would have struck
in quick strokes filled
with inertia and follow-through.
He would have hit at the precise
moment the direction of force

in the hammer exactly lined up
with the axis of the nail.

As friction tightened, he would have
hit harder, striking up
shock waves that struck back
in his elbow and shoulder.

Near the end, when his arm
grew weak and his hand
could barely hang on,
he would have gone
all out and clobbered
the nail, crushed it into itself,
with each blow knocking
off kilter every new tilt of the head.

I hack and scrape
but can't get the hammer's claw
to catch under the rim of the nail,
and I have no nail pull or pry bar.
But looking back in time, I see
my father, how he solved
it when in the same fix:
angling the claw of his hammer
like a chisel, he cozied it
up to the nail head, then taking
a second hammer, smacked
the face of the first, and kept on
smacking it, until the claw
gouged grooves for itself

in the bruised wood and grudged under.
So I do as my father did.

Now begins what could be called
carpenters' arm wrestling, and also,
in this case, transrealmic combat
between father and son.
We clasp right hands (the flared
part of the hammer handle,
his hand) and press right elbows
to the hemlock (the curved
hammer head, his steel elbow) and pull.
Or rather, I pull, he holds fast, lacking
the writ to drag me down where he lies.

A nail driven so long ago
ought to be allowed to stay put,
until the house it serves
crumbles into its ill-fitting cellar hole,
or on a freezing night flaps up
and disappears in a turmoil
of flame and smoke and
blackened bones; or until the nail
discovers it has become
merely a nail hole filled with rust.

A spike driven long ago
resists being pulled — worse
than a stupefied wisdom tooth
whose roots, which have screwed
themselves into the jawbone,

refuse to budge; worse even
than an old pig who hears
the slaughterer's truck pull up
and rasp open its gate and rattle
its ramp into place, and grunts,
and squeals, and digs in.

Slipping for leverage
a scrap of quarter-inch wood
under the hammer, I apply
a methodology I learned from
unscrewing stuck bottle lids:
first, put to it the maximum force
you think you can maintain,
and second, maintain it.

Just as when an earthworm
pulls itself out of a cul-de-sac,
cautious end pulling adventurous end,
stretching itself almost to breaking
until the stuck end starts to come free,
so this nail, stretched and now
starting to let go, utters a thick squawk —
first sound it has made since
my father brought down his hammer
full force on it, adding a grunt of his own,
and thudded it home — and a half-inch
of newly polished steel stutters
out of fibrous matter intended to grip it
a good long time, if not forever.

My fulcrum this time a chunk
of inch board, I pull again, again
raising a chaotic ruckus,
and another segment of bright
steel screeches free.

Helped along this time by
a block of two-by-four lying
on its inch-and-three-quarter side,
I leverage out another noisy half-inch.
At last, standing the block up
on its three-and-three-quarter-inch side,
I pull hard, hold the pressure,
and the entire rest of the nail,
almost too hot to handle, extrudes
in an elegant curve of defeated matter.

It seems I've won.
But in matters like this
winning doesn't often
feel exactly like winning.
It's only a nail, I know,
an earthen bit. Bent.
Very possibly torqued.
And yet my father drove it
to stake out his only hope
of leaving something
lasting behind. See,
there he is now, bent
at his workbench,

in the permanent
gloom of the basement
of the house on Oswald
Street that he built, as he did
everything he did, alone,
probably driving all but a few dozen
of its ten thousand nails himself.

A dark yellowish aura, like
the dead glow of earliest
electricity, unused to being
harnessed, hangs above
his head. He's picking over
a small heap of bent nails,
chucking some, straightening
others back into usefulness
in the rectilinear world.
At this one he pauses.
He lifts it to the light, sights
along it as if he doubts
it can ever be used again.
I take it from his hand just
as he fades out of sight.
In it I can feel the last heat
of our struggle. Thumb
and forefinger hold the nail
to the bench, bent side up,
forming a little wobbling
bridge between then
and now, between me and him,
or him and me, over which

almost nothing of what mattered
to either of us ever passed.
A hammer still floats in the space
he had been standing in.
I pluck it out of the air
and use it to hammer the nail
up and down its length, rotate it
to keep the bent part on top,
hammer it, rotate it,
hammer it, well into the night.
The cellar windows become light.
It is late. I don't think
I will ever straighten it out.

The Quick and the Dead

At the hayfield's edge, a few stalks
of grass twitch. Bending close,
I find the plump body of the vole.
I lobbed him here myself,
after snapping him in a trap to halt
his forays through the flower beds.
He's dead, and yet he lives,
he jerks, he heaves, he shudders,
as if something quickens in him.
Or does something unimaginable happen,
a resolution worse than death, after death?

I prog and tilt him and peer under him
to see why he twitches, and find

he's being buried, by beetles —
bright red or yellow chevrons
laid across their black wings —
carrion beetles, sexton beetles,
corpse-eating buriers who delve
and undergrub him and howk out
the trench his sausagy form settles into.

Now a large beetle spewing at both ends
moils across him, drouking him
in marinating juices. The reek
is heavy, swampy, undoubtedly savory,
luring from afar these several beetles
and also those freeloaders of the afterlife,
the midden flies, who arrive
just in time to drop their eggs in, too,
before the covering of the grave.

The vole by now has dwelt some while
in death, and yet somehow
he still is looking good. Mouth
gaped, teeth bared: uppers
stubby and old-folks yellow, inch-long
lowers curled inward, like uppers
of beavers when they must subsist on soft food.
Scummaging down into a last resting place,
at the last day, when souls go back
to their graves and resume the form
and flesh that once was theirs, this one
could jump and jig, as if freshly risen
from a full night's dead sloom.

When the flies' eggs hatch, larvae squirm
in and out of the eyeholes; in and out
of the ears; in and out of the snout,
which slorped the airy auras
of flowers; in and out of the mouth,
which, even cluttered with bent choppers,
snipped flowers and dragged blossoms
stem-first through gaps in the stone wall —
except for a large peony blossom that stuck
and stoppered the hole for a week
like a great gorgeous cork — while other larvae
wriggle in and out of the anus, like revenant
turds that go in to practice going out.

The last half of the vole's tail
still sticks out, like a stalk of grass,
as if it might be left that way
as camouflage. At the grave's edge
stands a cricket in glittering black,
ogling it all, like a Yankee town father
spectating at a cross-burning.

A larger beetle, the pronotum behind
her head brilliant red, noggles
into view. Pushing the grass down
on either side, she plouters
without pause past the curled teeth
and down into the underroom
of the self-digesting birth banquet
to deposit her eggs and then wait, and later

pick tidbits from the carcass and feed
her hatchlings mouth to mouth, like a bird.

Soon this small plot will be unfindable.
Every blade of grass will look
like a vole's tail, every smither
of ungrassed earth like burial ground,
day won't feel exactly like day, nor night
like night, and in the true night,
when we have our other, more lunatic day,
I may hear in the dunch of my own blood
a distant, comforting, steady shoveling.

But when the human body
has been drained of its broths and filled
again with formaldehyde and salts
or unguents and aromatic oils, and pranked
up in its holiday best and laid out
in a satin-lined airtight stainless-steel
coffin inside a leakproof concrete vault —
I know that if no fellow creatures
can force their way in to do the underdigging
and jiggling and earthing over and mating
and egg-laying and birthing forth, then for us
the most that can come to pass
will be a centuries-long withering down
to a gowpen of dead dust, and never
the crawling of new life out of the old,
which is what we have for eternity on earth.

III

When the Towers Fell

From our high window we saw them
in their bands and blocks of light
brightening against a fading sunset,
saw them in the dark hours glittering
as if spirits inside them sat up
calculating profit and loss all night, saw
their tops steeped in the first yellow
of sunrise, grew so used to them
often we didn't see them, and now,
not seeing them, we see them.

—————————

The banker is talking to London.
Humberto is delivering breakfast sandwiches.
The trader is working the phone.
The mail sorter starts sorting the mail.
The secretary arrives, the chef,
the gofer, the CEO... *povres et riches*
Sages et folz, prestres et laiz
Nobles, villains, larges et chiches
Petiz et grans et beaulx et laiz...

—————————

The plane screamed low, down lower Fifth Avenue,
lifted at the Arch, someone said, shaking the dog walkers
in Washington Square, drove for the North Tower,
struck with a heavy thud and a huge bright gush
of blackened orange fire, and vanished, leaving behind
a hole the size and shape a cartoon plane might make

passing through and flying away, on the far side,
back into the realm of the imaginary.

———————————

Some with torn clothing, some bloodied,
some limping at top speed like children
in a three-legged race, some half dragged,
some intact in neat suits and dresses,
many dusted to a ghostly whiteness
with eyes rubbed red as the eyes of a zahorí,
who can see the dead under the ground,
they swarm in silence up the avenues.

———————————

Some died while calling home to say they were OK.
Some called the telephone operators and were told to stay put.
Some died after over an hour spent learning they would die.
Some died so abruptly they may have seen death from inside it.
Some burned, their faces caught fire.
Some were asphyxiated.
Some broke windows and leaned into the sunny day.
Some were pushed out from behind by others in flames.
Some let themselves fall, begging gravity to speed them to the ground.
Some leapt hand in hand that their fall down the sky might happen
    more lightly.

———————————

At the high window where I've often stood
to think, or to elude a nightmare, I meet
the single, unblinking, electric glare
lighting the all-night lifting

and sifting for bodies, pieces of bodies, a thumb, a tooth, anything
that is not nothing.

———————

She stands on a corner holding his picture.
He is smiling. In the heavy smoke
few pass. Sorry sorry sorry.
She startles.
Suppose, across the street, that headlong stride . . .
or there, that man with hair so black it's purple . . .

And yet, suppose some evening I forgot
The fare and transfer, yet got by that way
Without recall — lost, yet poised in traffic —
Then I might find your eyes . . .

Sorry sorry good luck thank you.
On this side it is "amnesia," or forgetting the way home;
on the other, "invisibleness," or never entirely returning.
Hard to see past the metallic mist
or through the canopy of supposed reality
cast over our world, bourn that no creature ever born
can pry its way back through, that no love can tear.

———————

All day the towers burn and fall, and burn and fall.
In a shot from New Jersey they seem like smokestacks spewing
earth's oily remnants.
Schwarze Milch der Frühe wir trinken sie abends
wir trinken sie mittags und morgens wir trinken sie nachts
wir trinken und trinken

———————

They come before us now not as a likeness,
but as a corollary, a small instance in the immense
lineage of the twentieth century's history of violent death —
black men in the South castrated and strung up from trees,
soldiers advancing through mud at ninety thousand dead per mile,
train upon train of boxcars heading eastward shoved full to the
    corners with Jews and Roma to be enslaved or gassed,
state murder of twenty, thirty, forty million of its own,
state starvation of a hundred million farmers,
atomic blasts erasing cities off the earth, firebombings the same,
death marches, assassinations, disappearances,
entire countries become rubble, minefields, mass graves.

Wir schaufeln ein Grab in den Lüften da liegt man nicht eng.

———————

Burst jet fuel, incinerated aluminum, steel fume, crushed marble,
    exploded granite, pulverized drywall, mashed concrete, berserked
    plastic, crazed chemicals, scoria, rotting flesh, vapor
of the vaporized — draped over
our island up to streets regimented
into numerals and letters, breathed across
the great bridges to Brooklyn and the waiting sea —
astringent, miasmic, empyreumatic, sticky,
air too foul to take in, but we take it in,
too gruesome for seekers of lost beloveds
to breathe, but they breathe it and you breathe it.

———————

The man doesn't look up.
Her photograph hangs from his neck.
He stares at the sidewalk of flagstones

laid down in Whitman's century, curbside edges rounded
by the rasps of wheels of iron and steel:
the human brain envying the stones:
Nie stają, się, są.
Nic nod to, myślałem,
zbrzydziwszy sobie
wszystko co staje się.

———————

I thought again of those on the high floors
who knew they would burn alive and then, burned alive.
As if there were mechanisms of death
so mutilating to existence no one
gets over them, not even the dead.

———————

I sat down by the waters of the Hudson
and saw in steel letters welded to the railing posts
Whitman's words written when America
was plunging into war with itself: *City of the world!...*
Proud and passionate city — mettlesome, mad, extravagant city!
But when the war was over and Lincoln dead
and the dead buried, Whitman remembered:
I saw battle-corpses, myriads of them,
And the white skeletons of young men, I saw them,
I saw the debris and debris of all the slain soldiers of the war,
But I saw they were not as was thought.
They themselves were fully at rest — they suffer'd not,
The living remain'd and suffer'd, the mother suffer'd,
And the wife and the child and the musing comrade suffer'd.

———————

In our minds the glassy blocks succumb over and over,
slamming down floor by floor into themselves,
blowing up as if in reverse, exploding

downward and rolling outward,
the way, in the days of the gods, a god
might rage through the streets, overtaking the fleeing.

As each tower goes down, it concentrates
into itself, transforms itself
infinitely slowly into a black hole

infinitesimally small: mass
without space, where each light,
each life, put out, lies down within us.

IV

Middle Path

Let James rejoice with the Skuttle-Fish, who foils
   his foe by the effusion of his ink.
                              — Christopher Smart

In memory of James Wright, 1927–1980

One at a time your feet lift
and slide through the air, and stamp
down in the awkward gait
of someone who has been wound up
too tight somewhere and set down
pointed in two directions,
inner and outer, both at once —

past wind-fallen trees that hold up
their root systems for psychiatric inspection,
past singers who flash the pink of their tonsils,
past cash registers that cry *Treblinka!* when the drawer pops open,
past dogs who hoist a leg but dribble on themselves,
past Boeing wings that lower their landing flaps and reveal their tiny
   whirling gears —
everything found a way to show you its insides

in those days when you walked on Middle Path on fire
in the clear idea that it could be done,
but, since speech that expresses trouble
takes going through hell, also afraid
that it could not be done for long.

You of all of us were able
to sit down forever, almost without self,
with pencil and notebook, with second sight,
wherever life and death meet.

Today, this first day of spring,
I can see you stray off Middle Path,
lifting your feet high to clamber through
the last sooted remains of snow and move
among the ancient graves and hunker down
at a headstone and read the chiselings
time and the chemical rains have spared:

Alfred and [effaced]
Age 6   Age 4
Children of [effaced] and Elizabeth [effaced]
Of such is the kingdom of [effaced]

How Could She Not

In memory of Jane Kenyon, 1947–1995

The air glitters. Overfull clouds
slide across the sky. A short shower,
its parallel diagonals visible
against the firs, douses and then
refreshes the crocuses. We knew
it might happen one day this week.
Out the open door, east of us, stand
the mountains of New Hampshire.
There, too, the sun is bright,

and heaped cumuli make their shadowy
ways along the horizon. When we learn
that she died this morning, we wish
we could think: how could it not
have been today? In another room,
Kiri Te Kanawa is singing
Mozart's *Laudate Dominum*
from far in the past, her voice
barely there over the swishings of scythes,
and rattlings of horse-pulled
mowing machines dragging
their cutter bar's little reciprocating
triangles through the timothy.

This morning did she wake
in the dark, almost used up
by her year of pain? By first light
did she glimpse the world
as she had loved it, and see
that if she died now, she would
be leaving him in a day like paradise?
Near sunrise did her hold loosen a little?

Having these last days spoken
her whole heart to him, who spoke
his whole heart to her, might she not
have felt that in the silence to come
he would not feel any word
was missing? When her room filled
with daylight, how could she not
have slipped under a spell, with him

next to her, his arms around her, as they
had been, it may then have seemed,
all her life? How could she not
press her cheek to his cheek,
which presses itself to hers
from now on? How could she not
rise and go, with sunlight at the window,
and the drone, fading, deepening, hard to say,
of a single-engine plane in the distance,
coming for her, that no one else hears?

The Scattering of Evan Jones' Ashes

For Judith Jones

Judith moves like a dancer
on sea swells, in a cloud
of the dust of this ardent man
who, as he grew older, more and more
gave himself to his love of poetry.

The airiest of his relics take
to the breeze, the rest fall
of their own loyalty to earth. Each of us
scoops up a handful of this intimate
grit and follows in her wake.

Some fling the ashes, others
sift them slowly through their fingers
as if feeling for something lost. Finally

the bowl, as wide and shallow as
a primitive grail, is empty.

It is as if the Darwin Lime Enterprise
lime truck out of North Danville
had come and done its cloudy work
and had just now pulled away, leaving
the green slopes dusted white.

Now one of us, a tall red-haired boy,
trumpet in hand, comes running.
He lopes across the moat, plunges into the woods,
which open for him and shut behind him.
A minute later he reappears

in the clearing at the top of the hill.
His hair aflame in a ray of sunset,
he puts his trumpet to his lips and blows
the slow solo in each one of us.
Evan's Welsh warrior corgi Maduc,

giving a high-pitched howl, flops
on his back with stubby legs
in the air, and sleds himself head-first
down to the edge of the pond, on grass
quickened and alchemized by Evan's ashes.

The 26th of December

A Tuesday, day of Tiw,
god of war, dawns in darkness.
The short holiday day of talking by the fire,
floating on snowshoes among
ancient self-pollarded maples,
visiting, being visited, giving
a rain gauge, receiving red socks,
watching snow buntings nearly over
their heads in snow stab at spirtled bits
of sunflower seeds the chickadees
hold with their feet to a bough
and hack apart, scattering debris
like sloppy butchers, is over.
Irregular life begins. Telephone calls,
Google searches, evasive letters,
complicated arrangements, faxes,
second thoughts, consultations,
e-mails, solemnly given kisses.

Promissory Note

If I die before you
which is all but certain
then in the moment
before you will see me
become someone dead
in a transformation
as quick as a shooting star's

I will cross over into you
and ask you to carry
not only your own memories
but mine too until you
too lie down and erase us
both together into oblivion.

V

Shelley

When I was twenty the one true
free spirit I had heard of was Shelley,
Shelley who wrote tracts advocating
atheism, free love, the emancipation
of women, and the abolition of wealth and class,
a lively version of Plato's *Symposium,*
lyrics on the bliss and brevity
of romantic love, and complex
poems on love's difficulties, Shelley
who, I learned later — perhaps
almost too late — remarried Harriet,
then pregnant with their second child,
and a few months later ran off with Mary,
already pregnant with their first, bringing
along Mary's stepsister Claire,
who very likely also became his lover,

and in this malaise à trois, which Shelley
said would be a "paradise of exiles,"
they made their life, along with the spectres
of Harriet, who drowned herself in the Serpentine,
and of Mary's half sister Fanny, who, fixated
on Shelley, killed herself, and with the spirits
of adored but neglected children
conceived almost incidentally
in the pursuit of Eros — Harriet's
Ianthe and Charles, denied to Shelley
and sent out to foster parents, Mary's
Clara, dead at one, her Willmouse, dead at three,

Elena, the baby in Naples, almost surely
Shelley's own, whom he "adopted" but then
left behind, dead at one and a half,
and Allegra, Claire's daughter by Byron,
whom Byron packed off to the convent
at Bagnacavallo at four, dead at five —

and in those days, before I knew
any of this, I thought I followed Shelley,
who thought he was following radiant desire.

Sex

On my hands are the odors
of the knockout ether
either of above the sky
where the bluebirds get blued
on their upper surfaces
or of down under the earth
where the immaculate nightcrawlers
take in tubes of red earth
and polish their insides.

Insomniac

I open my eyes to see how the night
is progressing. The clock glows green,
the light of the last-quarter moon
shines up off the snow into our bedroom.

Her portion of our oceanic duvet
lies completely flat. The words
of the shepherd in *Tristan,* "Waste
and empty, the sea," come back to me.
Where can she be? Then in the furrow
where the duvet overlaps her pillow,
a small hank of brown hair
shows itself, her marker that she's here,
asleep, somewhere down in the dark
underneath. Now she rotates
herself a quarter turn, from strewn
all unfolded on her back to bunched
in a Z on her side, with her back to me.
I squirm nearer, careful not to break
into the immensity of her sleep,
and lie there absorbing the astounding
quantity of heat a slender body
ovens up around itself.
Her slow, purring, sometimes snorish,
perfectly intelligible sleeping sounds
abruptly stop. A leg darts back
and hooks my ankle with its foot
and draws me closer. Immediately
her sleeping sounds resume, telling me:
"Come, press against me, yes, like that,
put your right elbow on my hipbone, perfect,
and your right hand at my breasts, yes, that's it,
now your left arm, which has become extra,
stow it somewhere out of the way, good.
Entangled with each other so, unsleeping one,
together we will outsleep the night."

Field Notes

When we were out at dinner
last night and a dim mood
from the day hung on in me
that neither the quenelles
de brochet nor the Pignan
Châteauneuf-du-Pape
2000 could quite lift,
she disappeared and plucked
out of the air somewhere
some amusement or comfort
and, quickly back again,
laid it in our dinner talk.

When it was time to leave
and she scanned the restaurant
for the restroom, she went up
on her toes, like the upland plover,
and in the taxi home we kissed
a mint from the maitre d's desk
from my mouth to hers,
like cedar waxwings.

When I squished in bare feet
up to the bedroom, I found her
already dropped off, bedside lamp still on,
Theodore Xenophon Barber's
The Human Nature of Birds
lying open face-down under her chin.

Gazing at her I saw
that she was gazing back,
having been sleeping awake
as the tree swallow does.

I went around the foot
of the bed and climbed in
and slid toward the side lined
with the warmth and softness
of herself, and we clasped each other
like no birds I know of.

Our cries that night were wild,
unhinged, not from here,
as unearthly as the common loon's.

Walnut

On the potholed road from the Port
Authority Terminal the Newark Airport bus
sighs up and down as if moguling.
In my experience, motion of this kind
while sitting in a bus often increases
the size of the penis. It does so now.
A mixed sign. In certain operas
the desire for sex and the allure of death
seem to be present just before or just after
each other but occasionally simultaneously.

Consider the love life of the prostate.
During lovemaking this gland, which is,
as doctors like to say, the size of a walnut,
and has very few pleasure fibers in it
but a great many for pain, transmits
the sensation of pain with growing intensity,
until at last, when our walnut can no longer bear it,
the duct opens and semen bursts out and gives
shuddering relief or ecstatic joy, as you like.

Climbing the Pulaski Skyway on a faulty
pneumatic suspension, the bus gasps
and blows and develops a bucking rhythm
that lets me imagine what the fuck-
ing of buses might be like. Minutes later
I find myself thinking the bus moves
like an antediluvian mammal
being shoved to its grave without first
having been fully persuaded its time is up.
Though not kept informed explicitly, the penis
instinctively senses this turn of thought, and shrinks.

Pure Balance

Wherever we are is unlikely.
Our few kisses — I don't know if
they're of goodbye or of
what — or if she knows either.

Neither do I understand why it's
exhilarating — as well as the other things it is —
to know one doesn't have a future,
or how much longer one won't have one.

Future tramples all prediction.
Hope loses hope. Clarity
turns out to be
an invisible form of sadness.

We look for a bridge to cross
to the other shore where our other
could be looking for us
but all the river crossings

all the way to the sea
have been bombed. We look for a tree —
touch it — touch
right through it — sometimes nowhere

is there anything to hitch oneself to
and we must make our way by pure balance.
This is so and can't be helped
without doing damage to oneself.

Why Regret?

Didn't you like the way the ants help
the peony globes open by eating the glue off?
Weren't you cheered to see the ironworkers
sitting on an I-beam dangling from a cable,
in a row, like starlings, eating lunch, maybe
baloney on white with fluorescent mustard?
Wasn't it a revelation to waggle
from the estuary all the way up the river,
the kill, the pirle, the run, the rent, the beck,
the sike barely trickling, to the shock of a spring?
Didn't you almost shiver, hearing book lice
clicking their sexual dissonance inside an old
Webster's New International, perhaps having just
eaten out of it *izle, xyster,* and *thalassacon*?
What did you imagine lies in wait anyway
at the end of a world whose sub-substance
is glaim, gleet, birdlime, slime, mucus, muck?
Forget about becoming emaciated. Think of the wren
and how little flesh is needed to make a song.
Didn't it seem somehow familiar when the nymph
split open and the mayfly struggled free
and flew and perched and then its own back
broke open and the imago, the true adult,
somersaulted out and took flight, seeking
the swarm, mouth-parts vestigial,
alimentary canal come to a stop,
a day or hour left to find the desired one?
Or when Casanova took up the platter
of linguine in squid's ink and slid the stuff

out the window, telling his startled companion,
"The perfected lover does not eat."
As a child, didn't you find it calming to imagine
pinworms as some kind of tiny batons
giving cadence to the squeezes and releases
around the downward march of debris?
Didn't you glimpse in the monarchs
what seemed your own inner blazonry
flapping and gliding, in desire, in the middle air?
Weren't you reassured to think these flimsy
hinged beings, and then their offspring,
and then their offspring's offspring, could
navigate, working in shifts, all the way to Mexico,
to the exact plot, perhaps the very tree,
by tracing the flair of the bodies of ancestors
who fell in this same migration a year ago?
Doesn't it outdo the pleasures of the brilliant concert
to wake in the night and find ourselves
holding each other's hand in our sleep?

Last Poems

2010–2014

Turkeys

Sometimes we saw shadows of gods
in the trees; silenced, we went on.
Sometimes the dog would bound off
over the snow, into the forest.
Sometimes a tree had twenty
or more black turkeys in it, each
seeming the size of a small black bear.
We remember them for their care
for their kind ever since we watched the big hen
in the very top of the tree shaking
load after load of apples down to the flock.
Sometimes I felt I would never
come out of the woods, I thought
its deeper darkness might absorb me
or feed me to the black turkeys
and I would cry out for the dog
and the dog would not answer.

Jubilate

I

So from poet to poet we proceeded
in our celebration of Christopher Smart's
long lost poem *Jubilate Agno,* composed
by this profligate, drunken, devout, mad polymath
between 1759 and 1763, while locked up
in St Luke's Hospital for the Insane, and then

549

in the less bedlamic asylum at Bethnal Green.
Drawing on books he had brought along with him
or borrowed from other madhouse libraries —
to wit: an Authorized Bible, a Polyglot Bible,
Albin's *Natural History of Birds,* Walton's
Compleat Angler, Coxe's *Descriptions of Carolana,*
Pliny's *Natural History,* Anson's *Voyage Around
the World,* Ainsworth's *Thesaurus,* plus various popular
journals and occult writings — and availing himself also
of his own waggery, his own observations, and his wide
learning, prodigious memory, and excited imaginings
— *"For I am not without authority in my jeopardy"* —
he extracted out of his whirling brain, one, two,
sometimes three lines a day, to keep himself sane —
for a profound sanity underlay this project:
to repair our connection with the natural world
by joining person after person — a Joram or Caleb or Ehud
or Haggith or Bernice or Shobab or Joab — with an animal,
insect, tree, plant, flower, or precious stone — almost any
living, or nearly living, entity would suffice: from the Zoony
to the Great Flabber Dabber Flat Clapping Fish.
This grand but unfinished work, which Smart declared was his
"Magnificat," is witty and wild in its call-and-response,
and a long, healing roll-call of the earth.

2

And so, two hundred and fifteen years later,
on a February night, twenty-one poets gathered
in a little church on Lower Fifth Avenue
and one by one stood up and read or recited
to a large and ardent audience thirty lines

or so per poet from *Jubilate Agno* —
mere floccinaucinihilipilification
to the world — but to us a source of joy and truth,
the lung-ether of the living loving the long dead.
Some poets were attracted to passages they knew
for their own reasons, such as Etheridge Knight,
who, like Kit Smart, had done time:
"Let Andrew rejoice with the whale,
who is array'd in beauteous blue
and is a combination of bulk and activity,
for they work me with their harping-irons,
which is a barbarous instrument,
because I am more unguarded than the rest."
Or like Allen Ginsberg, who remembered
that in writing "Howl" he had communed
with the genius of Kit's madness, and chanted:
"Rejoice with Buteo who hath three testicles,
for I bless God in the strength of my loins
and for the voice which he hath made sonorous."
Whereupon Grace Paley, born Grace Goodside
to immigrant Ukrainian socialists — here present
in her earthly glory — betook herself to the podium
and most lovingly bronxed: *"Let Milcah rejoice*
with the Horned Beetle who will strike a man
in the face . . . for I am the Lord's News-Writer
— the Scribe-Evangelist." And then Philip Levine —
he too had drawn singing stinging breaths
into himself from those Smartian incantations
in his own great poem "They Feed They Lion" —
proclaimed: *"Let Philip rejoice with Boca, which is a fish*
that can speak. For the English tongue shall be

the language of the West." After him, came
elegant David Ignatow, followed by Allen Grossman,
our philosopher, and Nancy Willard,
our magician. Jane Cooper's tremulous piping
came floating back down from the vaulted ceiling
and reminded us: *"Earth which is an intelligence*
hath a voice and a propensity to speak in all her parts,"
whereupon Gerald Stern, with his own joyfully Smartian
super-exuberance cried out — as if, Eureka!
he had learned how to do it just yesterday: *"The Circle*
may be SQUARED by swelling and flattening!"
Joel Oppenheimer came next, followed
by Harvey Shapiro and Gregory Orr
and lion-tongued Thomas Lux, who roared:
"For the coffin and the cradle and the purse
are all against a man . . ." But Vertemae Grosvenor,
whose first language, Gullah, came
to her on the tongues of Sea Islanders,
called us back into happiness: *"Rejoice*
with the Pigeon, who is an antidote
to malignity and will carry a letter." Next Paul Zweig,
beautiful doomed disappearing spirit, told us:
"For harpsichords are best strung with gold wire,"
and from Allen Planz, fisherman by trade:
"Let Jude bless with the bream, who is melancholy
for his depth and serenity, for I have a greater
compass of mirth and melancholy than another."
Then Stanley Plumly recited, then David
Cumberland, and then me, and next
James Wright, who read a passage Gerald

Stern might have been hoping for: Kit's éloge
to his Cat Jeoffrey, his one faithful companion:
"For there is nothing sweeter than his peace
when at rest, there is nothing
brisker than his life when in motion."

3

Last to the podium went Muriel Rukeyser,
who once wrote her own Smartian vow:
"Never to despise in myself what I have been
taught to despise, and never to despise the other,"
and concluded her ode to cockroaches so:
"I reach, I touch, I begin to know you."
Muriel was soaring now, in full song,
and the faces in the nave all lifted as one,
amazed, all of them, by her huge head,
her heart-shaped face, her ferocious beauty,
and her voice lovely and growly at its edges:
"For I have a providential acquaintance
with men who bear the names of animals . . ."
And everyone present was with her in
the little church swelled with light. Indeed
the podium itself seemed to be attempting
to raise itself up — *"for I bless God*
for Mr Lion Mr Cock Mr Cat Mr Talbot
Mr Hart Mrs Fysh Mr Grub and Miss Lamb."
And now it became evident that our podium
was not rising, it was Muriel who was sinking,
toppling in fact, hauling down on herself
the microphone and amplifier and all their wires,

into a heap on the floor. From under this wreckage
her suddenly re-clarioned voice was heard: *"Let Zadok
worship with the Mole — before honour is humility!"*
And as we disentangled her, she sat up and scanned about
and said: *"She that looketh low shall learn!"* Suddenly
a young woman rushed out the door, shouting:
"I'm calling an ambulance!" Muriel called after her:
"No ambulances! I need a chair! A chair!"
A plump man came swiftly wriggling
through the audience, "I'm a doctor! A doctor!"
"No doctors!" Muriel shouted even louder,
"A chair! A chair!" Eased into a chair at last,
she smiled: *"Let Carpus rejoice with the Frog-Fish —
a woman cannot die on her knees!"*

4

For all those who were there, at the Church
of the Transfiguration, that evening in 1978,
and for those who may have heard about it later
and those of you coming upon it now
for the first time, and for Kit Smart who died
in debtor's prison in 1771 at forty-nine,
and for Muriel who would die two years after that evening,
and for these witnesses who are also gone:
Paul and Etheridge and Jane and Harvey and Allen
and Allen and Grace and David and James and Joel —
and the carrier pigeon too — and for the rest of us
still standing, or sitting — and before long to topple —
let all of us rejoice and be made glad.

The Sulphur Baths at Esalen

Those must be the two students I have not
yet met, sitting up to their necks
in sulphurous water, their heads distinct
but the sunken rest of them blurry,
like albumen of an egg poaching.
The shuddery oiliness of the water
slops with flashes of sky, and reeks
sweetly of the bowels of the sea.
When I reach them, and uncinch
my towel, and drop it onto the deck,
the two heads swivel as one, as if
on synchronized axes, and gaze at me
for a moment which goes on too long,
in my opinion, to still be called a moment.
Being writers, perhaps they form all things
they meet into words, such as, in this case,
"Navel squinting through nearly shut lids."
"Flesh falling in sweals as if partly melted."
"Cock which does not look as if it has been
up and crowing at first light lately."
I grope around mentally for a supposed self
that these two might have found in my poems,
to face them with. Gone.
I'm just a naked body, a body
not as it was, nor as it wishes to be,
but as it is. I sink slowly up
to my chin in the bath water and wonder
if I have ever written a truthful poem.

Astonishment

    Oarlocks knock in the dusk, a rowboat rises
    and settles, surges and slides.
    Under a great eucalyptus,
    a boy and girl feel around with their feet
    for those small flattish stones so perfect
    for scudding across the water.

§

    A dog barks from deep in the silence.
    A woodpecker, double-knocking,
    keeps time. I have slept in so many arms.
    Consolation? Probably. But too much
    consolation may leave one inconsolable.

§

    The water before us has hardly moved
    except in the shallowest breathing places.
    For us back then, to live seemed almost to die.
    One day a darkness fell between her and me.
    When we woke, a hawthorn sprig
    stood in the water glass at our bedside.

§

    There is a silence in the beginning.
    The life within us grows quiet.
    There is little fear. No matter
    how all this comes out, from now on
    it cannot not exist ever again.
    We liked talking our nights away

in words close to the natural language,
which most other animals can still speak.

§

The present pushes back the life of regret.
It draws forward the life of desire. Soon memory
will have started sticking itself all over us.
We were fashioned from clay in a hurry,
poor throwing may mean it didn't matter
to the makers if their pots cracked.

§

On the mountain tonight the full moon
faces the full sun. Now could be the moment
when we fall apart or we become whole.
Our time seems to be up — I think I even hear it stopping.
Then why have we kept up the singing for so long?
Because that's the sort of determined creature we are.
Before us, our first task is to astonish,
and then, harder by far, to be astonished.

I, Coyote, Stilled Wonder

When did I get this bejawed look,
that flashes up out of creeks and pools?
Was it when I fled across
pasture and through woods,
up to ledge, and came out
in the world to let myself think events

back into their right sequence again?
Man glaring into bloody mess on ground,
cow, who has birthed calf, I,
Coyote, actually tasted,
ate of it well past demarcating line
where calf becomes aftermatter.
I think it was then, when I fled
singing, happy, to wood's edge.
I could see Man raise arms,
steady his over-and-under, and squeeze.
I, Coyote, I was there, yes I saw it all,
even the flock of tiny lead
that went scattering past.
I felt in me all those that hit,
nearly shattered wraith, clinging
to crushed jawbone, invisibly
slickering through trees, from here on
alone, I, Coyote, stilled wonder.

The Silence of the World

I can imagine the silence when the world
will have stilled itself — no more poems tossed
off the tongue, no more screams
of raven lugging entrails of porcupine,
no more tales of the Navajo, or Louisiana black man, or
    old-time Vermonter,
no more breathing in the ear of last lover,
no more angelic beings left to be kissed

into the claustrophobia of flesh,
no more temples giving light
from open doors into bitter winter nights, no more
curious weasel who leaves
her black ring frozen in the air,
no more tooth that gnaws through gum and bones into the
    cathedral of the mouth.
No more *splat* when singer spits
mouthwash into the washbasin after the concert,
no more "Quit yer bawlin!"
from punk principal to slob schoolboy
when sore mother hauls
small boy into classroom by sore ear.
No more young woman in large hat in profile
in afternoon light saying, "So what, darling?
I don't hate you. I love you. So what?"
No more flutesman trudging through snow
on 125th Street on the last Sunday morning of his jeopardy.
No more husband saying, "Snack bar's the other way."
No more wife replying, "You aren't going to eat *again*, are you?"
No more husband replying, "I don't want to eat,
I was just telling you where the snack bar is."
No more wife replying, "For Chrissake! I know where it is."
No more caesura or else everything one endless caesura,
no more feminine rhyme such as "lattice" and "thereat is,"
no more *parallelismus membrorum* panting in one ear,
no more Neruda's slowly deepening voice saying,
"Federico, te acuerdas, debajo de la tierra . . ."

From across the valley the thud of an axe
arrives later than its strike

and the call of goodbye slowly separates itself
little by little from the vocal chords of everything.

Gravity

1

Upon the black hole Cygnus X-1 that wobbles
as if boffed by an invisible companion,
upon a silk stocking the color of bees
rolling itself up down a leg, upon the soft dip
over the clavicles, which accept only tongued kisses,
upon the tongue that slowly drifts
into the other's mouth and chats
there with her opposite number,
gravity exerts the precise force needed.

2

In the wings of the Eskimo curlew
flapping through the thin air of the Andes,
in the sacral vertebrae of the widow
who stoops at the window to peer
behind the drawn blind, in the saggy skin
under the eyes of the woman
who is in love with a man incapable
of love, who lives on in the heaviness
of emotional isolation, in the lavish
cascade of urine the rhino releases,
in the mouthwater of the child who waits
in shriek position for the dentist,

in the scradged skin dangling in shreds
from the children who lurched toward
the Nakashima River screaming, as if this were
the single aria they had ever rehearsed, gravity
shudders at its mathematical immensity.

3

As long as two kvetches remain alive,
because inside each is self-hatred so hardened
not even nonexistence can abide them,
as long as the hummingbird strikes
the air seventy-four times per second,
as long as the mound of earth remains heaped
beside the rectangular hole waiting to be filled,
gravity cannot be said to impose its will.

4

If the pilot ejects one second too late,
if the condemned man shrinks at seeing
the trapdoor give way, if the man who stands
with fire at his back and a baby in his arms
hears the near neighbors cry,
"Drop her! Don't worry! We'll catch her,"
if the juggler gets behind in her count
and the bright object flies past the spot
where the other hand was to snatch it,
gravity cannot pause to rectify matters.

5

When a deer kenning us stands immobile,
and for one moment we know we exist

entirely within her thoughts, when cichlid fry,
sensing danger, empty their air bladders
and drop to the river bottom like pebbles,
when the snow goes and millions of leaves
reveal themselves pressed down over the contours
of earth to create her hibernation mask,
when a person in a military cemetery
among grave markers that spread to all the horizons
understands that all of existence has been destroyed
again and again, when depression after mania
causes clock hands to stick and days to crawl,
when the full moon's light creeps across a sleeper
calling to her atavistic soul, when a soldier,
who has always known life is imperfect,
is wheeled to another hopeless attempt
at surgery — but, this time, resolves
to sleep and not wake again until such time
as time begins again — then gravity
grips us to the earth, and crosses its fingers.

6

In the case of the last ancient trees at Ypres
still turning out their terrified wood,
in the case of the concertina wire
hurled out in exuberant spirals and set down
between rich and poor, in the case of the howls
that fly off the earth through madhouse windows,
in the case of the word "heavenly"
when we remind ourselves that earth,
too, was a heavenly body once,
in the case of the numeral keys

totting up the number of humans
humans have killed, in the case of the man
who strays into a gravitational field where
the differential between the force on the scalp
and the force on the foot sole will stretch him
into an alimentary canal thin as a thread,
in the case of the child who has upset
his ink bottle while doing homework
and quickly snaps both arms down
to halt the lateral gush of the black juices,
gravity, if it could, would recuse itself.

Notes
Acknowledgments
Biographical Afterword
Index
Illustration Credits

NOTES

First Poems 1946–1954

First published in 1970 by The Perishable Press in an edition of 150 copies, the book was reproduced without revision in *The Avenue Bearing the Initial of Christ into the New World* (Houghton Mifflin, 1974; henceforth *Avenue C, 1974*). Four poems were included in *Selected Poems* with revisions in 1984. In 2002, *Avenue C* was reissued without *First Poems* and with the following note from GK: "I'm not really sure how *First Poems* got into that volume in the first place, unless the firm assertion in the title could, over time, have persuaded me that the book consisted of actual poems, rather than of first, frequently floundering efforts."

All versions are from *Avenue C, 1974,* except as noted:
"A Walk in the Country": *First Poems.*
"A Winter Sky": *Selected Poems.*
"The Gallows": *First Poems.*
"Conversation at Tea": section 3, stanza 6, last line: corrected presumed
    typo, "that" changed to "than."
"Meditation Among the Tombs": *Selected Poems.*

What a Kingdom It Was

All versions are from *Avenue C, 2002,* except as noted:

"First Communion": *Avenue C, 2002,* except line 12 reverts to *What a Kingdom It Was:* "Now we carry the aftertaste of the Lord."

"Burning": *Avenue C, 1974,* except first stanza reverts to *What a Kingdom It Was.*

"Westport": *Selected Poems.*

"A Toast to Tu Fu": *Avenue C, 1974.*

"For the Lost Generation": *Avenue C, 1974.*

"Alewives Pool": *Avenue C, 1974.*

"Across the Brown River": *Avenue C, 1974.*

"One Generation": *Avenue C, 1974.*

"The Supper After the Last": *New Selected Poems.*

Flower Herding on Mount Monadnock

All versions are from *Avenue C, 2002,* except as noted:

"Hunger unto Death": *Avenue C, 1974.*

"Last Spring": *Avenue C, 1974.*

"For Robert Frost": *Avenue C, 2002,* except the penultimate line in section 4 reverts to "broken lips" from *Flower Herding . . .* and *New Selected Poems.*

"Ruins under the Stars": *New Selected Poems.*

Body Rags

All versions are from *Three Books, 2002.*

The Book of Nightmares

All versions are from the paperback *Book of Nightmares,* except as noted:

"Under the Maud Moon": *New Selected Poems,* except the last two lines of
    section 3 revert to *Book of Nightmares.*

"The Hen Flower": *New Selected Poems.*

"The Dead Shall Be Raised Incorruptible": *New Selected Poems,* except
    section 4, stanza 5, lines 4 and 5 revert to *Book of Nightmares;*
    section 4, stanza 9 reverts to *Book of Nightmares;* section 7, line 8
    reverts to *Book of Nightmares.*

"Little Sleep's-Head Sprouting Hair in the Moonlight": *New Selected
    Poems,* except section 2, stanza 3, last line reverts to *Book of
    Nightmares;* section 3, stanza 2, penultimate line reverts to *Book of
    Nightmares.*

"Lastness": *New Selected Poems.*

Mortal Acts, Mortal Words

All versions are from *Three Books, 2002,* except:

"Wait": In giving readings in his last ten years, GK dropped the last
    two lines of the poem: "most of all to hear your whole existence, /
    rehearsed by the sorrows, play itself into total exhaustion." He also
    cut those lines in marked-up copies of his *New Selected Poems,* and in
    2012 Poets House published a broadside omitting those lines. This
    seemed a strong reason to omit them here.

"Blackberry Eating": *Mortal Acts, Mortal Words.*

The Past

All versions are from *Three Books, 2002.*

When One Has Lived a Long Time Alone

All versions are from the paperback edition of *When One Has Lived a Long Time Alone,* except as noted:

"The Tragedy of Bricks": *New Selected Poems.*

"The Cat": *New Selected Poems.*

"Oatmeal": *New Selected Poems,* except after line 11, where these lines are reinstated: "Oi 'ad a 'eck of a toime . . . through his porridge." And, after line 13: "An entire stanza . . . a hole in the pocket."

"The Perch": *New Selected Poems.*

"The Room": *New Selected Poems.*

"Last Gods": *New Selected Poems.*

"Farewell": *New Selected Poems.*

"When One Has Lived a Long Time Alone": *New Selected Poems.*

Imperfect Thirst

All versions are from the paperback edition of *Imperfect Thirst,* except as noted:

"My Mother's R & R": *New Selected Poems.*

"The Man in the Chair": *New Selected Poems.*

"The Cellist": *New Selected Poems.*

"Running on Silk": *New Selected Poems.*

"The Deconstruction of Emily Dickinson": *New Selected Poems.*

"Driving West": *New Selected Poems.*

"Passing the Cemetery": *New Selected Poems.*

"Parkinson's Disease": *New Selected Poems.*

"Rapture": *New Selected Poems.*

"Flies": *New Selected Poems.*

"Neverland": *New Selected Poems.*

Strong Is Your Hold

All versions are from the paperback edition of *Strong Is Your Hold*.

GK's notes on the poems:

"The Stone Table":
"I believe in the miracles of art, but what / prodigy will keep you safe beside me." — Jane Kenyon, from "Afternoon at MacDowell"

"It All Comes Back":
The lines ". . . those said to die miserably every day for lack of the small / clarifications sometimes found in poems" refer to the following passage in William Carlos Williams's poem "Asphodel, That Greeny Flower": "It is difficult / to get the news from poems / yet men die miserably every day / for lack / of what is found there."

"When the Towers Fell":
The lines beginning *"povres et riches . . ."* are from François Villon, "The Testament": ". . . poor and rich / Wise and foolish, priests and laymen / Noblemen, serfs, generous and mean / Short and tall and handsome and homely."

"And yet, suppose some evening I forgot . . ." — Hart Crane, from "For the Marriage of Faustus and Helen"

"Schwarze Milch der Frühe wir trinken sie abends . . .": "Black milk of daybreak we drink it at nightfall / we drink it at midday at morning we drink it at night / we drink it and drink it." — Paul Celan, from *Death Fugue*

"Wir schaufeln ein Grab in den Lüften da liegt man nicht eng":
"We're digging a grave in the sky there'll be plenty of room to lie
down there." — Paul Celan, from *Death Fugue*

"Nie stają, się, są . . .": "They do not become, they are. / Nothing
but that, I thought, / finally secretly loathing / everything that be-
comes." — Aleksander Wat, from *Songs of a Wanderer*

"City of the world! . . ." — Walt Whitman, from "City of Ships"

"I saw battle-corpses, myriads of them . . ." — Walt Whitman, from
"When Lilacs Last in the Door-yard Bloom'd"

Last Poems (2010–2014)

"Turkeys": 2010, *The New Yorker.*
"Jubilate": 2013, *Poetry Ireland.* First published in 2011 in *American Poetry
    Review.*
"The Sulphur Baths at Esalen": 2012, *Catamaran Literary Reader.* GK
    was never satisfied with the ending of this poem and published it only
    reluctantly.
"Astonishment": 2012, *The New Yorker.*
"I, Coyote, Stilled Wonder": 2013, *The New Yorker.*
"The Silence of the World": 2013, *The New Yorker.*
"Gravity": 2014, *The New Yorker.*

ACKNOWLEDGMENTS

MY DEEPEST GRATITUDE is to Galway Kinnell's family (and mine): to Maud Kozodoy, my stepdaughter and co–literary executor, who helped proofread the manuscript, searched long hours for uncollected poems, and was always available for consultation on any matter, inconsequential or immense; and to Neal Kozodoy, for his unfailing generosity and clarity in all things practical, contractual, editorial, and literary. And for their support and many kindnesses: Mirah Kozodoy, Inés Delgado de Torres, Fergus Kinnell, and Ephraim Kozodoy.

I am indebted to several dear friends for their inspiriting encouragement, guidance, and faithfulness, especially Edward Hirsch and Sharon Olds. Also: Margery Cantor, Virginia Carter, Pablo Conrad, Tune Faulkner, Alice Gordon, Donald Hall, Robert Hass, Katherine Hourigan, and Frank Lentriccia. Shortly after Galway's death in October 2014, two of his close poet friends, Philip Levine and C. K. Williams, also died. When I began work on the *Collected Poems,* I acutely missed their counsel — they had known his work so well — and I continue to feel their absence from our world.

Though our final decision was not to include any early uncollected poems that Galway had implicitly disavowed, we did try to track down every one of them. Erika Dowell, Associate Director and Curator of Modern Books and Manuscripts at the Lilly Library at Indiana University, and Bill Ross, Special Collections Librarian at the University of New Hampshire's Milne Special Collections and Archives, were tremendously helpful in locating copies of those poems residing in the Galway Kinnell collections there. Amanda Glassman at Poets House; James Maynard, Curator of the Poetry Collection of the University Libraries, University at Buffalo, State University of New York; and Mari Tsuchiya of Outreach, Learning, and Research Services at Rush Rhees Library at the University of Rochester also helped to find additional poems.

At Houghton Mifflin Harcourt, a long line of sympathetic (and often forbearing) editors going back fifty years brought Galway's poems into book form, and I am lucky to have been able to work with Larry Cooper, his longtime manuscript editor. My editor, Deanne Urmy, and her colleague, the dauntless Jenny Xu, have shown me much kindness and generosity (as well as their own share of forbearance).

Finally, I am grateful to have benefited from the vision, sensibility, and cheerfulness of Jennifer Keller, Galway's former graduate student, longtime assistant, and friend, who so quickly became an essential partner in the work on this volume that there was no question she should be its coeditor.

B. K. B.

BIOGRAPHICAL AFTERWORD

GALWAY KINNELL was born in Providence, Rhode Island, on February 1, 1927, the fourth child of Elizabeth Mills and James Scott Kinnell, immigrants from Londonderry, Ireland, and Edinburgh, Scotland, respectively. He was raised in Pawtucket, Rhode Island, a once-thriving mill town then in the depths of the Depression. His father worked odd jobs and taught woodworking at the local high school; his mother, who had been a bank clerk in London, lost all of her savings in the 1929 crash and went to work cleaning houses. Her disappointment in her life and circumstances infused much of Galway's childhood.

By his own description introverted and "mute," Galway, when not in school, spent much of his childhood wandering through the nearby Seekonk Woods, dreaming of life as a hobo. A copy of Palgrave's *Golden Treasury* on his mother's bookshelf revealed to him the hypnotic poems of Edgar Allan Poe, and he knew from age twelve that he had found his vocation. In poetry, he sensed, it might be possible to say the things that he couldn't otherwise express. By eighteen, he was writing with seriousness of purpose.

In 1943, a scholarship enabled him to attend Wilbraham Academy in Massachusetts. There he was encouraged in his earliest writings by a teacher, Roger Nye Lincoln, to whom he later dedicated his *Selected Poems.* He immersed himself in the poems of Poe, Emily Dickinson, Percy Bysshe Shelley, William Wordsworth, Rudyard Kipling, A. E. Housman, as well as James Whitcomb Riley and Robert Service, and the travel writings of the vagabond adventurers Richard Halliburton and Harry Franck. At Wilbraham, he acquired the nickname "Casey" for his baseball prowess.

Kinnell was admitted to Princeton on a scholarship in 1944, and shortly afterward enlisted in the navy. After basic training, he returned to Princeton to complete his studies and officer training. There he met W. S. Merwin, a classmate and fellow scholarship student, who arrived late one night, book in hand, and introduced him to W. B. Yeats by reading aloud until dawn. Merwin was perfecting his craft with the critic R. P. Blackmur and the poet John Berryman. But Kinnell (self-protectively, he later admitted) professed "a certain scorn that there could be a *course* in poetry" and studied instead with the humanist scholar Charles G. Bell, who became a lifelong mentor and close friend. In 1948, he graduated from Princeton summa cum laude.

In pursuit of his M.A. degree at the University of Rochester, he wrote a thesis on Hart Crane's *The Bridge.* There followed his first teaching job at Alfred University, and a position directing the Basic Program of Liberal Education for adults at the Downtown Center of the University of Chicago from 1951 to 1955. Kinnell spent the next several years abroad, first as a Fulbright scholar in Paris and later teaching at the universities of Grenoble and Nice, where he took flying lessons and earned his pilot's license. During that time, he began publishing in literary magazines: *Beloit Poetry Journal* and *Poetry* were among his early supporters.

While at Grenoble he taught the work of Walt Whitman for the first time. It was a conversion experience: As he later recalled in *The Essential*

Whitman: "Soon I understood that poetry could be transcendent, hymn-like, a cosmic song, and yet remain idolatrously attached to the creatures and things of our world. Under Whitman's spell, I stopped writing in rhyme and meter . . . and turned to long-lined, loosely cadenced verse and at once I felt immensely liberated."

In 1957, his older brother Derry was killed in an automobile accident. Kinnell moved back to the United States and lived for the next two years on New York's Lower East Side. A second Fulbright then took him to Asia and eventually to Iran, where he taught at the University of Tehran and worked as a journalist and photographer for an English-language newspaper. He was intrigued by the persistence of ancient Persian culture in the midst of a modernizing country, and Iran was to become the setting of his only novella, *Black Light* (1966).

On the Lower East Side, Kinnell had been transfixed by the multilingual, largely impoverished, teeming immigrant world of Avenue C. This poured into the making of "The Avenue Bearing the Initial of Christ into the New World." The long poem, published in 1960 in his first collection, *What a Kingdom It Was,* would stun many readers, critics, and fellow poets and lead to a first Guggenheim fellowship.

That same year, he bought an abandoned farmhouse outside Sheffield, Vermont, as a place to store his books while he traveled the world. "I started out in the southwest corner of the state," he later recalled, "and worked my way to the northeast corner until I found some land I could buy for the $800 I had in my pocket." Kinnell was an able draftsman and carpenter (a skill he had learned from his father), and he rebuilt much of the farmhouse in Sheffield, from floors and windows to a brick fireplace and furniture. The place became his second home for the rest of his life.

In the early 1960s, Kinnell traveled to Louisiana with the Congress of Racial Equality and the Student Nonviolent Coordinating Committee to work on black voter registration and desegregation, at one point landing in jail for five days. In March 1965, he and a group of student protesters from Juniata College were charged by mounted police in Montgomery, Alabama. Charles Moore's photograph of Kinnell's bloodied face was one of many graphic images in *Life* that helped to stir public outrage, leading to the passage of the Voting Rights Act later that year.

Kinnell's second collection, *Flower Herding on Mount Monadnock,* was published in 1964. Soon after came his translation *The Poems of François Villon* (a poet whose work he had discovered during a summer studying with his Princeton professor Charles Bell at Black Mountain College), followed by translations of Yves Bonnefoy and Yvan Goll.

The mid-to-late 1960s also saw his marriage to the Spanish-born editor Inés Delgado de Torres, in 1965, and the birth of their two children, Maud Natasha (1966) and Finn Fergus (1968). *Body Rags,* published in 1968, includes some of his most anthologized poems, among them "The Porcupine," "The Bear," and "Vapor Trail Reflected in the Frog Pond."

After *The Book of Nightmares* was published in 1971, he became a frequent presence on the poetry-reading circuit, taking several short-term teaching positions in the U.S. and abroad, among them at Reed College, UC Irvine, Sarah Lawrence, Columbia, and Macquarie University in Australia. He was awarded a second Guggenheim fellowship and the Poetry Society of America's Shelley Prize. Nearly a decade would pass without another collection, a difficult time of financial insecurity. He had been consumed by writing *The Book of Nightmares* and felt "an unsettling emptiness afterward." Even so, his children, his family life in Vermont, and the death of his mother brought forth some of his most admired poems, collected in *Mortal Acts, Mortal Words* (1980).

In 1983, Kinnell's *Selected Poems* won both the Pulitzer Prize and the National Book Award. After two years spent teaching at the University of Hawaii, he found a permanent academic home at New York University, where he cofounded the creative writing program and taught with Sharon

Olds. Eventually appointed the Erich Maria Remarque Professor of Creative Writing, he would remain at NYU for the rest of his teaching life.

Kinnell had great affection for the paraphernalia of writing, collecting fountain pens and antique typewriters. He cherished old dictionaries, too, especially a 1918 edition of *Webster's New International,* with its separate section of archaic and obsolete words to which he might give new life in his poems. He also took to the fax machine, and throughout the 1990s would exchange poems with Olds nearly every day. (In his early years, Charles Bell had been the first reader of his work; in later years, his friends John Logan, Donald Hall, Robert Bly, and later still, Philip Levine, C. K. Williams, and Olds took on that role.)

Over the years, Kinnell was resident at several writers' colonies and writing programs, including Yaddo and the MacDowell Colony, where he was taken in frequently during his early itinerant days before his Sheffield house was habitable. In the 1980s and 1990s, he had two residencies at the Rockefeller Foundation's Bellagio Center and taught at the Squaw Valley Community of Writers, where he was the director of the summer poetry program for seventeen years.

Kinnell's social activism and his engagement with the larger world remained strong. In 1982, he organized "Poetry Against the End of the World," a historic reading at Town Hall in New York City to protest the nuclear arms race. Feeling that building a global community of poets would benefit all, and in particular those who were unable to publish freely, he traveled to other countries, including to Japan for the Asian Writers Congress in 1983, to China to read at the Beijing Foreign Studies University in 1984, and to Czechoslovakia in the late 1980s.

In 1985, he and Inés were divorced; *The Past,* dedicated to her, was published that year. A MacArthur fellowship in 1984 eased Kinnell's financial situation, and he continued to give readings around the country and abroad for the next twenty-five years, splitting his time between Sheffield and New York. In 1989, he was appointed State Poet of Vermont, the first to hold that title since the death of Robert Frost. His two edited volumes — *The Essential Whitman* (1987) and *The Essential Rilke* (2000) — paid homage to poets who, with Emily Dickinson, had been his lodestars throughout much of his life.

In 1988, he met Barbara (Bobbie) K. Bristol, who became his editor for *When One Has Lived a Long Time Alone* (1990); they married in 1997 and began to spend more time in Vermont. Another collection, *Imperfect Thirst,* was published in 1994.

Recognition of Galway Kinnell's lifetime achievement came in 2002 in the form of the Frost Medal from the Poetry Society of America, and in 2010 in the bestowal of the Wallace Stevens Award by the Academy of American Poets, where he had been a Chancellor. His last collection, *Strong Is Your Hold,* was published in 2006.

Retiring from NYU that year, Kinnell, with Bobbie and their two dogs, made Sheffield his permanent home, leaving it less and less often. No longer able to play the game of tennis he loved so much, he took up croquet as the new arena for his competitive spirit. All were expected to pick up a mallet, even Ephraim and Mirah, his small grandchildren.

In increasingly ill health in the last years of his life, he continued to work every day on his poems. He died at home in Sheffield on October 28, 2014.

B. K. B.

INDEX OF TITLES
AND FIRST LINES

ILLUSTRATION CREDITS